...for BEC and BULATS

Business
BENCHMARK

Advanced

Higher

Teacher's Resource Book

CAMBRIDGE
UNIVERSITY PRESS

Guy Brook-Hart

CAMBRIDGE UNIVERSITY PRESS
Cambridge, New York, Melbourne, Madrid, Cape Town, Singapore, São Paulo

Cambridge University Press
The Edinburgh Building, Cambridge CB2 8RU, UK

www.cambridge.org
Information on this title: www.cambridge.org/9780521672962

First published 2007

Printed in the United Kingdom at the University Press, Cambridge

A catalogue record for this publication is available from the British Library

ISBN 978-0-521-67296-2 Teacher's Resource Book Advanced/Higher
ISBN 978-0-521-67295-5 Student's Book BEC Higher Edition
ISBN 978-0-521-67294-8 Student's Book BULATS Edition Advanced with CD-ROM
ISBN 978-0-521-67297-9 Personal Study Book Advanced/Higher
ISBN 978-0-521-67298-6 Audio Cassette BEC Higher Edition
ISBN 978-0-521-67299-3 Audio CD BEC Higher Edition
ISBN 978-0-521-67661-8 Audio Cassette BULATS Edition Advanced
ISBN 978-0-521-67662-5 Audio CD BULATS Edition Advanced

Contents

Acknowledgements

Author acknowledgements

The author would like to thank the editorial team for their help, advice, guidance, enthusiasm, feedback and ideas throughout the project, especially Charlotte Adams (Senior Commissioning Editor), Sally Searby (Publishing Manager), Jane Coates (Series Editor), Catriona Watson-Brown (Freelance Editor), Gemma Wilkins (Production Controller) and Michelle Simpson (Assistant Permissions Clearance Controller). Special thanks also to Susie Fairfax-Davies for using her compendious list of contacts to search out and interview business people for the book, and thanks to the following people for kindly giving up time and agreeing to be interviewed: Rachel Babington (Disney Channel), William Brook-Hart (Gifford Engineering Consultancy), Neil Ivey (MediaCom), Philip Franks and Richard Coates (Wolseley PLC).

Many thanks to Elaine Boyd for writing the BEC practice material for the BEC edition.

The author would also like to thank his Business English students at the British Council, Valencia, from 2004 to 2006, who kindly and good-humouredly worked through and trialled the materials, pointed out faults, suggested improvements and, by applying their business expertise, provided essential input.

The author would like to give his warmest thanks and love to his wife, Paz, for her help, enthusiasm and encouragement throughout the project. He dedicates the book to his son, Esteban, and his daughter, Elena, with much love.

The publishers would like to thank Elaine Boyd for her invaluable feedback when reviewing the course material.

Senior commissioning editor: Charlotte Adams
Publishing manager: Sally Searby
Project manager and editor: Jane Coates
Freelance editor: Catriona Watson-Brown
Production controller: Gemma Wilkins
Assistant permissions controller: Michelle Simpson
Design and layout: Hart McLeod Ltd

Text acknowledgements

The authors and publishers are grateful to the following for permission to reproduce copyright material. While every effort has been made, it has not always been possible to identify the sources of all the material used, or to trace the copyright holders. If any omissions are brought to our notice, we will be happy to include the appropriate acknowledgements on reprinting.

The publishers are grateful to the following for permission to reproduce copyright material:
For the information on p. 7 about Business English Certificate (BEC) Higher level and the Business Language Testing Service (BULATS) test. Reproduced by permission of University of Cambridge ESOL Examinations © UCLES; pp. 10–11: University of Nebraska-Lincoln Extension for the text 'Thirteen timely tips for more effective personal time management' by Kathy Prochaska-Cue. Taken from NEB Facts – Nebraska Cooperative Extension NF94-172. Used by permission; p. 20: Hilary Whitney for the text 'Don't be bullied by a big bad boss' taken from *The Guardian*, 17 July 2000. Used by permission of Hilary Whitney; p. 33: Pars International for the text 'Getting to know them' written by Meredith Levinson. Issue 15 February 2004 of *CIO Magazine*. Copyright CXO Media Inc. All rights reserved; pp. 38–39: *The Economist* for the text 'The price is wrong', 23 May 2002 and p. 108: 'The trouble with women', 23 October 2003. © The Economist Newspaper Limited, London; p. 74: Entrepreneur Media Inc. for the text 'Breakthrough performance', written by Barry Farber. Reprinted with permission from *Entrepreneur Magazine*, December 2003. www.entrepreneur.com; p. 98: Stanford Graduate School of Business for the text 'Negotiation Strategy: Six common pitfalls to avoid' written by Margaret Neale. Taken from the website: http://www.gsb.stanford.edu. news.research/hr_negotiation_strategy.shtml. Used by kind permission of Stanford Graduate School of Business, Stanford University; p.160: CILT, the National Centre for Languages for 'Can Do Statements'. Adapted from National Language Standards © CILT, the National Centre for Languages.

Illustrations

p. 26; p. 31; p. 57; p. 63: Tim Oliver

Introduction

Who this course is for

Business Benchmark Advanced/Higher is designed as an interesting and stimulating course in Business English for students at Common European Framework (CEF) level C1. It combines lively, authentic materials from a wide range of business sources and is suitable for people already working in business and pre-service students (younger people who are intending to work in business in the future).

The course provides the necessary practical writing, reading, speaking and listening skills for people who will need English in a business environment. It builds up students' knowledge of essential business vocabulary and grammar in 24 short units designed to take approximately three hours' classroom time each.

For students who require a Business English qualification, the course provides a thorough preparation for the Business English Certificate (BEC) Higher level, or the Business Language Testing Service (BULATS) test, including **one complete practice exam** for BEC and another for BULATS.

What the course contains

Student's Book

The Student's Book contains:

- **24 topic- or skills-based units** designed to cover a wide range of the main topic and skills areas required by people working in modern business. The units are organised in 'clusters' of four, each cluster covering a broad topic area. The first unit in each cluster is designed to place more emphasis on reading skills (though the other skills are covered), the second places emphasis on listening skills, the third on writing skills, and the fourth on speaking skills. All units, however, are designed to provide lively, stimulating and varied classroom work where all skills are required. The units contain:
  - **discussion and role-play activities** designed to build up essential business speaking skills such as those required for meetings, conferences, negotiations and presentations
  - step-by-step work on writing skills in order to be able to write **emails, memos, faxes, letters, reports** and **proposals**
  - a large number of authentic business articles from a wide variety of well-known business

publications, together with examples of letters, reports and proposals, all designed to teach essential business reading skills
  - specially designed listening materials and **authentic interviews** with business people, intended to improve students' listening proficiency and confidence
  - numerous vocabulary exercises so that students studying the course will have an **ample business vocabulary** for most general situations
  - **grammar explanations and exercises** to extend and revise students' knowledge of English grammar at this level in a business context.

  Many of the activities in the units are also designed to provide students with the skills and training necessary for either the **Business English Certificate (BEC) Higher level** or the **Business Language Testing Service (BULATS) test**.

- **Grammar workshops** with further grammar explanations and exercises related to grammar work arising from the units.

- **An Exam skills and Exam practice section** which provides detailed advice on what each section of the BEC Higher exam consists of, or what the BULATS test consists of, together with information about what each section of the exam is testing and detailed step-by-step advice on how to approach each question. The Exam skills section also contains exercises designed to build up students' exam skills. This section also contains a complete **BEC Higher exam (BEC Higher edition)** or the parts of the **BULATS test (BULATS edition)** which are designed for advanced students. The **BULATS test** is supplied by **Cambridge ESOL**.

- **Answer keys** to all the exercises in the book.

- **Transcripts** for all the listening materials.

Personal Study Book

The Personal Study Book contains:

- **24 units**, each relating to the 24 units of the Student's Book. These units contain:
  - vocabulary revision and consolidation work
  - grammar revision and consolidation work
  - further reading and writing exercises

- a **Word list** of the core business vocabulary and expressions which appear in the Student's Book.

Recorded materials

The recorded materials for the Student's Book are available either on audio CD or cassette.

Teacher's Resource Book

The Teacher's Resource Book contains:

- information about how the activities in each unit relate to the BEC exam and BULATS test
- notes on each unit in the Student's Book, with advice on how to handle activities in the unit and suggestions for alternative treatments for certain exercises
- a large number of extra **photocopiable activities**, including further **reading texts**, **discussion activities**, **games** and **case studies**, intended to supplement and extend the work done in the Student's Book units and to provide a wider range of activities or a more in-depth study of certain business topics. The photocopiable activities also provide **extra writing tasks**, all with a step-by-step approach and a sample answer for students or teachers to refer to
- answer keys to all exercises in the photocopiable activities
- answer keys to all exercises and activities in the Student's Book, including the Exam skills and Exam practice section
- complete Student's Book transcripts with the words or sentences giving the correct answer to the listening exercise underlined
- information about the **Common European Framework** and how this course relates to it
- a checklist of Can Do statements for students at C1 (advanced) level.

Website

Further information and resources can be found online @ http://www.cambridge.org/businessbenchmark.

BULATS CD-ROM (BULATS edition)

The BULATS edition of *Business Benchmark, Advanced* contains skills advice and exam practice for all parts of the BULATS test which are relevant to students at advanced level. A complete BULATS test is supplied free with *Business Benchmark BULATS Edition, Advanced* on CD-ROM for students wishing to familiarise themselves with all parts of the computer test.

Business English Certificate (BEC) Higher exam

BEC Higher assesses language ability used in the context of business at the Council of Europe's Effective Operational Proficiency Level (C1) for general language proficiency.

- In the **Reading** component, there are six tasks of the following types: multiple choice, matching, word level

gap-filling, sentence-level gap-filling, multiple-choice gap-filling and error identification. The Reading component is 25% of the total marks.

- In the **Writing** component, there are two tasks. In Part One candidates produce a short report (based on graphic input, approximately 120–140 words). In Part Two candidates choose whether to write a report, proposal or piece of business correspondence. The Writing paper is 25% of the total marks.
- In the **Listening** component, there are three tasks of the following types: gap-filling or note completion, matching and multiple choice. Texts used are monologues and dialogues, including interviews, discussions, telephone conversations and messages. The Listening paper is 25% of the total marks.
- The **Speaking Test** is conducted by two external examiners and candidates are tested in pairs. At centres with an uneven number of candidates, the last single candidate is examined with the last pair in a group of three. During the test each candidate responds to questions, gives a 'mini-presentation' lasting approximately one minute, takes part in a collaborative task with the other candidate and the interlocutor. The Speaking Test is 25% of the total marks.

Business Language Testing Service (BULATS) test

BULATS makes use of a number of specially designed tests:

- **The Computer Test**
- **The Standard Test**
- **The Speaking Test**
- **The Writing Test**

Each test can be used independently of the others, or they can be used in various combinations. All the tests aim to be relevant to people using the language at work. They cover areas such as descriptions of jobs, companies and products, travel, management and marketing, customer service planning, reports, phone messages, business correspondence and presentations. The tasks in the test are generally practical ones, e.g. taking a phone message, checking a letter, giving a presentation, understanding an article, writing a report.

All the tests aim to assess candidates across the six levels of the ALTE Framework, i.e. the same test is used for all candidates whatever their level. (0–5 of the ALTE Framework correspond to the Council of Europe Framework levels A1–C2.) See the Appendix on page 159 for more information about the Council of Europe Framework.

Corporate culture

This unit teaches language and vocabulary connected with company culture, phrasal verbs and defining and non-defining relative clauses.

Although none of the tasks in the unit exactly replicate exam questions, some are designed to give students the skills and practice needed to deal with them (see table below).

	BEC	BULATS
Talking point: *Aspects of corporate culture*	Speaking Part 1	Speaking Part 1
Listening: *Aspects of corporate culture*	Listening Part 2	Listening Part 3
Reading: *Creating a corporate culture*	Reading Part 2	
Talking point: *Creating a corporate culture*	Speaking Part 3	Speaking Part 3
Photocopiable activity 1	Speaking Parts 1 & 2	Speaking Parts 1 & 2

Notes on unit

Getting started

As a further extension, you can get students to brainstorm other typical characteristics of corporate culture.

You could also discuss the relationship between national cultures and corporate cultures if you think your students have the background to do this.

Talking point: *Aspects of corporate culture*

Pre-service students who have no close acquaintance with a company can be asked to talk about the culture of a college or school where they have studied.

Listening: *Aspects of corporate culture*

All audio material in this book is intended to be listened to twice.

If students are new to this type of listening activity, allow them to check their answers by looking at the transcript for Track 2 to see how the activity works.

If you wish to make the activity more challenging, Exercise 1 can be done after, rather than before, Exercise 2.

Reading: *Creating a corporate culture*

As a warmer before the reading passage, ask students to do Exercises 1 and 2.

When students do Exercise 3, they should read the whole text again when they have finished to make sure that it reads logically.

As an alternative approach to this and other tasks, you can discuss the best approach with students and get their ideas. Different students, or different groups of students, can try different ways, e.g. reading the list of sentences carefully first and then finding gaps for them, or reading to the first gap and then looking through the list of sentences, etc. They can then compare which method was most effective.

Vocabulary: *Creating a corporate culture*

If your students have a copy of the Personal Study Book, you can point out that it contains exercises which recycle vocabulary and grammar encountered in the unit and, in some units, gives extra reading and writing tasks.

You can also point out that the Personal Study Book contains a Word list which they can consult when doing vocabulary exercises.

Photocopiable activity

This activity is intended as an ice-breaker at the beginning of the course (perhaps before students have had time to buy their course books) and will take about an hour of class time.

Getting started

Time management is about managing your time efficiently so that you achieve the most effective use of your working day, and also have time for free-time activities and interests. Courses in time management are also offered in many universities to help students manage their time efficiently. This activity is intended to analyse how you spend your day and suggest some time-management methods.

Work with a partner and complete this questionnaire for each other. (Ask each other complete questions to obtain the information, e.g. *How long is your working day?*)

Job/Occupation/Studies:

Summary of duties and responsibilities / What course consists of:

Length of working day / time each day spent in class or studying:

Starts work/studies at:

Length of lunch break:

Finishes work/studies at:

Time per day spent travelling to work/college/university:

How time spent while travelling to work/college/university (e.g. reading the newspaper):

Takes work home? Yes/No
If *Yes*, give details:

Works/Studies at weekends? Yes/No
If *Yes*, give details:

Working time spent in meetings/classes/tutorials:

Working time spent on phone:

Time spent per day on enjoyable non-work/non-study activities:

Time spent per day on household chores, childcare, etc.:

Do you think you make efficient use of your time? Yes/No
If *Yes*, give details:

Talking point

> Time management experts list a number of common activities or circumstances which waste people's time. These are often called *time thieves*.

Work in groups of three. Discuss these questions.

1 How do the *time thieves* listed below waste people's time?
2 Which ones waste your time?
3 How can people reduce their vulnerability to these *time thieves*?

Time thieves

- Telephone interruptions
- Interruptions from visitors
- Meetings
- Not delegating tasks
- Crisis management (i.e. spending your day dealing with problems that arise)
- Poor communication

- Lack of training
- Unclear objectives
- Poor planning
- Stress and fatigue
- Inability to say 'No'
- An untidy desk/computer filing system
- Being a perfectionist

Reading

1 Work in groups of three. You will each read a different text giving advice on how to manage time better.

2 Read your text and make brief notes on the main points.

3 Talk to your partners and explain the main advice and the reasons for it. When speaking, refer to your notes rather than the original text.

4 When you have finished, discuss which were the best pieces of advice.

Writing

Work with a partner. Write one more piece of advice for good time management like the ones you have just read.

✂ -

A

SPEND TIME PLANNING AND ORGANISING. Using time to think and plan is time well spent. In fact, if you fail to take time for planning, you are, in effect, planning to fail. Organise in a way that makes sense to you. Some people need to have papers filed away; others get their creative energy from their piles. So forget the 'shoulds' and organise *your* way.

SET GOALS. Goals give your life, and the way you spend your time, direction. When asked the secret to becoming so rich, one of the famous Hunt brothers from Texas replied, 'First, you've got to decide what you want.' Set goals which are specific, measurable, realistic and achievable. Your optimum goals are those which cause you to 'stretch' but not 'break' as you strive for achievement. Goals can give creative people a much-needed sense of direction.

PRIORITISE. Use the 80–20 rule originally stated by the Italian economist Vilfredo Pareto, who noted that 80 per cent of the reward comes from 20 per cent of the effort. The trick to prioritising is to isolate and identify that valuable 20 per cent. Once identified, prioritise time to concentrate your work on those items with the greatest reward.

USE A 'TO-DO' LIST. Some people thrive using a daily 'to-do' list which they construct either last thing the previous day or first thing in the morning. Such people may combine a 'to-do' list with a calendar or schedule. Others prefer a 'running' 'to-do' list which is continuously being updated.

B

BE FLEXIBLE. Allow time for interruptions and distractions. Time management experts often suggest planning for just 50 per cent or less of one's time. With only 50 per cent of your time planned, you will have the flexibility to handle interruptions and the unplanned 'emergency'. When you expect to be interrupted, schedule routine tasks. Save (or make) larger blocks of time for your priorities. When interrupted, ask Alan Lakein's crucial question, 'What is the most important thing I can be doing with my time right now?' to help you get back on track fast.

CONSIDER YOUR BIOLOGICAL PRIME TIME. That's the time of day when you are at your best. Are you a 'morning person', a 'night owl', or a late-afternoon 'whiz'? Knowing when your best time is and planning to use that time of day for your priorities (if possible) is effective time management.

DO THE RIGHT THING RIGHT. Noted management expert Peter Drucker says 'doing the right thing is more important than doing things right'. Doing the right thing is effectiveness; doing things right is efficiency. Focus first on effectiveness (identifying what is the right thing to do), then concentrate on efficiency (doing it right).

ELIMINATE THE URGENT. Urgent tasks have short-term consequences, while important tasks are those with long-term, goal-related implications. Work towards reducing the urgent things you must do so you'll have time for your important priorities.

C

PRACTISE THE ART OF INTELLIGENT NEGLECT. Eliminate from your life trivial tasks or those tasks which do not have long-term consequences for you. Can you delegate or eliminate any of your 'to-do' list? Work on those tasks which you alone can do.

AVOID BEING A PERFECTIONIST. In the Malaysian culture, only the gods are considered capable of producing anything perfect. Whenever something is made, a flaw is left on purpose so the gods will not be offended. Yes, some things need to be closer to perfect than others, but perfectionism, paying unnecessary attention to detail, can be a form of procrastination.

LEARN TO SAY 'NO'. Such a small word – and so hard to say. Focusing on your goals may help. Blocking time for important, but often not scheduled, priorities such as family and friends can also help. But first you must be convinced that you and your priorities are important – that seems to be the hardest part in learning to say 'no'. Once convinced of their importance, saying 'no' to the unimportant in life gets easier.

REWARD YOURSELF. Even for small successes, celebrate achievement of goals. Promise yourself a reward for completing each task, or finishing the total job. Then keep your promise to yourself and indulge in your reward. Doing so will help you maintain the necessary balance in life between work and play. As Ann McGee-Cooper says, 'If we learn to balance excellence in work with excellence in play, fun, and relaxation, our lives become happier, healthier and a great deal more creative.'

From *Thirteen timely tips for more effective personal time management* by Kathy Prochaska-Cue

Answer key

Student's Book activities

Getting started

1 1 b   2 g   3 e   4 d   5 f   6 c   7 a

2 1 mentor   2 dress code   3 goals   4 autocratic
5 bonuses   6 do things by the book   7 vision
8 entrepreneurial

Aspects of corporate culture

Listening

1 1 g   2 j   3 a   4 i   5 d   6 e   7 c   8 b   9 f
10 h

2 Candela: 5   Henry: 4   Sonia: 7   Omar: 3

Vocabulary

1 out   2 through   3 up with   4 to   5 turn
6 getting   7 down

Creating a corporate culture

Reading

1 1 The board of directors
2 It can affect ethics, risk-taking and bottom-line performance.
3 Board members often lack an understanding of corporate culture.

3 1 G   2 F   3 D   4 C   5 A   6 E

Vocabulary

1 b   2 g   3 c   4 a   5 d   6 f   7 e

Grammar workshop: *defining and non-defining relative clauses*

1 How should a director think about the "corporate culture" of the company on **whose** board he or she serves?

2 Consult a management text on organizational culture and you'll find a chapter or more of definition **which**/that boils down to something like "a pattern of shared basic assumptions."

3 Every organization has a culture **which**/that manifests itself in everything from entrepreneurship to risk-taking all the way down to the dress code.

4 An understanding of corporate culture is one of the main things missing on boards, but they really need it if they're going to monitor **what**'s going on inside the corporation.

5 Nucor's culture, **which** he describes as "extraordinarily powerful, effective, and unique," can be traced back to the values and vision of its legendary founder, F. Kenneth Iverson.

Transcript

2 Listening page 11

Omar: So, Candela, what's it like working for a large car manufacturer?

Candela: You'd be surprised, actually. You hear so much about cut-throat competition amongst managers in my type of company, but in fact, as someone starting out on the management ladder, I get a lot of back-up from senior staff. We have twice-weekly get-togethers where we talk through our difficulties and come up with ideas and solutions. It's great. I don't get the feeling that it's 'sink or swim' at all.

Omar: And you, Henry?

Henry: Well, as you'd expect working in hospital administration, there's plenty of red tape. We have to stick to the rules fairly carefully because at the end of the day, people's health's involved, and we're publicly accountable. But that doesn't mean there's no room for inventiveness. We're always looking for ways of streamlining procedures and making efficiency gains.

Omar: And saving taxpayers' money.

Henry: That's right.

Omar: Now, Sonia, what's it like working for a dotcom?

Sonia: It's not exactly a dotcom. As a matter of fact, it's more a software developer. And it really suits me, you know, I nearly always turn up at work wearing jeans and a T-shirt, which is great for a manager, and everyone talks to everyone else in a really relaxed way. There's none of that 'them-and-us' feeling between management and staff that you get in other industries. I mean, in most ways the staff are more expert than the managers! And what about you, Omar?

Omar: My company, as you know, is a consumer products company, and we're all organised in divisions, and the divisions in teams, and we're all competing against each other. Our pay is performance-related, and nobody gets the same. Getting ahead and even keeping your job depends on your performance.

Sonia: Um, and how's performance measured, Omar? Is there a yardstick?

Omar: Not really. In the end, it boils down to performance in comparison with other teams and divisions.

Henry: Sounds quite a rat race.

Omar: For me, that's business!

2 Leaders and managers

This unit studies language and vocabulary related to the functions and qualities of leaders and managers. It revises the grammar of *as* and *like* and teaches a number of management collocations.

Although none of the tasks in the unit exactly replicate exam questions, some are designed to give students the skills and practice needed to deal with them (see table below).

	BEC	BULATS
Getting started	Speaking Part 2	Speaking Part 2
Reading: *Great leaders and great managers*	Reading Part 3	Reading Part 2 Section 5
Listening: *Great leaders and great managers*	Listening Part 1	Speaking Part 1
Listening: *Managing staff*	Listening Part 1	
Talking point 2: *Managing staff*	Speaking Part 3	Speaking Part 3

Notes on unit

Getting started

Giving short talks of this type is a useful business skill: business people are often asked to talk in meetings about their ideas, activities or projects.

If you want to extend the discussion, you can:
- ask students about well-known business leaders from their country
- ask which qualities are most valued by business leaders and managers in their country, or if some of these qualities are not considered important in their country.

Talking point: *Great leaders and great managers*

As an alternative task, ask your students to work in small groups. Tell them each to:
- pick out three sentences from the text whose ideas made an impression on them
- read each sentence to the others in their group, who then give their reaction to it
- if appropriate, ask them to compare Branson's attitude to managing people with the attitudes in the companies where they work.

Listening: *Great leaders and great managers*

The task tip suggests students should try to predict the type of information they will need to complete the notes. You can help them by eliciting:

- gap 1: *Do you think you need a noun, verb, adjective or what? What qualities might help the business progress?*
- gap 2: *What part of speech do you need? What is the essential difference between managers and leaders, and what is their relationship?*, etc.

Vocabulary 2: *Great leaders and great managers*

As a follow-up to this activity, you can:
- ask students if they can identify two different **types** of collocation with *management* (**answer**: types or categories of management, and things which are managed)
- ask them to brainstorm two or three other collocations for each category.

Talking point 1: *Managing staff*

If you have pre-service students, ask them:
- if teachers fill a similar role to managers
- what teachers can do to optimise the performance of their students
- what aspects of their education might prepare them for management roles.

Photocopiable activity

This is intended as a fun approach to some people-management issues and practises related vocabulary.

Encourage students to give reasons for their answers. When they come to score their answers, encourage them to disagree with the interpretations if they wish, since these are intended to be mildly provocative.

This activity will take more than an hour of class time.

Photocopiable activity

Reading

What sort of people manager are you / would you be? Do the quiz to find out.

1 Work in pairs. Read each question and then tell each other:

  • the answer you would choose

  • the reason why you would choose that answer.

2 When you have finished, add up your partner's score and give him/her the appraisal which follows.

✂ ---

How to score

1 a 1 **b** 7 **c** 1 **d** 3

Even if he's a brilliant and valuable worker, you're not doing him a favour letting him get away with working in an undisciplined way – and it's bad for the morale of other staff, who might feel he's being treated too kindly.

2 a 5 **b** 5 **c** 1 **d** 6

If she's been in the department for 20 years, she probably has more 'ownership' of the job than you. On the other hand, she may benefit from a change of scene. The personal interview is brave, but may be counter-productive.

3 a 1 **b** 5 **c** 1 **d** 1

All options except (b) may show weakness on your part. At least (b) shows a constructive approach to a human problem.

4 a 1 **b** 5 **c** 2 **d** 0

More money won't solve work-related stress. The only sensible solution is (b), though you will have to justify it to your boss.

5 a 6 **b** 2 **c** 1 **d** 3

The only sensible option is (a).

6 a 3 **b** 7 **c** 1 **d** 7

If your team is doing well, it reflects the fact that you are a good leader. The only absurd reaction is (c). Although taking the kudos is a very natural reaction in an ambitious manager, it can have a damaging effect on staff motivation.

7 a 0 **b** 0 **c** 6 **d** 3

Option (c) is reasonable, but (d) is possible in some circumstances; some customers are wrong and need to be told so. Loyalty to your staff is also a good quality in a manager.

8 a 5 **b** 1 **c** 0 **d** 4

Surely this is none of your business unless passions start affecting productivity.

9 a 0 **b** 3 **c** 0 **d** 4

Your team's poor performance can reflect badly on your boss as well as on yourself, so the best answer is to get her involved in actively finding a solution.

10 a 8 **b** 3 **c** 0 **d** 0

See how he manages with more challenge before doing anything else. You can't move everyone every time they complain.

✂ ---

Results

1–18: You may not be cut out to be a manager and perhaps a little more management training would be useful.

19–35: As a manager your skills are average. You may well get to the top of your profession, but not because of your skills in managing people.

35+: You are clearly one of those rare individuals – a good manager of people. Show the results of this test to your Human Resources Director and see if he/she is equally impressed!

✂ ---

Vocabulary

Find words or phrases in the quiz which mean the following.

1 amount of work to be done (question 2)
2 reaching an acceptable standard (question 3)
3 dismissal (question 3)
4 admiration that a person receives as a result of a particular achievement (question 6)
5 extra amount of money that is given to you as a reward for good work (question 6)
6 people who are at the same level in an organisation (question 7)

7 person in a less important position in an organisation (question 7)
8 ignore something that you know is wrong (question 8)
9 stop it (question 8)
10 watch (question 8)
11 difficult, in a way that tests your ability or determination (question 10)
12 moving to a new job (question 10)

From *Business Benchmark Advanced/Higher* by Guy Brook-Hart © Cambridge University Press 2007 　**PHOTOCOPIABLE**　**UNIT 2**

What sort of people manager are you?

1 **One of your staff often arrives late for work. He's a good worker – efficient, brilliant and original – but arriving late means that he often misses the beginning of team meetings, or other people have to answer his phone calls. Do you …**

a write him a letter threatening him with dismissal if he doesn't improve?

b have an informal private chat with him where you suggest he pulls his socks up?

c make sarcastic comments about his poor time-keeping in front of the team?

d ignore the problem – he's a good worker after all?

2 **There's a member of your staff you just don't like. She often openly disagrees with your decisions, and you're sure she criticises you constantly behind your back. Do you …**

a put up with her because she's been in the department for 20 years?

b transfer her to another department where someone else will have the pleasure of her company?

c increase her workload in the hope that she will leave?

d have a personal interview with her where you talk over the problems between you?

3 **A new recruit to your department is not learning the job as quickly as you had hoped, and you consider him to be a weak link in your team. Do you …**

a tell him he's not up to scratch and threaten him with the sack?

b tell him your opinion and offer him further training?

c pretend there's no problem – if you take action against this person, it may upset other members of your team?

d offer him a transfer to another department where he may be more at home?

4 **You've noticed signs of stress in your team: people are irritable, complaining of headaches, taking sick leave. Do you …**

a offer to give them a pay rise?

b take on more staff to ease their workloads?

c try to do more of their work yourself?

d carry on as if the situation was normal?

5 **Your divisional boss has asked you and your team to take on an extra project. You're already working flat out on a current project. Do you …**

a explain the situation and ask for another solution?

b accept the extra work because you're afraid to say 'no'?

c accept the extra work because you're ambitious and it could eventually mean promotion?

d tell your boss he must be joking – your people are under enough pressure as it is?

6 **Your team is doing extremely well – you're exceeding all your targets and easily meeting all your deadlines. Your divisional boss recently called you in to congratulate you. Do you …**

a take all the kudos – after all you're the leader?

b pass on the praise to your team and suggest they be paid a bonus?

c ask your boss to set even higher targets?

d hold a team party to celebrate?

7 **An important customer has complained that one of your staff was very rude to him. Do you …**

a confront her during a team meeting and then reprimand her in front of her peers?

b fire her on the spot?

c ask her for her version of events and take it from there?

d stand by your subordinate and tell the customer he was wrong?

8 **You've noticed that two of your team are getting more than friendly. You imagine that there's an office romance under way. Do you …**

a turn a blind eye?

b get involved in the office gossip to find out what's happening?

c tell them to put an end to it?

d keep an eye on the situation in case it has an effect on team efficiency?

9 **Your divisional manager has told you that your team's performance is not up to scratch. Do you …**

a blame the team?

b blame outside circumstances which are beyond your control?

c take the blame yourself?

d tell her it's her fault for not giving you the necessary resources?

10 **One of your staff tells you he doesn't find his job sufficiently challenging. Do you …**

a offer him more responsibility and empowerment in his current job?

b promote him to a position of greater responsibility?

c tell him it's time he was moving on?

d tell him he should be happy he's got a job at all?

Answer key

Photocopiable activity
Vocabulary
1 workload   2 up to scratch   3 the sack   4 kudos
5 bonus   6 peers   7 subordinate   8 turn a blind
eye   9 put an end to it   10 keep an eye on
11 challenging   12 moving on

Student's Book activities

Getting started
1 1 h   2 f   3 b   4 c   5 e   6 g   7 a   8 d

Great leaders and great managers
Reading
3 1 D … says his goal is to turn Virgin into 'the
      most respected brand in the world'.
      (paragraph 1)
   2 B 'I think being a high-profile person has its
      advantages,' he says. 'Advertising costs
      enormous amounts of money these days. I
      just announced in India that I was setting up
      a domestic airline, and we ended up getting
      on the front pages of the newspaper.'
      (paragraph 2)
   3 C I have to be willing to step back. The
      company must be set up so it can continue
      without me. (paragraph 4)
   4 D For the people who work for you or with
      you, you must lavish praise on them at all
      times (paragraph 5)
   5 A Employees often leave companies, he
      reasons, because they are frustrated by the
      fact that their ideas fall on deaf ears.
      (paragraph 6)
   6 B … then give chief executives a stake in the
      company (paragraph 7)

Vocabulary 1
1 founder   2 venture   3 underlying   4 flamboyant
5 from scratch   6 lavish praise on   7 slipped up /
made a mess of something   8 firing   9 immersed
10 the ins and outs   11 stake

Listening
1 vision   2 implementation   3 hands-on
4 experienced, good people   5 opportunity to develop

Grammar workshop: *as* or *like*?
1 b   2 a (like)   3 c   4 a (as well as)
5 d (as … as)

Vocabulary 2
1 g   2 d   3 a   4 c   5 b   6 e   7 f

Managing staff
Listening
2 1 directional strategy   2 (responsibility and)
   ownership   3 superficial level   4 opportunities
   5 (kind of) mentor

Transcripts

3 Listening page 16

I = interviewer; RB = Rachel Babington

I: What do you think makes a great leader as opposed to a great manager, because they're quite different things, aren't they?

RB: I think I've worked in a lot of places where a lot of senior people haven't really been leaders, they've been managers, and I think I'd say probably a … a good leader has <u>vision</u> and can see how to develop and take things forward and is inspirational. Really, a manager, I think, is more about the <u>implementation of that vision</u>, and I think too many people who are in leadership roles get bogged down with the nitty-gritty management side, which is probably not what they should be doing, but I suppose it takes a strong leader and a confident one who believes in their team to take a step back, um, and I think really they should. I don't think they should be too <u>hands-on</u>.

I: Can you describe a bad leader to me?

RB: I think someone who … has a team of quite <u>experienced</u>, <u>good people</u> who won't give them the space to get on and do their job and is overbearing and involved, um, and doesn't take a step back and give … give people the responsibility to get on with their role, and I suppose who doesn't give a person room to grow and the <u>opportunity to develop</u> their career, because I think that happens a lot, that you just are expected to tick along and not expect anything back from your job. Whereas if you're good at it and reasonably ambitious, you want to know you're going somewhere.

4 Listening page 17

I = interviewer; RB = Rachel Babington

I: What … How would you describe empowerment? And how can workers be empowered, do you think?

RB: I think empowerment is … um … giving someone the opportunity to decide the <u>directional strategy</u> of a job and agreeing on it, and then leaving them to get on and do it and be in the background to help them if they need it, but not to be breathing down their neck. Um, and I suppose it is that feeling of <u>responsibility and ownership</u> that makes people feel empowered. I think if you work with someone who really lacks confidence to give their team responsibility, it's very difficult to break out of that cycle.

I: And has managing techniques, or have managing people, changed over the last … in the last ten years?

RB: I don't know, I'm probably a bit cynical, but I think there's a lot, certainly, that I have noticed in the organisations I've worked in, there are a lot of steps that are taken to be seen to be empowering individuals, and so I think things … probably at a <u>superficial</u> <u>level</u> look to have changed, but whether they really have deep down, I'm not so sure.

I: How do you think people could be managed in order to get the very best from them?

RB: I think to get the most out of them, you want them to feel empowered, that they're achieving, that they're, they're um, developing, that there are <u>opportunities</u> ahead of them that they can strive to work to, that they're … um … under a manageable amount of pressure, um, that they're getting the right kind of support. I think what a lot of people lack is a <u>kind of mentor</u> and someone that'll help them develop in their career, and you can become very stale if you don't have that. So I'd say that would be important to people as well.

UNIT 3 Internal communications

This unit works on writing for communication inside a company or organisation – memos, emails, notes and notices. It studies differences in style and format for what, for many business students, is a major part of their work activity in English. The unit also revises the future simple and future continuous.

Although none of the tasks in the unit exactly replicate exam questions, some are designed to give students the skills and practice needed to deal with them (see table below).

	BEC	BULATS
Reading: *Internal messages*	Reading Part 1	Reading Part 2 Section 1
Writing: *Internal messages*		Writing Part 1
Listening: *Advice for communicating with colleagues*	Listening Part 2	Listening Part 3
Writing: *Advice for communicating with colleagues*		Writing Part 1
Talking point: *Advice for communicating with colleagues*	Speaking Part 3	Speaking Part 3
Photocopiable activity	Reading Part 2	Reading Part 2 Section 5

Notes on unit

Getting started
Possible areas for discussion if students have enough business experience are:
• how frequently an unsuitable medium of communication is chosen for internal 'messages'
• why this is
• what the consequences of this may be (in a general sense).

Reading: *Internal messages*
Although email is often the usual medium, a memo is a message to all staff, or to a group of staff such as a department or a team. An email may be more directed to an individual or a number of named staff.

As a lead-in to the reading activity, you could ask students (both in-service and pre-service) to say what sort of messages are passed on in their organisation by memo, and what sorts of communication are put on notice boards. You could also ask them what advantages notice boards have as a medium of communication.

Writing: *Internal messages*
You should try to ensure equal numbers of students for each of the four writing tasks, so that the format, language and style of all can be discussed afterwards.

Go through the Useful language with your students before they start.

If you have access to networked computers and a data projector, this activity could be done using them, and then projected and analysed afterwards by the whole class.

Phrases for internal communications:
• you can elicit other typical phrases from students
• ask them to write their phrases on the board. Then discuss with the class when they would be used, their register, etc.

Listening: *Advice for communicating with colleagues*
As a pre-listening task, you could ask students what extra advice they would give apart from the advice listed.

Writing: *Advice for communicating with colleagues*
This activity is best done on networked computers and the results projected afterwards for students to comment on.

Talking point: *Advice for communicating with colleagues*
Ask students to give examples of:
• when managers (or teachers) have communicated well
• when communications have been mishandled
• how communications could have been handled better.

Photocopiable activity

Getting started

1 Work in pairs. Match these phrases to make possible characteristics of bad bosses.

1 They are bad at	a rude and aggressive language.
2 They ask people to do things which are not in	b communicating with staff.
3 They continually interrupt	c their job descriptions.
4 They pretend other people's good ideas	d people's work.
5 They put the blame for their mistakes	e on their staff.
6 They refuse to speak	f to more junior members of staff.
7 They take decisions	g were their own.
8 They use	h without consultation.

2 Add three more characteristics to the list.

3 Discuss what workers can do if they have a bad boss.

Reading

1 Read the article your teacher will give you fairly quickly (in about three minutes) and find six suggestions it gives for dealing with bad bosses.

2 Work in pairs. Without looking back at the article, try to remember and write a list of all the suggestions the article contained for dealing with bad bosses.

3 When you have finished, check back in the article to see if your list is complete.

4 Work alone. Read the article again and answer these questions.

1 What is the main point of the first paragraph?
A In general, managers are better now than in the past.
B Managers nowadays find it easy to improve their performance.
C There is an increasing number of bad managers.
D Although help is available, there are still many bad managers.

2 What reason is given for bosses treating their staff badly?
A They believe their staff will be more obedient.
B They want to appear more competent themselves.
C They believe it improves staff performance.
D They want to encourage incompetent staff to leave.

3 What, according to the writer, is the result of a bullying manager?
A It is something other workers find amusing.
B It reduces productivity.
C It demoralises other managers.
D It means the company will become unprofitable.

4 What is the main piece of advice offered by McFarlin and Sweeney?
A Pay no attention to a boss who bullies.
B Ask for help from your co-workers.
C Keep a record of incidents.
D Leave the company.

5 According to Angela Ishmael, who should you discuss the problem with first?
A a co-worker
B your personnel manager
C one of your boss's colleagues
D a lawyer

6 According to McFarlin and Sweeney, if you decide to leave the company, what should you do when you leave?
A Leave without making a fuss.
B Explain why you are leaving to the senior managers.
C Make the top managers feel guilty about you leaving.
D Make your boss realise how he or she has failed.

Talking point

Discuss these questions in small groups.

1 Which suggestions given for dealing with bad bosses do you think are more useful and which suggestions are not so useful?

2 Do you think the following is true?

> The Peter Principle is a theory originated by Dr Laurence J. Peter which states that employees within a hierarchical organisation advance to their highest level of competence, are then promoted to a level where they are incompetent, and then stay in that position.

✂ -

Don't be bullied by a bad boss
by Hilary Whitney

How do you become a good manager? Judging by the abundance of information, from books to CD-ROMs to residential courses, on how to become a better boss, one might suppose that there was no reason for anyone to suffer from bad management any longer. However, the unfortunate reality, according to a recent survey carried out by the University of Manchester Institute of Science and Technology, is that you are as likely to encounter a bad boss as a good one.

Everyone would like to work for a focused and dynamic boss who is secure enough to encourage the careers of colleagues without feeling threatened in his or her own career. Unfortunately, many employees have to deal with a lesser breed of managers who use bullying and manipulative methods to get their own way and show themselves in the best light.

This is where incompetent management becomes actively malevolent. Take your pick from a catalogue of sins: criticising competent staff, taking away responsibilities and assigning trivial tasks instead, shouting at staff, picking on people in front of colleagues, blocking promotion, setting impossible deadlines, and regularly making the same person the butt of jokes. Sound familiar? If so, you are likely to appreciate the devastating effect this kind of behaviour can have on employees – both physically and psychologically. A demotivated workforce simply does not perform as effectively, and there is the risk of a huge loss of resources as experienced staff leave the organisation in despair.

Perhaps surprisingly, unless you can prove that the motivation behind the behaviour is sexually or racially motivated, there is no law against bullying. But that doesn't mean you should give in without standing your ground. A new book, *Where Egos Dare* by Dean B. McFarlin and Paul D. Sweeney, argues that while ignoring the problem may seem the easiest solution, in the long term it may not be the wisest way to proceed. The book is packed with depressing examples of atrocious managers, but the authors – both academics – offer plenty of constructive advice on how to handle them, ranging from getting the support of colleagues to making contingency plans and, in particular, putting everything in writing. You may ultimately decide you will be happier elsewhere, but making a positive decision to move is at least preferable to being signed off sick because of stress and depression.

Angela Ishmael from the Industrial Society stresses that, however malevolent your manager, it is important not to lose your personal power. She agrees that it is important to keep a diary of aggressive incidents and suggests confiding in a colleague you trust who might be able to help you develop a strategy to cope. Don't be afraid to contact your HR department or another manager if that is unsuccessful, she says – that's what they are there for after all – but if you still feel unsupported, it might be worth talking to a solicitor.

If all else fails and you feel you really must move on, don't let it shake your own self-esteem, say McFarlin and Sweeney. 'On your way out, demand exit interviews with top managers and tell anyone who will listen about what has happened. Doing so will allow you to leave with a clear conscience.' And you'll probably feel a lot better for it.

From *The Guardian*

From *Business Benchmark Advanced/Higher* by Guy Brook-Hart © Cambridge University Press 2007   PHOTOCOPIABLE

Answer key

Photocopiable activity

Getting started
1   1 b   2 c   3 d   4 g   5 e   6 f   7 h   8 a

Reading
1   • Get support from colleagues / Confide in a colleague
    • Make contingency plans
    • Put everything in writing / Keep a diary of incidents
    • Change jobs – and if you move on, demand an exit interview to explain why
    • Contact your HR department or another manager
    • Talk to a solicitor

4   1 D Judging by the abundance of information … no reason for anyone to suffer from bad management … However, you are as likely to encounter a bad boss as a good one.
    2 B … show themselves in the best light.
    3 B A demotivated workforce simply does not perform as effectively
    4 C … in particular, putting everything in writing.
    5 A … suggests confiding in a colleague
    6 B … demand exit interviews with top managers

Student's Book activities

Getting started
2   Suggested answers
    1 memo
    2 memo or email
    3 email or suggestion box
    4 interview
    5 memo or informal chat
    6 meeting
    7 note

Internal messages
Reading
1   1 C   2 B   3 A   4 C   5 A   6 D   7 B   8 B
2   1 D   2 B, C   3 B, C, D   4 A, B   5 C   6 C
    7 D

Writing
1   Suggested answers
1   Dear Max,
    Apologies for my lack of punctuality recently. This has unfortunately been due to roadworks on the way in to work, which are making journey times rather unpredictable at the moment and, although I'm leaving home earlier, sometimes I'm delayed in traffic jams for as much as 40 mins.
    Can I suggest that we start team meetings half an hour later from now on? This should ensure that no one is kept waiting.
    Best wishes,
    Angela
2   Hi, Mohammed,
    Thanks for this summary of our meeting. Just a brief note to say that there are a couple of things which I think we agreed slightly differently:
    • Staff will have Fri p.m. free from 2 p.m. onwards.
    • We agreed to one more part-time post to provide extra cover at peak times and on Saturday mornings.
    Do call me if you'd like to discuss this further.
    Best wishes,
    Jenny
3   Janice – envelopes as requested – haven't posted letters 'cos I've got an urgent meeting. Phil fixed yr printer – it was unplugged!
    Cheers – Carl
4   Dear Melanie,
    I would be interested in attending the coffee morning on Thursday for the delegation from the Haneul Corporation. This is because I am hoping in the future to form part of our sales team in East Asia.
    Although I am not a member of the management team, I wonder if it would be possible for me to do so.
    Yours,

Vocabulary
1   1 Best wishes   2 minutes   3 please   4 could
    5 your (can also be year, but not here)
    6 as soon as possible   7 Personal Assistant
    8 Chief Executive Officer
2   1 reference   2 Further   3 Good; input   4 know
    5 note   6 answer   7 advance   8 details
    9 hearing

Grammar workshop: *future simple or future continuous?*
1   Future simple: will help (A), will advertise (B), will … know (D), will all make (D), will include (D)
    Future continuous: will be visiting (D), shall also be showing (D), will be meeting (D)

Answer key

2 1 d   2 b/c   3 c/b   4 a

3 1 d   will be visiting, shall also be showing,
            will be meeting
   2 b   will advertise, will include
   3 c   will help, will all make
   4 a   will … know

Advice for communicating with colleagues
Listening
1 Larry: **G**   Marina: **D** or **H**   Magdi: **A**   Thérèse: **B**

Vocabulary
1 overdo   2 knock off   3 barging into   4 query
5 courtesy   6 overworked

Writing
2 Suggested answers
Task A

> To: Customer Services Department
> From: Customer Services Manager
> Subject: Change to customer complaints procedure
>
> Dear colleagues
> Following a couple of incidents last month where customer-service staff gave inappropriate replies to customer complaints, I have decided to change the procedure for handling such complaints. In future, the procedure will be as follows:
> 1 Staff will continue to reply to written complaints in writing, but all replies must be signed by me personally. This is to ensure that answers to customer complaints and suggestions are handled in the same way and written in the same style. As you know, model letters are available on file for you to use when drafting your reply.
> 2 Spoken complaints, either when talking directly to customers or by telephone, will be dealt with following existing procedures.
> Thank you for your co-operation in this matter. Please let me know if you have any further suggestions for improvements in procedures.
> GC

> To: Giovanni Castelli
> From: Franz Craven
> Subject: Change to customer complaints procedure
>
> Dear Giovanni
> With reference to your memo about changes to the customer complaints procedure, could I just point out that many staff will probably find these changes demotivating, as it appears we cannot be trusted to handle complaints responsibly? I would also like to point out that the incidents in question were the fault of one temporary member of staff who is now no longer with us and therefore the change is not necessary.
> May I suggest instead that all written complaints are handled by permanent members of the customer-service team, rather than temporary workers?
> Best wishes
> Franz

Task B

> To: Nagwa Moulid
> From: Kamal Salim
> Subject: Post of Human Resources Manager
>   (Recruitment)
>
> Dear Nagwa
> As you may know, the HR Department is advertising internally for a Human Resources Manager responsible for recruitment. Although I'm happy working in my present department, I'd like to apply for this post, as it represents an opportunity for promotion within the company and is also the type of challenging administrative post which I think I'm now ready for.
> The application form states that applications should be accompanied by recommendations from the applicant's line manager, and I'd be very grateful if you could do this for me.
> Many thanks
> Kamal

> To: Kamal Salim
> From: Nagwa Moulid
> Subject: Re: Post of Human Resources Manager
>   (Recruitment)
>
> Dear Kamal
> Thank you for this. I regret to say, however, that I don't consider you ready for the post you mention, as you've only been in your present post for six months. I believe, both for your own benefit and for the benefit of the department, it would be better if you stayed with us and built up your experience and competencies for at least another six months, after which time we could review the situation.

Answer key

I would be very happy to discuss this with you when I return next week. I'm sorry to give you this disappointing news and would like to add that I consider your work to be satisfactory and that you are a valuable member of our team.
Best wishes
Nagwa

Task C

Contract with Haneul Corporation
Following the very successful visit of the delegation from the Haneul Corporation last week, I'm delighted to announce that they have signed a contract with us for the purchase of 40 of our SN printing machines for a total price of €72 million, including installation and after-sales service. This is excellent news for the company, as it represents a major breakthrough for our marketing effort in East Asia. It will also allow us to expand our production facilities here at home, as we had hoped.
I would like to thank all of you for the part you played in landing this contract, both those who contributed directly to the marketing effort and negotiations with Haneul, and those of you who, through the high quality of your work, have made us the supplier of choice for Haneul.
On Friday lunchtime, we will be holding a brief celebration of this good news in the Directors' Boardroom. You are all most welcome to join us there.
Manfred Schüller
CEO

Dear Manfred,
Just a brief note to congratulate you on this important new contract. It really is splendid news! I'll be delighted to attend the celebration.
See you then,
Sofia

Transcript

5 Listening page 20

Trainer: So, we've seen a bit about how internal communications is quite a neglected area in business. Now I'd like to go over to you and ask you if you have any ideas how it can be improved. Larry, what about you?

Larry: Well, I guess we all have a tendency to overdo things a bit. I mean, we think we have to reply immediately to everything that comes in, and it becomes a bit of a time-waster, always sending off messages left, right and centre. I think it's probably better to have a fixed time – you know, that quiet time just after lunch or just before you knock off for the day – and deal with them then.

Trainer: Erm, well, possibly. I guess this might depend on the type of job you're doing. Er, still, that's something we can discuss in a minute. And you, Marina?

Marina: I'm very interested in the quality of the message – it says so much about the person – and if it's well written, it's a good deal easier to understand, so I'd say to people that they should avoid incomplete sentences or sentences without verbs – when writing, of course. Good English creates a good impression.

Trainer: Um, an interesting point and that's another one we can come back to. I mean, it might depend who you're writing to and what you're writing about. What's your advice, Magdi?

Magdi: Mine's a question of respect for colleagues and basic working formality. If you're busy, you can be sure that most of your colleagues are too, so they don't want you barging into their offices without warning with some minor query or being continually phoned up. Let them get on with their work and, if they're not urgent, save your queries for coffee time.

Trainer: Um, thanks, Magdi, that's partly a time-management question, isn't it? Er, now you, Thérèse?

Thérèse: I just think common courtesy is such an important part of office life – greeting people when you arrive at the office, not losing your temper or shouting at people, however overworked you may feel. You have to work with each other and you might as well make the circumstances as pleasant as possible.

Trainer: Um, I absolutely agree ... um, so now let's take those points one by one and see how you all feel about them. Now, the first one was about ...

UNIT 4 Chairing meetings

This unit presents language functions and vocabulary for chairing business meetings.

Although none of the tasks in the unit exactly replicate exam questions, some are designed to give students the skills and practice needed to deal with them (see table below).

	BEC	BULATS
Reading: *Advice for chairs*	Reading Part 4	Reading Part 2 Section 2
Listening: *Key phrases for chairs*	Listening Part 2	Listening Part 2
Speaking: *Holding meetings*	Speaking Part 3	Speaking Part 3
Reading: *Summarising action points*	Reading Part 6	Reading Part 2 Section 2
Writing: *Summarising action points*		Writing Part 1
Photocopiable activity	Reading Part 6 Writing Part 1 Speaking Part 3 Speaking Part 2	Reading Part 2 Section 2 Writing Part 1 Speaking Part 3 Speaking Part 2

Notes on unit

Getting started
Chairman has been replaced by the non-gender-specific (but slightly clumsy) *chairperson* or the increasingly popular term *chair*.

Reading: *Advice for chairs*
Before doing this activity, ask students:
• if they ever chair meetings / have chaired meetings
• what mistakes chairs make.
Ask them to form groups and discuss what general advice they would give to people who are going to chair meetings.
   When they finish, they can check the text to see if their ideas coincide.

Speaking: *Holding meetings*
Make sure students spend two or three minutes preparing before they hold each meeting to ensure that they practise the language which has just been presented and that the meetings are more realistic.
   If you are pressed for time, some of the meetings can be put off to a later class.

Vocabulary: *Holding meetings*
An alternative approach is to ask students:
• to work in groups and brainstorm ways of evaluating meetings
• what comments people often make after meetings, e.g. 'It was a waste of time', 'It was really useful', and ask them to think of others.

Writing: *Summarising action points*
This exercise can be given for homework if you wish. Tell students to invent action points if necessary (in case the meeting they chaired did not produce any).

Photocopiable activity
The case study is intended to integrate a number of different skills. It will take up to 90 minutes of class time.
   For the discussion of the agenda, you could act as chair or secretary and note the points for the agenda on the board.
   For the role-play, if there are not enough students to form groups of six, drop Role F first and then Role E.

Photocopiable activity

Getting started

1 Work in small groups. Read this statement, then brainstorm a list of things bosses (don't) do which cause people to leave companies.

'Studies show that 70 to 80 per cent of the reasons why people leave companies are related to bosses.'

2 Discuss this question.

Which is more important: keeping bosses or keeping workers?

Reading and writing

Spenfeld is a high-technology company specialising in printing, graphic design and software solutions for industry. It employs 2,500 people, generally highly skilled, in offices in many countries in Asia and Europe. Its head office is in Copenhagen, Denmark. At its divisional headquarters for Eastern Europe, based in Krakow, Poland, the following confidential memo has recently been circulated.

1 Read the memo. In most lines, there is one extra word. Write the extra word in the space provided. If a line is correct, put a tick (✓).

From:	HR Director	**To:**	Management team
Subject:	Highly confidential: staffing problems **Attachments:**		Chart 1.xls, Chart 2.xls, Table.xls

Dear all,
Please see the attached charts and accompanying report which they show   1 *they*
figures for staff turnover in our company, with particular attention is being   2 ....
paid to our Bratislava office. As a result of these figures, I have recently been   3 ....
conducting the exit interviews with staff who are leaving in order to   4 ....
determine the reasons for the high turnover.   5 ....
   As you are all made aware, staff turnover represents a significant cost to our   6 ....
organisation because in terms of loss of skilled workers and recruitment   7 ....
expenses. However, I should add that in Bratislava, we are experiencing   8 ....
difficulties in recruiting people of the calibre we require them.   9 ....
   I would also like to point it out that in February of last year, our very   10 ....
experienced managing director at Bratislava, Birgit Larsen, who was   11 ....
promoted to Head Office and replaced by Simon Horvak. This fact may have   12 ....
a bearing on to the attached table.   13 ....
   I suggest that we ought hold a meeting next week to review the situation and   14 ....
consider our options. What I suggest Wednesday at 9.30 a.m. In the   15 ....
meantime, I would welcome making any comments.   16 ....
   I would like to remind that you to treat this matter as strictly confidential.   17 ....

Many thanks,

Gizela Dembkowski
Gizela Dembkowski
Human Resources Director

2 Write a brief email to Gizela confirming that you will be attending the meeting.

Photocopiable activity

Speaking and reading

1 Work in pairs. Study these charts. Discuss what they show.

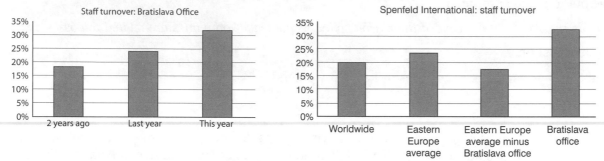

2 Complete this extract from Gizela's report by writing one word in each space.

Staff turnover at Bratislava office

Staff turnover in Bratislava has risen steeply over the **1** ………… three years from 18 per cent two years ago, **2** ………… was below average for our company, to 32 per cent this year, which is well **3** ………… average. This is also true **4** ………… comparison with our organisation worldwide, **5** ………… staff turnover stands **6** ………… 20 per cent, and in relation **7** ………… our East European offices, **8** ………… average is 22 per cent including Bratislava and just 17 per cent **9** ………… Bratislava.

Speaking and writing

1 Work in pairs. Study this table and discuss what it shows.

Reasons for leaving Spenfeld International Results of exit interviews				
Main reason	**Bratislava**		**Eastern Europe average**	
	this year	last year	this year	last year
Personal reasons	18%	24%	47%	38%
Working conditions in general*	22%	31%	33%	28%
Dissatisfaction with management**	56%	35%	10%	16%
Other reasons	4%	10%	10%	18%

* including: offered better salary elsewhere, better working conditions elsewhere

** including: limited career options, lack of responsibility, lack of recognition for work, etc.

2 Write the extract from Gizela's report for this table. Use the extract above as a model.

3 Discuss and agree on an agenda for the management meeting with the whole class.

Role-play

You are going to hold a management meeting to discuss the situation at the Bratislava office.

1 Work in groups of five or six. Study the agenda that you have just agreed on and each take one of the roles your teacher gives you.

2 When you finish, work with a partner from another group. Present the solution to the problem which your group came up with.

Role A: Head of Division, Spenfeld Eastern Europe

Your job is to chair the meeting. You should:
- start and administer the meeting
- keep the meeting focused
- make sure everyone has a chance to express their opinions
- summarise discussion and take the final decision.

Additional information
- You personally selected Simon Horvak for the job and would like to see him succeed.
- However, you are under pressure from Copenhagen to make the Bratislava office profitable.

Role B: Divisional Human Resources Director, Eastern Europe

You collected the information in the confidential memo. You should be prepared to present or repeat this information.

Additional information
- The cost of recruiting a new employee is on average €20,000.
- You have talked to other employees in Bratislava and you know that staff dissatisfaction is high – people don't feel empowered, they don't get recognition for their work.
- You would like to see the local manager, Simon Horvak, replaced.

Role C: Divisional Finance Officer

Until last year, Simon Horvak worked in your department. As well as being a colleague, he was a friend and you personally recommended him for the job.

Additional information
- You are convinced that Simon is a good, efficient manager.
- You believe a lot of the problems are because he has been introducing changes which are intended to make the Bratislava office more efficient.
- Under its previous manager, the Bratislava office was the least profitable in Eastern Europe. Profits have since fallen further, but you are convinced that in the next year or so, when the changes are implemented, they will rise again.

Role D: Marketing Director, Eastern Europe

You have worked closely with Simon Horvak on designing a new strategy for the Bratislava office. You know he takes a long-term view of the situation and you believe that, given time, he will implement the strategy successfully.

Additional information
- The Bratislava office has always been a problem for the marketing department because its products do not fit with general company style.
- Many of the products have been brilliant and innovative in the past, but difficult to sell.
- You hoped that the appointment last year of Simon Horvak would bring Bratislava into line with the rest of Eastern Europe and there are some signs that this is happening.
- While profitability at the Bratislava office may be falling, it is producing significant savings in the marketing budget.

Role E: Systems Director

You work quite closely with the Bratislava office on developing new software and other product lines.

Additional information
- You think Simon Horvak is an excellent technical worker (that is why he was originally promoted to a managerial position), but perhaps not a first-class manager because he is too hands-on and doesn't delegate enough.
- You like the input which Simon is bringing to the office and think that, with training and experience, he can learn to become a great manager.
- You also believe that it would be expensive to replace Simon, demoralising for other managers if you did so, and difficult to find an adequate replacement.

Role F: Chief Human Resources Director

You've noticed that the Divisional HR Director, who is your subordinate, tends to sympathise with staff more than management when there is a dispute.

Additional information
- You think that the high staff turnover in Bratislava may reflect the tight labour market in the area more than the situation in the Bratislava office.
- You would like to improve salaries and other benefits to attract and keep good workers.
- You would like to resolve the situation by sending Simon Horvak on a management training course.

Answer key

Photocopiable activity

Reading and writing

1 1 they 2 is 3 ✓ 4 the 5 ✓ 6 made
7 because 8 ✓ 9 them 10 it 11 who 12 ✓
13 to 14 ought 15 What 16 making 17 that

2 Sample answer
Dear Gizela,
Thanks for your memo with the attached charts
and report. I'll be happy to attend the meeting next
Wednesday at 9.30 and will offer my comments and
suggestions then.
Best wishes,

Speaking and reading

2 1 last/past 2 which 3 above 4 in 5 whose/
where 6 at 7 to 8 whose 9 excluding

Speaking and writing

2 Sample answer
During the last two years, we have conducted exit
interviews with all staff leaving our Eastern
European Division in order to ascertain their
reasons for leaving and to take suitable measures to
improve staff retention.
Our main findings are as follows:
• While last year 24% of those leaving our
Bratislava office did so for personal reasons, this
year that figure fell to 18%. This is in contrast to
the rest of Eastern Europe, where the figure
actually rose from 38% to 47%.
• Whereas last year 31% of staff leaving Bratislava
did so on account of working conditions, this figure
actually declined this year to 22%, unlike the rest
of Eastern Europe, where it rose from 28% to 33%.
• The most significant figure in Bratislava concerns
dissatisfaction with management, which 56% of
staff gave as their reason for leaving, as opposed
to 35% last year. In Eastern Europe as a whole,
this figure fell over the same period from 16% to
10%. Particular causes of dissatisfaction appear to
be limited career options, lack of responsibility
and lack of recognition for their work.
• In Bratislava, other reasons for leaving fell from
10% to 4%, while in Eastern Europe generally
they fell from 18% to 10%.
It seems therefore, in conclusion, that there is a
particular problem with management in the
Bratislava office which it would be advisable to
investigate and, if possible, remedy.

Student's Book activities

Advice for chairs

Reading

3 1 B 2 C 3 D 4 B 5 A 6 B 7 A 8 D
9 A 10 D 11 B 12 D

Key phrases for chairs

Listening

1 1 D 2 A 3 H 4 C 5 G

2 1 get 2 copy 3 minutes 4 purpose 5 views
6 sum 7 have 8 to 9 what 10 about
11 break 12 look 13 summary 14 other

4 Starting and managing a meeting: 1, 2, 3, 4, 10, 11,
12, 14
Asking for other opinions: 3, 5, 7
Keeping the meeting focused: 8
Summarising: 6, 9, 13

Holding meetings

Vocabulary

1 1 h 2 a 3 g 4 b 5 c 6 f 7 e 8 d

Summarising action points

Reading

1 to 2 also 3 more 4 were 5 correct 6 of 7
you 8 time 9 correct 10 at 11 intending
12 correct 13 down 14 made 15 up 16 for

GRAMMAR WORKSHOP 1

Defining and non-defining relative clauses

1 1 which 2 whose 3 –/that/which 4 which
5 –/that/which 6 who/whom 7 who/that
8 who 9 when 10 –/that/who/whom

2 1 Thank you for circulating the report (which/
that) you wrote.
2 The head of the department where I work would
like to discuss it with you.
3 She would like several of the marketing people
whose input you obtained to be present at the
meeting.
4 Could you suggest a time when it would be
convenient for us to meet?
5 Please pass my congratulations to Andy Drake,
who did the graphics.
6 The report contained a number of statistics
(which/that) I thought were surprising.
7 I had an interesting conversation with Maria
Kalitza, whose comments you included in the
conclusion.

Some meanings of as and like

1 as (a) 2 as (b) 3 as (a) 4 like (h) 5 as (g) 6 as (b)
7 like (h) 8 as (f) 9 like (i) 10 as (c) 11 as (d)

Future simple or future continuous?

1 will be giving 2 she'll make 3 will be producing
4 we'll be discussing

Transcripts

6 Listening page 23

1

Chair: OK, let's get started. Has everyone got a copy of the agenda?

Other participants: Yes. / Thanks.

Chair: Great. Would anyone like to take minutes, or shall we just keep a list of action points?

Piotr: Action points would be fine, Mat.

Chair: OK, Piotr, would you like to do that, then?

Piotr: Sure, no problem.

Chair: Thanks. So, anyway, thank you all for coming. The purpose of this meeting's to discuss how we go about investigating the East European market and seeing whether our products would have an outlet there, so the first point today is who should actually go and have a look around. I, personally, am pretty tied up till the end of May, so it might be better if it were someone else. Jane, could you give us your views on this?

Jane: Sure, thanks, Mat. Um, I honestly don't think it's that urgent. I mean, it can easily wait till June, which is less than a couple of months away and then we can make sure we have enough time …

7 **2**

Chair: So, if I could just sum up, what you think is that even if he hasn't been on time this time, as a customer he's too valuable to lose, so we should remind him, but in a very friendly and polite way.

Woman: That's right. I mean, he really does give us a lot of business, although as you can see from the books, if something doesn't happen soon, we're going to have problems with our cashflow. I mean, we've got our invoices to pay as well.

Chair: Point taken. Let's remind him and give him another week, then.

Woman: Fine.

Chair: Anything else to be said on this, or can we move on to the next point?

8 **3**

Salim: … so, quite frankly, I don't think it's good enough. I mean, we agreed to have the new procedures in place by the end of the month, which is in two weeks' time, and we're going to be nowhere near that target because the people responsible for training haven't even scheduled the training yet.

Chair: Thanks very much for that, Salim. Now, can we hear what other people have to say?

Woman: Yes, it's all very well to criticise, but we've had plenty of problems, you know. In my last job, people used to just criticise. I had a boss who …

Chair: Look, that's all very interesting, but can we keep to the issue in hand? The point is, there is a risk, and it would be bad to have an accident just when we've fallen behind with our training schedule, so let's get to the reasons for it and see how we can get things back on the rails.

9 **4**

Chair: … so, we clearly all agree on this, so let's not waste any more time and move on to point number five, which is whether the component really meets our specifications. Any thoughts on that? Anyone? Martin?

Martin: It clearly performs to specifications. All the tests I've run so far show that. It's just that we might have difficulty fitting it into the space we thought we had for it. It might mean we have to do a little bit of redesigning.

Chair: So, in a nutshell, what you think is that it's too large.

Martin: Well, it might be, but if they can't make it smaller, then we'll have to make do with it.

Liang: But that would add to our costs. I mean, redesigning our machine at this stage has all sorts of other implications.

Martin: I know, but the alternative is to source the component elsewhere, and I don't even know if that'll be possible.

Alex: I wonder whether it'd be worth it just for one relatively minor component.

Martin: Um, we'd have to look into that.

Chair: Well, we don't have to decide on this today. Let's think about it a bit more and come back to it if necessary next week. Now, let's take a five-minute break and then start on point number six.

10 **5**

Chair: So we need more information on this issue. Sandra, can you look into it for the next meeting?

Sandra: Sure.

Chair: So, in summary, we've agreed about where we're going to stay and Sandra's going to investigate prices, which potential customers we're inviting and what entertainment we're going to give them, so we're just left with the question of the timing of the event. Any ideas, anyone?

Man: Um, I don't think we want to get everyone together when it's too hot, so I guess spring would be most suitable.

Woman: Yes, because if we're going to do it in January or February, really that's too soon.

Man: Yes, if it was up to me, I'd go for April.

Chair: OK. Let's come to a quick decision on this. How many people are in favour of April? Five. Anyone against? No? Well, thanks all of you for your time. I think this has been very profitable, and we'll meet again to talk about the other points on Wednesday the 4th at the same time. See you all then.

UNIT 5 Customer relationships

This unit teaches language and vocabulary connected with customer relations and Customer Relationship Management (CRM). The unit concentrates particularly on reading skills.

Although none of the tasks in the unit exactly replicate exam questions, some are designed to give students the skills and practice needed to deal with them (see table below).

	BEC	BULATS
Getting started	Speaking Parts 1 & 2	Speaking Parts 1 & 2
Reading: *Problems with customer relations*	Reading Part 3	Reading Part 2 Section 5
Talking point: *Problems with customer relations*	Speaking Part 3	Speaking Part 3
Listening: *Customer Relationship Management*	Listening Part 1	Listening Part 2
Reading: *Customer Relationship Management*	Reading Part 1	Reading Part 2 Section 1
Talking point: *Customer Relationship Management*	Speaking Part 3	Speaking Part 3
Photocopiable activity	Writing Part 1	Speaking Parts 2 & 3
	Reading Part 2	Writing Part 1
	Speaking Parts 2 & 3	

Notes on unit

Getting started

Possibly before they open their books, elicit from students what different types of customers companies in general are likely to have, e.g. regular, occasional or one-time customers; private individuals, i.e. consumers, or corporate customers, etc.

Reading: *Problems with customer relations*

As a possible warmer to this reading activity, you can ask students:
- if they have ever phoned a company helpline
- whether this solved their problem
- what goods/services have given them problems in the past
- what methods companies have for solving the problems.

Talking point: *Problems with customer relations*

You could ask students these follow-up questions.
- Can you think of any other 80–20 rules, e.g. 20 per cent of customers generate 80 per cent of complaints? (The rules may be fictional.)
- Why is it so much more expensive to gain new customers than retain existing ones? (If students have experience of this, encourage them to talk about it.)

Listening: *Customer Relationship Management (CRM)*

Ask students to study the spaces first (perhaps in pairs) to try to predict the type of a) information and b) words they will need for each space.

A possible follow-up to this listening activity is to ask students what other applications of information technology they are familiar with, for example for:
- tracking shipments
- credit control
- processing orders
- keeping staff informed of developments.

Put students with similar knowledge in pairs to each prepare a short talk on the subject which they can then give to the rest of the class.

Photocopiable activity

This activity will probably take about two hours of class time and can be divided between two lessons if necessary.

Getting started

Imagine you work for Curiosity Tours, a travel company which organises tours to unusual destinations in Asia. Work in small groups. Brainstorm what sort of information it would be useful to have on your database about your customers. Then discuss how you could use this information.

Reading and writing

1 Read this information and label Charts 1 and 2.

Chart 1 shows our customers by age group. Our largest market is for people aged 66 and over, who make up 30% of our total customers. This is followed by 26–35-year-olds, who constitute 25% of our market. Our third most numerous category is 51–65-year-olds, who form 20% of the total, while 36–50-year-olds and 18–25-year-olds represent 15% and 10% of our customer base respectively.

Chart 2 shows that while 35% of our business comes from repeat customers, 65% are new customers.

Chart 1

Curiosity Tours
Customers by age group

18–25
1.............%

Over 66
5............%

26–35
2.............%

51–65
4   %

36–50
3............%

Chart 2

Curiosity Tours: Customers

6.............
35%

7...........
65%

2 Complete the paragraph below describing Chart 3 by writing a word from the box in each space. You can use some of the words more than once.

base	bring	constitute	finally	form	over
~~percentage~~	range	represent	total		

Chart 3

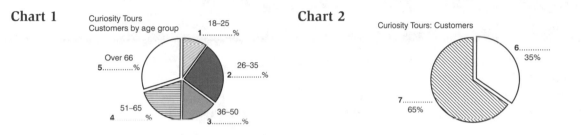

Curiosity Tours
Breakdown of customer base

customers by age group
revenues by age group

18–25 26–35 36–50 51–65 66+

Chart 3 compares our customers by age group and by the **1** _percentage_ of revenue which they **2** .... for the company. While the largest group of customers are aged 66 and **3** .... , they make up just 20% of our revenues. Similarly, although our second largest group, aged 26–35, **4** .... 25% of our customer base, they **5** .... in just 10% of our revenues. On the other hand, the 51–65 age **6** .... , who are 20% of our **7** .... customers, form 40% of our revenues, while the 36–50-year-old age group form 15% of our clients and 25% of our revenue. **8** .... , the 18–25-year-old age group, who **9** .... 10% of our customer **10** .... bring in just 5% of our revenue.

Chart 4

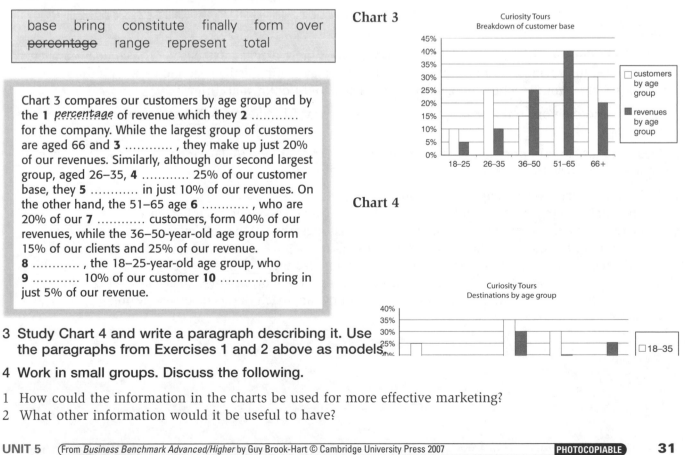

Curiosity Tours
Destinations by age group

18–35

3 Study Chart 4 and write a paragraph describing it. Use the paragraphs from Exercises 1 and 2 above as models.

4 Work in small groups. Discuss the following.

1 How could the information in the charts be used for more effective marketing?
2 What other information would it be useful to have?

Talking point 1

You recently employed a market-research firm to find out from customers why they were not booking further holidays with Curiosity Tours.

Read the comments below from some of the customers who were contacted and discuss:

- what Curiosity Tours could have done to keep each of these customers
- what Curiosity Tours should have done to avoid these problems.

1 *'There were several people on the bus which took us round Siberia who smoked heavily and spoiled the holiday for the rest of us.'*

2 *'I'm a vegetarian and I told them this when I booked the holiday, but when we were travelling around the Middle East, it was really difficult to get a completely vegetarian meal.'*

3 *'Curiosity Tours lost my luggage, so I had no change of clothes when I arrived in India. To make matters worse, no one even apologised.'*

4 *'We were promised first-class hotels, but quite frankly some of the accommodation was pretty low standard.'*

5 *'I have an intolerance to air-conditioning and I told them this when I booked. However, when I got to Indonesia, I found all the hotels had air-conditioning, and it really spoilt my holiday because I suffer badly from asthma.'*

6 *'The high point of our trip was supposed to be a visit to the Chen Hoon Teng Temple in Malaysia, but the weather turned bad and we never saw it. The holiday was a great disappointment to me.'*

> **Useful language**
> We could have laid on (a no-smoking bus if there had been sufficient demand for it).
> We should have steered them in the direction of (a no-smoking holiday).
> We should have advised them that (all first-class hotels in Indonesia are air-conditioned). There's little we could have done about (the weather in Malaysia).

Reading

The board of directors has asked you to investigate how a more detailed database of the company's clients could be used to provide a more effective marketing strategy and particularly to increase the numbers of repeat customers. Your teacher will give you an article about Continental Airlines.

1 **Skim the article your teacher gives you to find out what Continental Airlines' customer service strategies consist of.**

2 **Read the article and complete it by choosing the best sentence (A–G) for each space. There is one sentence you will not need.**

A Before, the person who complained the loudest got the best service.

B Continental's bottom line has not been made healthier by competition from low-cost rivals.

C In fact, Continental says that revenue from those passengers who received letters jumped 8 per cent.

D Not only that, the data staff didn't know what to tell them.

E Now, when a cancellation or delay occurs, the system does the work for them.

F The airline thinks being proactive will mitigate passengers' annoyance over their bags being lost.

G Armed with this information, flight attendants can now approach these customers during the flight to apologise for the inconveniences.

Getting to know them

Wouldn't it be nice if, just once, one of those airline employees offered an apology for losing your luggage or for a delayed flight? If you fly first class with Continental Airlines, you may finally get that apology.

Since 2001, the airline has been enhancing the in-flight reports it provides to flight attendants with more detailed information on passengers. For example, in addition to indicating which passengers ordered special meals, the expanded reports flag the airline's high-value customers and detail such things as whether they've had their luggage lost in the recent past or experienced a delayed flight. **1** ...... Such personalised service increases customer loyalty, particularly among Continental's most valuable patrons, and that loyalty in turn drives revenue. Continental categorises customers into different levels of profitability: since building its new system, the airline reports earning an average of $200 in revenue on each of its 400,000 valuable customers, and an additional $800 in revenue from each of the 35,000 customers it places in its most profitable tier – all because it accords them better service.

The company has used its data systems to determine if customer loyalty initiatives really affect revenue. By testing a sample of 30,000 customers who experienced delays, Continental found that those individuals to whom the airline sent a letter of apology and some sort of compensation (either in the form of a free cocktail on their next flight or extra frequent flier miles) forgot the event and didn't hold a grudge. **2** ......

When members of Continental's data staff first approached gate agents with freshly minted info on the company's most valuable customers, the airport staffers didn't understand how they could use this information. **3** ...... So after doing some research, the data staff went back to the drawing board armed with new insights about the work the gate agents do and the pressures they're under.

The data team developed a solution to one of the biggest headaches gate agents face: accommodating passengers inconvenienced by a cancellation or delay. The team created a program that automates the rebooking process. Before the program was developed, gate agents had to figure out on their own how to reroute passengers. **4** ...... For example, when the system identifies a high-value customer whose flight has been cancelled, the gate agent may decide to put that traveller on a competitor's flight just to make the individual happy and to get him on his way as fast as possible.

Currently, Continental is trying to use customer and operational data to come up with a way for flight attendants to get information about baggage that's been mislaid and to inform passengers while they're still on the plane that their luggage has gone astray. **5** ...... If flight attendants have a way to tell an individual not to bother going to baggage claim and to take the person's address so that Continental can send her suitcase when it arrives, the airline will save that person the time and frustration associated with filing a claim for lost luggage.

'**6** ...... Now our most valuable customers get the best service,' says Alicia Acebo, Continental's data director. That strategy is helping the company narrow its losses during a period of great instability in the airline industry.

From *CIO Magazine*

Talking point 2

1 Work in groups of four. Read the article and discuss these questions.

- What parts of Continental Airlines' experience with CRM (Customer Relationship Management) could be used by Curiosity Tours to their advantage?
- How could CRM be used to deal with the problems which arose in Talking point 1?
- Which customers should Curiosity Tours target for this kind of treatment?

2 Change groups and take turns to present your ideas. Decide which ideas are the best.

Task tip
Before you present your ideas, make a few brief notes of the main points you want to make. Then present your ideas to your group, referring to your notes from time to time.

Writing

Write a memo to the board of directors in which you present your main ideas for increasing the number of repeat customers.

Useful language
One thing that might be worth considering is …
I would also strongly recommend + –ing
It might be a good idea to …
A further suggestion would be to …
I would suggest you look into + –ing
You might also consider + –ing

Answer key

Photocopiable activity

Getting started
Useful information for database:
- Where customers have been with Curiosity Tours before
- Age, tastes, any previous complaints
- Vegetarian, non-smoker, etc.
- How much they have spent on previous trips
- Addresses
- Retired or working

How this information could be used:
- Target customers for specific publicity
- Tailor holidays for existing customers
- Advise them on holiday choices
- Determine prices of holidays
- Avoid incompatibilities between different customers on the same tour

Reading and writing
1 1 10%   2 25%   3 15%   4 20%   5 30%
   6 repeat customers   7 new customers
2 1 percentage   2 represent   3 over
   4 form/constitute/represent   5 bring   6 range
   7 total   8 Finally   9 represent/form/constitute
   10 base
3 Sample answer
   South-East Asia is the most popular destination for all our customers, as it is chosen by 35% of those under 35 and 30% of those aged 36 and over. Our second most popular destination for the younger age range is India, which attracts 30% of customers under 36, but only 20% of those aged 36 and over. On the other hand, older customers prefer Central Asia, where 25% of them choose to go. This contrasts with the 18–35 age range, only 5% of whom opt for this destination. The Middle East attracts 25% of the younger age range and just 15% of the older age range. The least popular destination is Siberia and Mongolia, with just 5% and 10% of those age ranges respectively.
4 Suggested answers
   1 • by designing holidays to fit these tastes
      • adapting holidays and activities to suit age ranges
      • targeting customers with specific publicity
      • investigating how to increase the proportion of repeat customers
   2 • a breakdown of how much different ages of customers spend per holiday

- information about what attracted groups of customers to buy particular packages
- reasons why customers do/don't repeat bookings with Curiosity Tours

Talking point 1
Suggested answers
1 Curiosity Tours could have organised smoking and no-smoking buses/holidays. They should have pointed out in advance that it was a smoking bus.
2 They should have informed the restaurants in advance, or they should have told the customer that this was going to be problematic.
3 They could at least have apologised and helped the customer to re-equip himself/herself with clothes.
4 Something went wrong with the quality-control system. Curiosity Tours should double-check the quality of the hotels and make sure they are up to client expectations, or else warn customers that hotel star ratings are not the same in all countries.
5 They should have discouraged this particular customer from taking this particular holiday.
6 Here the only possibility is if there are alternative activities available for when the weather is not suitable, and to warn customers that the company is not responsible for cancellations due to circumstances beyond its control, such as the weather.

Reading
2 1 G   2 C   3 D   4 E   5 F   6 A

Student's Book activities

Getting started
Suggested answers
1 a loyalty, information about future needs
   b after-sales service, information about product updates
   c cost savings, personalised treatment
2 Other activities can include: interactive websites, after-sales services, call centres and helpdesks, regular updates on products by direct mail or email, loyalty cards, discounts for existing customers, clubs and competitions

Problems with customer relations
Reading
3 1 B (the whole paragraph)
   2 C … and that gap is the next big business opportunity.

Answer key

3 A When firms cut costs, … they put pressure on frontline staff who handle complaints, cutting the time each call-centre operative is allowed to spend on a pacifying call

4 D The difficulty begins with companies promising customers support that they cannot deliver. Electronic networks mean that firms now know more about their customers than ever before, so they believe that they can treat customers as individuals.

5 D … because it knows that retaining existing customers costs far less than recruiting new ones.

6 B That depends on whether consumers are willing to pay for support.

Vocabulary

1 helpdesk   2 shipped   3 reliability   4 handle
5 retaining   6 outsourcing   7 redundant

Customer Relationship Management (CRM)

Listening

2 1 profitability   2 (their) competitors
    3 information systems   4 (marketing) budget
    5 sales process   6 loyalty (and) satisfaction
    7 (the) Internet

Reading

3 1 E Such an organisational structure makes it difficult to comprehend the total value of a customer and therefore can't capture important opportunities such as cross-selling.

2 A While providing customer service, clever companies are also gathering data on their customers' buying habits and needs

3 D (the whole extract)

4 B It simply can't be the 'project of the month'.

5 A … businesses can transform themselves into the proverbial friendly general store – to provide the same levels of customer service that were typical decades ago.

6 A … with the ultimate aim of turning consumers into customers for life.

7 C The customer is more interested in service than the technology that delivers it.

8 D While investors implicitly value product-development and R&D expenditures, considering them assets that are potentially useful over a long period of time, they undervalue marketing and customer-acquisition costs.

Interviewer: Boris Shulov, we hear a lot nowadays about Customer Relationship Management, or CRM for short. Can you tell us what it is?

Boris: Er, yes, in simple terms, Customer Relationship Management is the process of integrating marketing, sales and after-sales service within a business or other organisation with the objective of ensuring that customer relationships generate maximum profitability for the company. While, in the process, maintaining and enhancing those relationships. In other words, by working on these relationships, we can produce more revenues for the company and provide a mechanism which permits companies to stand out or differentiate themselves from their competitors. What I mean by this is that nowadays, as we all know, the products companies produce are frequently almost identical – at least in the eyes of the consumer – and what gives a company a competitive edge is the difference in the quality of service it offers.

Interviewer: This is achieved largely by the use of computer technology, isn't it?

Boris: Um, that's right. At the centre of CRM are information systems; with computer technology, it's now possible to store and transmit huge amounts of data about individual customers – you know, their preferences, their free-time activities, the make-up of their families and any other details which you think are interesting or useful. And all this information can, at least theoretically, be acted upon by organisations to give their customers personalised individual treatment. Er, to give you a … rather basic example, your customer, Mrs X, buys cosmetics from you. You know from information you have gathered that she has a teenage daughter. Perhaps she'd also like to buy cosmetics for her daughter – you could interest her in a younger range of products maybe.

Interviewer: In which areas of an organisation is CRM most likely to be used?

Boris: Well, clearly in those areas which have most contact with customers. Er, to give you a few details, er, there's Marketing Automation, which allows you to concentrate your marketing efforts on your most profitable customers and manage your campaigns so that your marketing budget is spent in the most cost-efficient and profitable way. Er, you've perhaps heard of the 20–80 rule, which says that 20% of your customers generate 80% of your profits. The common-sense conclusion to be drawn from this statistic is that we should be spending a larger proportion of our marketing budget on that 20% of customers to keep them happy, to encourage them to spend more with us – and proportionately less on the remaining 80%.

Interviewer: Interesting. I've also heard of Sales Automation. Er, can you explain for all of us what that is?

Boris: Sure. Sales Automation is information systems providing key back-up for the sales process, for example, products a particular customer has bought in the past, discounts they've been given, problems that have arisen when selling to that client, etc. All this makes the sales staff's task much easier. They can offer similar discounts; they're not going to make a mess by offering a far larger or far smaller one – at least, not unless it's part of an informed strategy. They know about problems which have arisen in the past and they can avoid irritating the customer by repeating them. Then there's the final area …

Interviewer: Customer Service, isn't it?

Boris: That's right.

Interviewer: Can you explain it a little, please?

Boris: Yeah, Customer Service, as a part of CRM, is being able to deal efficiently with problems and queries when they arise in such a way that they actually enhance the customer's feelings of loyalty and satisfaction. After all, the main thrust of CRM is to have loyal and satisfied customers. These are the ones who are most profitable to a company and who pass the company's reputation on by word of mouth to other potential customers.

Interviewer: The process must be very complex. How is all this data collected and transmitted with a large organisation?

Boris: The most normal way nowadays is via the Internet because this allows both employees and customers to access information and communicate with each other efficiently.

Interviewer: Very interesting. But, I wonder, do organisations manage to handle these vast amounts of data efficiently and effectively? I would have thought these systems are fraught with pitfalls.

6 Competitive advantage

This unit teaches language and vocabulary connected with a company gaining advantage over its competitors, particularly with pricing. The unit also introduces grammar connected with expressing hypothetical ideas (which is developed further in the Grammar workshop).

Although none of the tasks in the unit exactly replicate exam questions, some are designed to give students the skills and practice needed to deal with them (see table below).

	BEC	BULATS
Listening: *Submitting tenders*	Listening Part 1	Listening Part 2
Speaking: *Submitting tenders*	Speaking Part 2	Speaking Part 2
Reading: *Submitting tenders*	Reading Part 5	Reading Part 2 Section 3
Listening: *Winning contracts*	Listening Part 3	Listening Part 4
Talking point: *Winning contracts*	Speaking Part 3	Speaking Part 3
Photocopiable activity 1	Reading Part 1	Reading Part 2 Section 1
Photocopiable activity 2	Speaking Part 2	Speaking Part 2

Notes on unit

Getting started

If your students have the Personal Study Book, and are experiencing problems with vocabulary in this exercise, you can refer them to the Word list.

In answer to the question 'Which do you think is the most effective?', the most logical answer is perhaps, 'It depends'. Ask students what it depends on and tell them to suggest examples to back up their cases.

Listening: *Submitting tenders*

When students have done the listening exercise, play it again and ask them to follow the transcript. This will help them to see how the questions are constructed paraphrasing the speaker's actual words: you can ask students to compare the words of the questions with the speaker's words.

An interesting point made during the interview is how Gifford tries to project an image of quality through the quality of its documents. This is a point which, after the listening activity, you could develop into a class discussion. You could ask:

- In what way can quality documents reflect quality engineering or quality products and services?
- What implications does this have for learning Business English? (Perhaps the quality of your employees' English and other languages reflects the quality of the company's products and services.)

Speaking: *Submitting tenders*

In both the BEC exam and the BULATS test, candidates are asked to speak for one minute to answer a question.

It is worth pointing out that this activity reflects a very real business requirement.

As a warmer, you could ask students to brainstorm occasions when business people might have to speak/present for a minute or more, e.g. when answering a question from a visiting journalist or when answering a job interview question.

Reading: *Submitting tenders*

As a warmer for this exercise, ask students what sort of companies have to submit tenders for contracts and what steps are involved (or what steps they imagine are involved). If students are working, ask them if any of them have experience of preparing tenders.

Listening: *Winning contracts*

The bridge featured in the photographs has an interesting website at http://www.gateshead.gov.uk/leisure%20 and%20Culture/bridge/Background.aspx for students who want to find out more.

Talking point: *Winning contracts*

This section asks students hypothetical questions, which they have just studied in the Grammar workshop. It's worth pointing this out, and encouraging them to speak in hypothetical terms where appropriate.

UNIT 6 Competitive advantage   **37**

Getting started

Discuss these questions in small groups.

1 Which of these is most important when deciding what price to give a product?
- covering costs
- what the market will bear
- competitors' prices
- maximising profits
- giving the customer a good deal
- signalling quality
- maximising sales
- giving distributors a good deal
- attracting new customers

2 Decide on the right retail price for these items.

a **New mid-range car from Ford**
- Costs of production, distribution and marketing per unit: €7,000
- Equivalent Volkswagen retails at €15,000
- Equivalent Daewoo retails at €8,000

b **200g perfume**
- Costs per unit: €1.50
- Equivalent drugstore's own brand retails at €3
- Equivalent from Chanel retails at €50

Reading

1 Work in pairs. Read these sentences and check that you understand them.

1 Attention to pricing can have a greater effect on profitability than attention to costs.   [B]
2 Cutting prices often entails extra expenses. [ ]
3 Information technology has led to downward pressure on prices. [ ]
4 It is not necessarily correct to reduce prices during slumps. [ ]
5 Most companies do not use the software available to help determine prices. [ ]
6 Prices are likely to rise less regularly in the future. [ ]
7 Prices can also be increased using methods which confuse the purchaser. [ ]
8 Pricing policy is being affected by increased competition. [ ]
9 Some companies increase prices by adding extra accessories. [ ]

2 Read these four paragraphs. Match each of the sentences from Exercise 1 with one of the paragraphs.

A

Raising prices is likely to remain tough, even as the world economy rebounds. Inflation is likely to remain low in rich countries, for several reasons. Globalisation has increased the number of competitors. The Internet has made it easier for buyers to shop around and to compare prices. The euro has made prices more transparent in Europe, even if consumers worry that retailers have used its introduction to mark up their goods. And big buyers, such as Wal-Mart, are squeezing ever more from their suppliers. The days of annual (upward) revisions to price lists look to be over.

B

Most bosses still worry more about their overheads than about the prices they charge. One survey found that managers spent less than 10% of their time on pricing. Henry Vogel of the Boston Consulting Group likes to remind clients that raising prices by 1% can boost profits by up to four times as much as a 1% cut in overheads. Today's managers, unlike those emerging from previous recessions, have no end of fancy technology to help them. Supermarket chains, for example, can quickly and easily track customers' 'elasticity' – how their buying habits change in response to a price rise or a discount. But although firms can now measure this sort of thing in a more sophisticated way, basic rules of thumb are still the most common way of setting price.

C

A popular – and rather crude – technique is hidden or 'stealth' increases. Mr Vogel points to car companies, which may charge extra for features such as anti-lock brakes and passenger-side airbags, instead of offering them as standard features. A slightly more subtle approach is to offer a huge menu of margin-enhancing financing schemes. Give your customer plenty of choices, and he will struggle to find the deal with the cheapest price.

D

Better organisation has helped some consumer-goods companies to set prices. Martin Smith of Whirlpool, an American white-goods maker, says his company overhauled its pricing two years ago by thinking of prices themselves as a product, much like a dishwasher. Despite the recession, when steep price cuts looked like the only way to go, Whirlpool last year reduced the frequency of its discounts, which it says are costly to communicate to salespeople, and can confuse customers if they are changed too often.

From
The Economist

3 Read the article again and answer these questions in your own words.

1 What pressures are there on companies to keep their prices low?
2 What relationship between prices, overheads and profits is mentioned?
3 What methods for deciding prices are mentioned, and which is the most popular?
4 How do car companies go about raising prices?
5 How did Whirlpool avoid introducing price reductions?

Vocabulary

Find words or phrases in the extracts which mean the following.

1 look for the best deal (extract A)
2 increase the price of (extract A)
3 forcing better and better deals from (extract A)
4 the regular and necessary costs involved in operating a business (extract B)
5 a lot of (extract B)
6 follow someone's progress (extract B)
7 practical and approximate ways of doing something (extract B)
8 simple and not skilfully done (extract C)
9 improving the profit that can be made after the costs have been subtracted (extract C)
10 improved something so that it worked better (extract D)

Talking point

Discuss these questions.

• How important is the price for you when you are deciding whether to buy a product or not?
• Does it depend on whether the product is something essential or a luxury?
• Do you look at the price more when the purchase is something big, such as a car, or when it is some small, everyday item?
• How does your company (or a company you know well) go about setting prices?
• Have you ever stopped buying something because the manufacturer put up the price?
• Do you ever buy things because they are more expensive?

Photocopiable activity 2   The competitive advantage game

Work in groups of four. Each of you is the manager of one of four large upmarket luxury hotels situated in the country beside a clean blue lake and surrounded by spectacular mountains. You all compete fiercely for the same customers. You have all been invited to a radio programme where you get points for explaining how you can gain a competitive advantage.

Rules

1 You need a die and counters.

2 The person who throws the highest number starts.

3 When you land on a square which says **Talk**, you must talk for one minute to answer the question given. During your talk you must:

  • express up to three ideas

  • give a reason for each idea

  • give an example for each idea.

4 The other players will listen and give you 1 point for each idea, 1 point for each reason, and 1 point for each example. Maximum points per talk = 9.

5 If you land on another square, add the points it gives.

6 If you land on a square where someone has already given a talk, move to the next square. Don't repeat the talk.

7 The winner is the person who achieves the highest score when everyone has passed **Finish**.

From *Business Benchmark Advanced/Higher* by Guy Brook-Hart © Cambridge University Press 2007   PHOTOCOPIABLE   UNIT 6

Photocopiable activity 2   The competitive advantage game

1 START	**2** Explain how a good location can give a hotel a competitive advantage. TALK	**3** Your hotel has been chosen for a business conference. Add 4 points and go to square 7.	**4** Fire in the kitchen. Go back to square 1.	**5**
10 How can a hotel achieve an edge over its competitors by being environmentally friendly? TALK	**9** Receptionist shouts at a guest. Go back to square 7.	**8** Your restaurant has been given five forks in a respected guide. Add 10 points and go to square 17.	**7**	**6** Marlon Brando once stayed at your hotel. Add 1 point and go to square 11.
11	**12** How can a manager motivate his/her staff to excel? TALK	**13** A guest saw a rat in the restaurant. Go back to square 7.	**14** Your hotel has been mentioned in a celebrity gossip magazine. Add 6 points and go to square 21.	**15** The printers have not delivered your brochure on time. Miss a turn.
20 How can proximity to your principal markets give you a competitive advantage? TALK	**19**	**18** Your hotel has been chosen for a political conference. Go back to square 11.	**17** Explain how attracting celebrity guests can give a hotel an advantage. TALK	**16** Your hotel has won the *Best-Kept Hotel Garden* competition. Add 2 points and go to square 21.
21	**22** How can CSR be used by a hotel to its advantage? TALK	**23** Your cook has been headhunted by one of your competitors. Go back to square 19.	**24** Your barman has been named Barman of the Year. Add 3 points and go to square 30.	**25** How can the latest technology give a hotel a competitive advantage? TALK

30	**29** Your hotel has been chosen for the opening night of a film festival. Add 10 points and go to square 35.	**28** There's a glitch in your wireless Internet connection. Go back to square 21.	**27** How can you achieve a competitive advantage by exceeding your customers' expectations?	**26** Problems with the air-conditioning in the indoor tennis court. Go back to square 21.
31 How can you go about recruiting staff who will put your hotel ahead of the competition?	**32** Fire inspectors give your hotel the thumbs down. Go back to square 21.	**33** You change the décor of your hotel every two years. Add 6 points and go to square 39.	**34** Real Madrid are going to use your hotel for their summer training camp. Add 5 points and go to square 42.	**35**
40 How can you train staff to give the sort of service which gives a competitive advantage?	**39**	**38** Your hotel features in a published list of the 100 best companies to work for. Add 3 points and go to square 44.	**37**	**36** How can you turn customer feedback to your advantage?
41 Your best rooms are being redecorated. Miss a turn.	**42**	**43** How can a hotel use special events to gain a better reputation?	**44**	**45** Your hotel has featured in a Sunday newspaper. Add 4 points and go to square 50.
50	**49** How does being different from one's competitors give a hotel an advantage?	**48**	**47** In what ways can the quality of your company literature give your hotel an advantage over the competition?	**46** Your staff are unhappy because your competitors pay 10% more. Go back to square 42.

Photocopiable activity 2   The competitive advantage game

51 A journalist from another Sunday newspaper visited your hotel, but she didn't include it in her article. Miss a turn.	**52** A famous international design company are using your hotel to show their spring collection. Add 5 points and go to square 57.	**53** Your hotel is the venue for a vintage car rally. Add 1 point and go to square 57.	**54**	**55** You've just added a golf course to your facilities. Add 8 points and go to square 63.
60 Is price a key factor in giving a luxury product a competitive edge? TALK	**59** Your hotel appeared in a dance competition on television. Add 2 points and go to square 68.	**58** Hollywood megastar Penelope Smith had her diamonds stolen from her room. Go back to square 48.	**57**	**56** What factors do you need to consider when pricing your hotel to give it a competitive advantage?
61 A scene from a blockbuster movie is being filmed by your swimming pool. Go to square 73.	**62** Your hotel is the first one people come to when they drive down to the lake. Add 6 points and go to square 72.	**63**	**64** What promotional activities could a hotel use to give itself an edge over the competition?	**65** The roof has been blown off the hotel in a storm. Go back to square 50.
70 What part does word-of-mouth play in keeping a hotel ahead of the pack? TALK	**69** You allow smoking in the bar and restaurant. Guests complain. Go back to square 63.	**68**	**67** Why is market research essential to competitive advantage? TALK	**66** Which three facilities at your hotel do you think are most important for attracting more customers than your competitors?
71 What types of publicity are most effective in attracting more visitors to stay at a luxury hotel?	**72**	**73**	**74** What sort of staff give a hotel a competitive advantage? TALK	**75** Add 10 points to your score if you arrived first. FINISH

Answer key

Photocopiable activity 1

Reading
2 1 B   2 D   3 A   4 D   5 B   6 A   7 C   8 A
   9 C
3 Suggested answers
   1 Increased competition due to globalisation, the
      ability of customers to compare prices using the
      Internet, the increased transparency of prices in
      Europe following the introduction of the euro,
      and pressure from supermarkets on their
      providers.
   2 A 1% price increase can increase profits by four
      times the increase generated by a 1% reduction
      in costs.
   3 Computer technology for tracking customers'
      changes in buying habits in response to price
      changes and discounts, and rule of thumb. The
      latter is the most popular.
   4 By making customers pay for extra non-
      standard features when they buy cars, and by
      offering financing schemes which confuse the
      customer and which increase profit margins.
   5 By reducing the frequency of its discounts.

Vocabulary
1 shop around   2 mark up
3 squeezing (ever more) from   4 overheads
5 no end of   6 track   7 rules of thumb   8 crude
9 margin enhancing   10 overhauled

Student's Book activities

Getting started
1 1 e   2 g   3 a   4 d   5 b   6 c   7 f

Submitting tenders
Listening
1 1 d   2 e   3 g   4 h   5 c   6 a   7 b   8 f
3 1 sufficient quality   2 value (for money)
   3 documents   4 past projects

Reading
3 1 By looking at recent contracts and comparing
      revenues with costs, and by matching tenders to
      business objectives.
   2 By being members of relevant professional
      bodies, monitoring the trade press, attending
      networking events and using an online tracking
      tool for public contracts.

3 People with suitable skills, who have not too
   great a workload.
4 They hold meetings at key stages and map
   critical paths.
5 They study budget briefs and compare their
   prices with other similar agencies.

2 1 set   2 as   3 so   4 being   5 At   6 if
   7 their   8 what   9 on   10 which   11 each
3 1 e   2 g   3 h   4 c   5 d   6 a   7 f   8 b

Winning contracts
Listening
2 1 C   2 B   3 A   4 C   5 B   6 A

Vocabulary 1
1 1 d   2 f   3 a   4 b   5 g   6 e   7 h   8 c
2 1 go for   2 teamed up with; came out with
   3 go about   4 work out; comes to   5 bid for
   6 Putting together

Grammar workshop: *speaking hypothetically*
1 1 We'd expect, we would hope
   2 To say this is an imaginary rather than an
      actual situation.
   3 Present simple and present continuous.
   4 None really; the time is indefinite.
2 1 don't land   2 doesn't happen / hasn't happened
   3 have   4 would approach   5 'd ask   6 is
   7 'd hope   8 would give   9 ('d) manage
   10 relies   11 ('d) do

Vocabulary 2
1 assessing; submitting   2 devote   3 compete
4 cover; go   5 itemise; establish

Transcripts

I = interviewer; WBH = William Brook-Hart

I: How does your company achieve the … an advantage over its competitors?

WBH: Well, I suppose the prime way you'd get an advantage is by offering, um, sufficient quality at the lowest price. And clients are always looking for the, er, lowest-price tender, and nowadays designers and consulting engineers have to compete a lot more on price than they had to maybe 30, 40 years ago, so price is certainly probably the major element. Um, but in more recent years, there's been far more recognition by clients that actually the quality dimension is also needed. If you go for the lowest price, you may not get the best value, the best value for money. Um, so now client procurement is much more directed towards getting the right match of quality and price. Um, the result of that being … is that when we're submitting tenders to clients to win work, um, we have to devote a lot of time to demonstrating the quality that we can bring to a particular project, and ways of doing that include the quality of our documents and what we say in our documents. Um, it's also, um, developing a reputation and having past projects that we can show clients and say, look, there's a fantastic quality of job we did on that one, um, why don't you employ us because we've got the track record and experience.

I = interviewer; WBH = William Brook-Hart

I: So how would you describe the Gifford's brand?

WBH: Er, the Gifford's brand, well, that's quite a tricky one. I think we're branded a lot by the … the projects, the past projects that we've worked on, so very much in projecting what we're about, we look towards recent projects which have been particularly successful, and, um, one of those has been the Gateshead Millennium Bridge, which … for which Gifford had to enter a design competition which was, which was supervised by the Gateshead Metropolitan Council, and there were about 200 entrants. And, um, Gifford teamed up with a leading architectural practice, Wilkinson Eyre and Associates, and jointly we came out with a completely new concept for a bridge. I don't think this type of bridge has ever been constructed before … Um, this bridge had a horizontal axis so that the entire bridge rotated horizontally to lift over the river to pass, um, ships underneath. And this particular structure's got a lot of international attention since it's been built and has been quite successful in promoting an image of Gifford, er, more widely.

I: So you'd use this project as a means of, um, obtaining further contracts, possibly?

WBH: Yes, I think it's demonstrated our, er, creativity and potential for innovation and problem-solving, in a way which others couldn't do.

I: That's very good. Just tell me, how do you or Gifford's go about getting new contracts?

WBH: Well, um, I suppose one prime route is to look at advertisements, and, um, nowadays within the European Union, um, all contracts or all public works over a certain size have to be advertised in the 'Journal of the European Union'. So we keep an eye on that and identify contracts which look, er, look interesting to us. Um, other routes apart from advertisements – and really a very important route – is through personal contact and, um, preferably through having done previous contracts with a client and establishing a relationship, er, and particularly if they are a private client, or a private company, er, if they like the work that you've done previously, then they may feel there's no need to advertise. They'll come back to you for future work. And, um, establishing those business relationships and friendly partner relationships with clients is … is really vital.

I: And how would you go about deciding a price for your bid when you're in competition with others?

WBH: Well, with great difficulty. There's … there's two, well, there's a number of ways you look at it. One is to assess what the value of the constructed works would be and assess in percentage terms what a reasonable fee for a designer would be in relation to the ultimate value, er, of the works as constructed, so that would be, er, on a percentage basis or a top-down basis. Um, the other main route would be bottom-up in terms of … you're itemising the work and all the tasks that you have to do in order to prepare and design, um, prepare the contract document, the specifications and probably also supervise the construction and the works or supervise the works construction contract, um, so you'd work out all the time on a spreadsheet from the bottom up and see what it comes to.

I: How many of the contracts that you bid for do you expect to win?

WBH: We'd expect to win about one in three, one in four of straight competitive bids where … where we're competing against maybe six other similar consultants. And we would hope to achieve that rate.

I: Putting together a proposal or bid must be expensive and time consuming. How do you cover the costs of this if you don't win the contract? Or is that just absorbed into a future contract?

WBH: The only way you can absorb the cost is out of fees earned on other contracts, so all … all tenderers have to effectively either recover their costs on other contracts or go out of business. It's as simple as that.

7 A proposal

This unit focuses on writing proposals and the language connected with this. Students also study linking words and phrases, compound nouns used in a business context and revise the passive.

Although none of the tasks in the unit exactly replicate exam questions, some are designed to give students the skills and practice needed to deal with them (see table below).

	BEC	BULATS
Listening: *Extending the product range*	Listening Part 1	
Reading: *Extending the product range*	Reading Part 4 Writing Part 2	Reading Part 2 Section 2
Reading: *Writing a proposal*	Reading Part 5	Reading Part 2 Section 3
Writing: *Writing a proposal*	Writing Part 2	

NB The BEC Higher exam always contains an optional question in the writing paper which takes the form of a proposal. The BULATS test does not ask students to write proposals.

Notes on unit
Getting started
This activity may be quite challenging for students with little business background, and you may have to elicit or suggest a few ideas to get them started.

You could do this by asking them additional questions such as:

1 Why would a company which produces soap also decide to produce washing-up liquid and shampoo? Some possible answers:
   • these are extensions of the same basic product and therefore relatively easy to produce with the existing skills base and technology
   • if your company doesn't do it, your competitors will
   • diversification insures against changes in the market, i.e. if a company just relies on one main product and that product goes out of fashion or becomes uncompetitive, then the company may go out of business.
2 What might happen if a very specialist company decided to move into areas where it didn't have the necessary expertise?

Another area you might explore in this context is the danger of loss of brand identity.

Listening: *Extending the product range*
Encourage students to study the spaces beforehand and predict the type of words and information which might be needed to complete them.

Writing: *Writing a proposal*
For students who are unfamiliar with writing proposals, point out that they have a similar style and format to a report, but:
• proposals concentrate on suggestions and recommendations for future activity
• reports may concentrate more on past and current situations
• reports may contain a number of recommendations, but they will probably not form the main body of the report.

Photocopiable activity 2
Put your students in groups of three or four and give each of them one of the question cards. Explain these rules to them:
• Students should take turns to read out a question (but not the answer) to the people in their group.
• They should not show their cards to their partners.
• The student who answers the question correctly first gets one point.
• The winner is the student with the highest score.

Photocopiable activity 1

Relocating

Getting started

Discuss these questions in small groups.

1 What are the advantages for a company of having its main offices in:
   - the city centre?
   - an out-of-town site?
2 In which would you prefer to work?

Reading

In most lines of this proposal there is one extra word which is either grammatically incorrect or does not fit with the sense of the text. Some lines are correct. Cross out the extra words and write them in the space. Put a tick (✓) if the line is correct.

Proposal for relocation of offices

The purpose of this proposal is to put forward the case for relocating our offices to an out-of-town site and ~~for~~ to suggest how this could be financed.

1 ✓.........
2 *for*.....

Our current premises

At present, our offices that are situated in the centre of Southampton, occupying a two-storey building which we own near of the port. They are located in an area where:
- rates are high
- property prices have been risen by 100% in the last seven years
- parking for staff and customers is expensive and access at the peak travelling times is much problematic.

3 ....
4 ....
5 ....
6 ....
7 ....
8 ....

The need for new offices

There are several reasons for needing our new offices:
- Our staff were surveyed earlier this year and were overwhelmingly favoured a move to a new site on the outskirts of Southampton in an area surrounded by countryside.
- Overheads such like as rates would be drastically reduced.
- Our present offices are urgently in need of the renovation.

9 ....
10 ....
11 ....
12 ....
13 ....

Costs

There are a number of rising costs involved in moving. The main ones are:
- the actual cost of the move and the loss of time and operational efficiency during make the move
- the cost of changing addresses on stationery, informing to customers and suppliers of our new address, etc.

14 ....
15 ....
16 ....
17 ....
18 ....

Recommendations

I recommend that we do go ahead with the change of offices for the following reasons:
- It would be so welcomed by our staff.
- By selling our present offices and moving out of town, then we would make a considerable profit, which would finance more than suitable, purpose-built offices.
- Our costs in the medium-term period would be appreciably lower.

19 ....
20 ....
21 ....
22 ....
23 ....

Speaking

Work in small groups. Imagine your company, or the place where you study, is thinking of relocating. Discuss these issues and note your decisions.

- Why it might be necessary to relocate.
- Which area you think the company/school/college should relocate to.
- What sort of building would be suitable.
- The costs and the benefits of doing this.

Writing

Write a proposal suggesting the relocation of your company offices/school/college. Use the proposal you read earlier as a model and the notes from your discussion.

Write 200–250 words.

Photocopiable activity 2   Compound nouns quiz

Question card A

1 What do you call the percentage of interest that a bank will charge when it lends you money? (*interest rate*)

2 What is the name of the room where the top directors of a company meet? (*boardroom*)

3 What do you call an expert who gives you advice about how to manage your company better? (*management consultant*)

4 What do you call the set of accounts which show a company's profits and losses? (*profit-and-loss account*)

5 What do you call the process when companies start competing by trying to offer their products at lower and lower prices than their competitors? (*price war*)

6 What is the name of the telephone service which companies sometimes offer to customers who need help with a product or service? (*customer helpline*)

7 What is the name of the activity or skill by which you use your time most effectively? (*time management*)

8 What would you call the person in charge of sales in a company? (*sales manager / sales director*)

9 What do you call a small booklet which contains blank cheques? (*cheque book*)

10 What do you call the department responsible for employing, training and looking after employees? (*human resources / personnel department*)

Question card B

1 What do you call the person who manages a bank? (*bank manager*)

2 What do you call the process of studying the market? (*market research*)

3 What phrase means 'how well consumers know your brand'? (*brand awareness*)

4 What do you call the interview someone leaving a company has with a senior manager? (*exit interview*)

5 What do you call the time you have to rest in the middle of the morning with a cup of coffee? (*coffee break*)

6 What do you call a party you might have with the people from the office? (*office party*)

7 What do you call the process by which a new product is launched onto the market? (*product launch*)

8 What do marketing people call a shop (a place where products reach consumers)? (*retail outlet*)

9 What do you call a complaint from a dissatisfied customer? (*customer complaint*)

10 What title is often given to the person in charge of production in a manufacturing company? (*production/operations manager*)

Question card C

1 What do you call the instructions for operating a machine? (*operating instructions*)

2 What do you call the process by which you deal with disasters or crises which affect your company? (*crisis management*)

3 What do you call costs which don't change (*fixed costs*)

4 What do you call the amounts of money (cash) going in and out of a company? (*cashflow*)

5 What do you call the person in charge of the way a company operates, often also known as the 'CEO' or 'chief executive officer'? (*managing director*)

6 What do you call a prediction of sales for a particular period? (*sales forecast*)

7 What would you call a letter you might write resigning from a job? (*resignation letter / letter of resignation*)

8 What compound noun would you use for when an employee's salary goes up? (*pay/wage rise / salary/wage increase*)

9 What compound noun can be used for when a price is lowered? (*price cut/reduction*)

10 What phrase describes the total value of a brand? (*brand equity/value*)

Question card D

1 What do you call a very profitable part of a business which produces plenty of cash for the company? (*cash cow*)

2 What do you call people who own shares in your company? (*shareholders*)

3 What do you call the place where stocks and shares are bought and sold? (*stock market / stock exchange*)

4 What would you call a meeting where members of a team talk about things? (*team meeting*)

5 What do you call a bonus which is given at the end of the year? (*end-of-year bonus / Christmas bonus*)

6 What do you call a set of different products produced by a company? (*product range*)

7 What do you call the difference between the price a company sells a product at and the cost of producing the product? (*profit margin*)

8 What do you call a message using text which is sent using a mobile phone? (*text message*)

9 What do you call the money which is allocated to be spent on marketing during a particular period? (*marketing budget*)

10 What do you call the desk where the receptionist sits? (*reception desk*)

 From *Business Benchmark Advanced/Higher* by Guy Brook-Hart © Cambridge University Press 2007   **PHOTOCOPIABLE**   UNIT 7

Answer key

Photocopiable activity 1

Reading

1 ✓ 2 for 3 that 4 of 5 ✓ 6 been 7 the
8 much 9 our 10 were 11 ✓ 12 like 13 the
14 rising 15 ✓ 16 make 17 to 18 ✓ 19 do
20 so 21 then 22 than 23 period

Student's Book activities

Extending the product range

Listening

1 1 board of directors 2 range of software
3 (our) existing clients 4 types of product
5 resources 6 extra costs 7 next board meeting

Reading

1 Yes, he has.
2 1 C 2 D 3 C 4 A 5 D 6 B 7 B 8 D
9 C 10 D
3 1 It has a title, and it's divided into sections with
section headings.
2 Yes.
3 Future activity.
4 Formal.

Vocabulary

1 1 a 2 b 3 a 4 c 5 f 6 g 7 d 8 c 9 e
2 1 Since 2 While 3 in turn 4 at the same
time 5 Therefore; in turn 6 in response to
7 apart from 8 in connection with
9 Furthermore
3 1 existing 2 identify 3 retail outlets
4 VAT returns 5 payroll 6 updates 7 generate
8 envisage/foresee

Grammar workshop 1: *compound nouns*

1 1 product range 2 accounting software
3 small retail outlets 4 existing products
5 client satisfaction 6 market research
7 recruitment requirements 8 marketing costs
2 1 customer service(s) manager
2 suggestion(s) box 3 holiday pay
4 resource management 5 job satisfaction
6 candidate selection process 7 client response
8 complaints procedure

Grammar workshop 2: *the passive*

1 The market research, which **was carried out** in
Liverpool between May and September, revealed
that **the price could be raised** by 50% with only a
5% loss of market share.
2 **Twenty-seven candidates have been interviewed**
for the job, but **none of them are considered** to be
suitable.
3 **Your order was received** the day before yesterday,
and **the goods have just been dispatched**, so they
should be delivered within the next 24 hours.
4 **No more goods will be supplied (to you)** until **the
outstanding invoice has been paid**.

Writing a proposal

Reading

1 to 2 take 3 had/received 4 if 5 which/that
6 In 7 done 8 out 9 soon 10 advance

Transcript

14 Listening page 36

Naseem: Naseem Bakhtiar.

Devika: Hi, Naseem. Devika here.

Naseem: Hi, Devika. What's up?

Devika: I think it's time to get that proposal together for the board of directors. You know, we were talking around the subject last month when we were having our round-up of points arising from the sales conference – at least, it was one of the things that we were talking about.

Naseem: That's the proposal for a wider range of software, isn't it? Let me just note that down.

Devika: That's right. I've just been talking to Lena and we were both saying that now could be the right time …

Naseem: Right, well, Lena's the finance director. Does she reckon we've got the budget for it?

Devika: Yes, that's the point. She says that since profits are definitely up this year, we should be looking to plough something back and reduce our tax exposure.

Naseem: OK, but the main reason for getting into a new project like this – and it would be a pretty big one – is that our existing clients have been asking for it. That would be the main selling point, er, in the proposal. Our clients want a whole range of compatible applications – compatible with the stuff we're selling them at the moment.

Devika: Exactly.

Naseem: OK, and what do you want to see in the proposal, Devika?

Devika: The reasons for adding to the product range, I guess. I mean, our existing products do well enough, but with the cut-throat market we're in, it wouldn't look too good if we spent a lot of cash developing a whole load of new products which just lost us money.

Naseem: Well, that doesn't sound too likely at the moment.

Devika: No. And could you also specify the types of product we are going to work on, you know, especially stock-control tools and applications for automatic online ordering, that sort of thing.

Naseem: OK. Those will do for a start anyway.

Devika: And you'll also have to cover resources in the proposal.

Naseem: Yes. Right.

Devika: I mean, this will mean quite a lot of people working on it and it will swallow a fair amount of cash before we start getting any return on our investment. Fortunately Lena will be keeping us to a tight budget, though.

Naseem: Quite. But it would be useful to know what the extra costs involved in this are likely to be.

Devika: OK, so you'd better include a section on them in your proposal, and then hopefully we should have everything pretty clear.

Naseem: Great. When's the next board meeting?

Devika: Wednesday of the week after next. Do you think you can get your proposal together by then?

Naseem: I'll try to get it ready by Friday of next week if possible so we can mull it over a bit before giving it to the board, though I can't promise that. Otherwise, definitely by the Wednesday.

Devika: That sounds fantastic. Thanks a lot, Naseem.

Naseem: My pleasure. I'll get cracking on this right away. I've been wanting it to happen for some time now.

Devika: Sure.

Naseem: Anything else, Devika?

Devika: Not just now, Naseem. Thanks.

Naseem: OK, bye, then.

Devika: Bye.

Naseem: Bye.

8 Presenting at meetings

This unit focuses on how to make short, comparatively informal presentations at meetings – a frequently needed business skill. Students also study how to describe charts and statistics, linking phrases in spoken discourse, the use of discourse markers to signal where they are in their presentation, and revision of indirect/embedded questions.

Although none of the tasks in the unit exactly replicate exam questions, some are designed to give students the skills and practice needed to deal with them (see table below).

	BEC	BULATS
Listening: *The Chinese ice-cream market*	Listening Part 1 Writing Part 1 Speaking Part 2	Speaking Part 2
Speaking: *More on the Chinese market*	Writing Part 1 Speaking Part 2	Speaking Part 2
Reading and speaking: *Trends in the ice-cream market*	Speaking Part 2	Speaking Part 2
Speaking: *Helsingor Foods: meetings*	Speaking Parts 2 & 3	Speaking Parts 2 & 3
Writing: *Helsingor Foods: meetings*	Writing Part 2	

Notes on unit

Helsingor Foods is a fictional company, but all the other players in the Chinese ice-cream market mentioned in the unit are real companies, and the statistics and other information presented in the unit were based on research and were true at the time of writing.

Listening: *The Chinese ice-cream market*

If you have Chinese students in your class, ask them what they know about the subject – the brands, the producers, the prices and the consumption habits.

This can be extended into a comparison with other students about their national ice-cream markets.

At the time of writing, €1 was worth approximately 10 yuan.

Speaking: *More on the Chinese market*

As an extension to this activity, if appropriate, ask your students to prepare charts which show the division of the market for a product and country they are familiar with. The charts and the information do not have to be too accurate. Students can then present this information either to another group or to the whole class.

Before students give their presentations, draw attention to the Useful language as a way of structuring a talk.

Reading and speaking: *Trends in the ice-cream market*

This activity gives further practice of giving short informal presentations, this time of more complex and varied information on the same subject. Encourage students to make notes of the salient points and to speak from their notes rather than look back at the text when giving their presentation.

When they have finished, if they have the Personal Study Book, you can draw their attention to Vocabulary Exercise 1 (page 20), which deals with the vocabulary in these three texts.

Speaking: *Helsingor Foods: meetings*

Before students hold their meetings, ask them to choose a chair and remind the chair of his/her duties (see Unit 4). If you wish, give them a time limit of ten minutes for Exercise 2.

Writing: *Helsingor Foods: meetings*

You will find a sample proposal on the same subject in Photocopiable activity 2. You can give this to students either as an example before they do the writing task (which is probably best done for homework) or afterwards, so that they can compare their writing with the sample.

Photocopiable activity 1   Catalina's presentation

Reading and listening

15 Work in pairs. Complete these sentences from Catalina's presentation using the phrases from the box. When you have finished, check your answers by listening again.

> along with   also   apparently   as to the second   but anyway   ~~in terms of~~
> So you can imagine that   to be exact   to give you a bit more background   you can see that

---

Right, well, I've got three main points to make: firstly, the Chinese market, unlike markets here in Europe or the US, is growing steadily and rapidly, so it represents a major business opportunity. Last year, the total market **1** *..in terms of..* ice-cream sales was 23 billion yuan – that's about 2.3 billion euros – so pretty considerable. I've been reading recently that China is likely to overtake the USA as the leading market for consumer goods within the next 25 years, and when you take into account that the market growth rate is a steady 10% a year, **2** .... there's an opportunity there, if we can get in. Now, my second point: at the moment, there are five major players selling in the Chinese market, **3** .... a lot of smaller local companies. These big ones have a market share between them of rather more than half – 57% **4** .... – and that's split up between our usual competitors: Nestlé, Wall's – that is, Unilever – and Meadow Gold, with 30% of the market, and a couple of local companies: Yili and Mengniu – I'm not sure I've got the right pronunciation there – **5** .... they've got about 27% of the market.
And now my third and final point: **6** .... , in China, on average people buy far less ice-cream than in Europe – the annual purchase is about 1 litre a head which is still a lot less than the 23 litres per head of the Europeans, so you can see that, as Chinese incomes rise, ice-cream consumption is a pretty hot prospect.

Sure, Paul. I've got something on the biggest national manufacturer – that's Yili. **7** .... , they recently announced plans to build more production facilities in different parts of the country. The reasoning behind this is logical. China is a huge country – the distances between major centres such as Shanghai, Beijing and Hong Kong are vast – so they'll then be able to save a lot on transportation costs. **8** .... , if you have a factory in each region along with a regional product development team, you can adapt your ice-creams to regional markets more easily and thereby satisfy local tastes. That, I think, answers the first part of your question as far as I can; **9** .... , while companies have been advertising pretty heavily, their main tactic for gaining more market has been to fight a fierce price war. Most products sell at about 1 to 2 yuan which is between 10 and 20 euro cents. **10** .... , even with cheap production costs, no companies as yet have been announcing big profits there.

From *Business Benchmark Advanced/Higher* by Guy Brook-Hart © Cambridge University Press 2007   PHOTOCOPIABLE   UNIT 8

Reading and speaking

1 Complete this proposal for marketing ice-cream in China by choosing the best word, A, B, C or D, for each space.

Helsingor Foods: Proposal for marketing ice-cream in China

Introduction

China is an increasing economic **1** ...A..... , and its growing affluence means that it **2** .... a major business opportunity for producers of consumer products. The aim of this proposal is to suggest how to **3** .... the Chinese market.

The existing situation

The Chinese ice-cream market is currently dominated by five major **4** .... : three multinational ice-cream producers (Nestlé, Wall's and Meadow Gold) and two national ice-cream companies (Yili and Mengniu). Since these companies have been waging a price **5** .... in an effort to maximise market share, prices are **6** .... , and competition for the mass market is **7** ....

Positioning our products

The majority of ice-cream products are sold at low prices, which means that profit margins are **8** .... and companies rely on high-volume sales to break **9** .... I suggest that we should target our products at the growing urban middle classes by offering extra quality and appreciably higher prices.

Initial distribution outlets

Distributing ice-cream on a national basis in a country the size of China would require considerable **10** .... in production facilities and infrastructure. Initially, it would be wise to test the market in two or three major cities, which would allow us to bring our products to our target customers in **11** .... conditions. Hong Kong, Shanghai and Beijing would be ideal for this (as our market research demonstrates) and I suggest we start by selling **12** .... top-quality restaurants and specialist food stores in those cities.

Advertising

Our initial entry onto the Chinese market will be on a modest **13** .... and therefore would not **14** .... the expense of mass-media advertising. I recommend **15** .... advertising in upmarket food and housekeeping magazines and also suggest we should rely on word of mouth to **16** .... our product known in our target market.

Conclusions

I recommend that we should proceed along the **17** .... indicated above and suggest that the next step should be to produce a **18** .... for our launch and operations in China.

1	A force	B strength	C potential	D weight
2	A shows	B displays	C represents	D manifests
3	A push in	B take over	C strike up	D break into
4	A competitors	B rivals	C players	D operators
5	A fight	B war	C battle	D contest
6	A down	B low	C scarce	D marginal
7	A fierce	B wild	C hostile	D cruel
8	A short	B thin	C narrow	D close
9	A flat	B even	C level	D steady
10	A spending	B expenditure	C expenses	D investment
11	A optimum	B best	C top	D finest
12	A by	B through	C over	D across
13	A amount	B quantity	C account	D scale
14	A pay	B allow	C justify	D repay
15	A few	B limited	C little	D restricted
16	A get	B have	C ensure	D allow
17	A ways	B methods	C manners	D lines
18	A cost	B account	C budget	D breakdown

2 **Discuss these questions in small groups.**

- Do you think that Helsingor Foods' strategy as outlined in the proposal is reasonable?
- Is there anything they have overlooked?
- What are the best methods for foreign companies to break into the market in your country?
- If you work for a company, how does your company go about selling its products abroad?
- Do you think companies should always be trying to expand their activities and looking for new markets, or are there circumstances when this is not a good idea?

Answer key

Photocopiable activity 1

Reading and listening

1 in terms of   2 you can see that   3 along with
4 to be exact   5 but anyway   6 To give you a bit
more background   7 Apparently   8 Also
9 as to the second   10 So you can imagine that

Photocopiable activity 2

Reading and speaking

1 1 A   2 C   3 D   4 C   5 B   6 B   7 A   8 C
   9 B   10 D   11 A   12 B   13 D   14 C   15 B
   16 A   17 D   18 C

Student's Book activities

The Chinese ice-cream market

Listening

2 1 market   2 (market) growth rate   3 market
   share   4 annual purchase/consumption
   5 production facilities   6 transportation costs
   7 regional markets / local tastes
   8 (fierce) price war

3 1 23 billion yuan (2.3 billion euros)   2 foreign
   companies (30%)   3 national companies (27%)
   4 others (43%)   5 market growth (rate)

4 1 True   It is, however, very informal and fairly
           brief.
   2 False She uses contractions, informal phrasal
           verbs (e.g. *get in*) and adverbs (e.g.
           pretty) and asides (e.g. *I'm not sure I've
           got the right pronunciation there*).
   3 False See above.
   4 True   She says *you can see that, as Chinese
           incomes rise, ice-cream consumption is a
           pretty hot prospect.*
   5 True   She says how many points she is going to
           make and uses markers (e.g. *firstly; Now,
           my second point; And now my third and
           final point*) to indicate where she is in
           her talk.
   6 True   She says *That, I think, answers the first
           part of your question as far as I can; as to
           the second, …*

Grammar workshop: *embedded questions*

1 I'd just like to know what the total sales for the
   Chinese market are.
2 Can you tell me how Chinese companies are
   reacting to this competition from abroad and also
   how these competitors are going about increasing
   their market share?
3 I wonder what sort of price you think we could
   sell our products at.
4 How do you think we would position them?

GRAMMAR WORKSHOP 2

Speaking hypothetically

1 1 advertised; would/'d find   2 hadn't/had not
   managed; 'd/would have gone   3 had; would …
   be   4 had/'d stayed; would/'d have known
   5 were/was; wouldn't/would not mind; had /'d
   realised; would/'d have left   6 had/'d put;
   would/'d have landed   7 taught; would be
   8 had/'d ordered   9 had not/hadn't won;
   would/'d probably be   10 did not/didn't have;
   would not/wouldn't have sold

2 1 'd/would first have   2 would also need
   3 had budgeted   4 wouldn't/would not have
   bought   5 (would) look   6 (would) even assess
   7 would/might/may/could cause   8 wouldn't/
   would not want

Compound nouns

1 an accounting procedure   2 a car manufacturer
3 a negotiating session   4 a rival firm
5 the finance director   6 a price list
7 a market research survey / a market-research survey
8 (job) application forms   9 a motorcycle delivery
service   10 a typing error

Embedded questions

1 1 I wonder when the new factory site will become
      operational.
   2 Do you have any idea how long the
      construction work is expected to take?
   3 Could you please tell me why the goods
      couldn't have been delivered on time?
   4 Several people have asked me if we have to
      send the invoice with the goods.
   5 Tell me what time you finally finished writing
      the report.
   6 I'd be grateful if you could tell me when we
      must have the work completed by.
   7 I'd like to know if they brought the samples
      with them.
   8 I'd appreciate it if you could answer a few
      questions for me.

Nils: Good, thank you all for coming. Shall we get started, then? <u>As you know, the purpose of our meeting is to start thinking about expanding our operations to China.</u> Before getting down to the finer details, please remember that our discussions in this meeting are confidential, OK? So, Catalina's going to get the ball rolling by giving us a brief run-down of the Chinese market. OK, Cati?

Catalina: Sure, Nils, thanks. Now, I'm just going to give you a number of key facts, which should help you to concentrate your minds on the opportunities and difficulties of breaking into China, OK?

Nils: Sure, go ahead.

Catalina: Right, well, I've got three main points to make: <u>firstly</u>, the Chinese market, unlike markets here in Europe or the US, is growing steadily and rapidly, so it represents a major business opportunity. Last year, the total <u>market</u> in terms of ice-cream sales was 23 billion yuan – that's about 2.3 billion euros – so pretty considerable. I've been reading recently that China is likely to overtake the USA as the leading market for consumer goods within the next 25 years, and when you take into account that the <u>market growth rate</u> is a steady 10% a year, you can see that there's an opportunity there, if we can get in. <u>Now, my second point</u>: at the moment, there are five major players selling on the Chinese market, along with a lot of smaller local companies. These big ones have a <u>market share</u> between them of rather more than half – 57% to be exact – and that's split up between our usual competitors: Nestlé, Wall's – that is, Unilever – and Meadow Gold, with 30% of the market, and a couple of local companies: Yili and Mengniu – I'm not sure I've got the right pronunciation there – but anyway they've got about 27% of the market.

<u>And now my third and final point</u>: to give you a bit more background, in China, on average people buy far less ice-cream than in Europe – the <u>annual purchase</u> is about 1 litre a head which is still a lot less than the 23 litres per head of the Europeans, <u>so you can see that, as Chinese incomes rise, ice-cream consumption is a pretty hot prospect</u>.

Nils: Thanks, Cati. That was interesting. Now, any of you got any questions?

Paul: Yes, Cati, can you tell me how Chinese companies are reacting to this competition from abroad and also how these competitors are going about increasing their market share?

Catalina: Sure, Paul. I've got something on the biggest national manufacturer – that's Yili. Apparently, they recently announced plans to build more <u>production facilities</u> in different parts of the country. The reasoning behind this is logical. China is a huge country – the distances between major centres such as Shanghai, Beijing and Hong Kong are vast – so they'll then be able to save a lot on <u>transportation costs</u>. Also, if you have a factory in each region along with a regional product development team, you can adapt your ice-creams to <u>regional markets</u> more easily and thereby satisfy <u>local tastes</u>. <u>That, I think, answers the first part of your question as far as I can; as to the second</u>, while companies have been advertising pretty heavily, their main tactic for gaining more market has been to fight a <u>fierce price war</u>. Most products sell at about 1 to 2 yuan which is between 10 and 20 cents. So you can imagine that, even with cheap production costs, no companies as yet have been announcing big profits there.

Nils: Any more questions? Yes, Tanya?

Tanya: Our products, as you know, are a bit more upmarket than the companies you've mentioned so far. I wonder what sort of price you think we could sell them at. What I want to know is how we would position them.

UNIT 9 Advertising and customers

This unit teaches language and vocabulary connected with advertising and the effectiveness of advertising. Students also study the grammar of adverbs.

Although none of the tasks in the unit exactly replicate exam questions, some are designed to give students the skills and practice needed to deal with them (see table below).

	BEC	BULATS
Reading: *The effectiveness of advertising*	Reading Part 1 Reading Part 4	Reading Part 2 Section 1 Reading Part 2 Section 2
Listening: *The effectiveness of advertising*	Listening Part 1	
Talking point: *Measuring the effectiveness of advertising*	Speaking Part 3	Speaking Part 3
Photocopiable activity	Reading Part 6 Reading Part 5 Writing Part 2	Reading Part 2 Section 6 Reading Part 2 Section 3 Writing Part 2

Notes on unit

Getting started

As an alternative, you could ask students to work in pairs and to do the following (with their books closed):

  1 brainstorm the objectives companies have when advertising
  2 discuss the effectiveness of advertising for meeting each of these objectives.

- As a follow-up to this, they could give a short presentation of their conclusions either to the whole class, or to a group of students.
- Another possible follow-up is to ask them how consumer advertising differs from business-to-business advertising.

Reading: *The effectiveness of advertising*

A possible follow-up to this activity is to ask students:

- if they can think of other examples of strong brands which have used their brand strength to move into new sectors (examples in the text were Apple, Starbucks and Dell)
- what risks companies face when they do this
- why it is that consumers' buying patterns change so quickly (as mentioned by Mike George) and what business conclusions can be drawn from this (e.g. the importance of pricing, the effectiveness of a good website, etc.).

Listening: *The effectiveness of advertising*

You could use this alternative approach to the note-taking exercise:

- write these three questions from the interview on the board before you play the recording:
  1 What in your experience is the best way to advertise?
  2 Is advertising always the most successful way of promoting a product?
  3 Who decides where something should be advertised?
- ask students to look at the questions and the notes and suggest possible answers
- do the listening exercise and follow it up by asking them to suggest other questions they would ask Neil Ivey if they were interviewing him.

Reading: *Measuring the effectiveness of advertising*

Alternatively, you can treat this reading exercise as exam practice, in which case:

- ask your students to read statements 1–8 first
- give them approximately ten minutes to find the answers in the extracts.

You could also ask this follow-up question to the reading exercise:

- Do you think these methods of measurement give information about the effectiveness of *particular* advertisements and advertising campaigns, or can they give information about the effectiveness of advertising *in general*, do you think?

Getting started

1 In small groups, discuss whether you agree or disagree with the following statements.

1 'Word of mouth is not enough: every business needs to advertise.'
2 'Business owners should never write their own advertisements: they should employ a professional to do this.'
3 'Advertising is not a cost – it's an investment.'
4 'Businesses should spend at least five per cent of turnover on advertising.'
5 'If your advertising is right, you can sell almost anything – the advertising may be more important than the product itself.'
6 'Business-to-business advertising is very different from consumer advertising.'

2 Which forms of advertising do you think would be most suitable for business-to-business advertising?

Reading

You work for Ascendisa, an advertising agency with offices in different parts of Europe. Read this letter from Country Club 366. For lines 1–11, there is one extra word in most lines. However, some of the lines are correct. Find the extra words and write them next to the line numbers. If there is no extra word, put a tick (✓). For lines 12–17, there are some gaps. Write one word in each gap.

Dear Sir/Madam,

Three years ago we ~~have~~ inaugurated the Country Club 366, a luxury country club in Slovenia, is located in unspoilt countryside 50 miles east of Ljubljana, specialising in corporate customers. As our facilities include exclusive accommodation for up to 50 guests, a nightclub and discothèque, swimming pools, a golf course, also and a variety of activities and entertainment at all times of the year. Special events are also organised on request.

Until recently we have marketed our services exclusively all through a corporate travel company who included us in their brochures as was one of their destinations. Also, all bookings were made through them.

Unfortunately, the company in question is undergoing its financial difficulties and has been unable to send us sufficient numbers of customers for to fill our capacity. We have, **12** ...., decided to market our company ourselves and to introduce our **13** .... booking system. We are also investigating the possibility of advertising our business and your company was recommended to us by **14** .... of our suppliers, Fendara S.A.

As you will see from the accompanying chart, the majority of our guests come from Europe and particularly Germany, Austria, Switzerland and Italy, and it is in **15** .... markets that we believe our main opportunities lie. We have provisionally earmarked an advertising budget of €250,000 **16** .... the next financial year and we **17** .... very much welcome your proposals for advertising activities and an advertising campaign.

I look forward to hearing from you.

Yours sincerely,

Antonija Dolenc

Antonija Dolenc
Marketing Manager

1 *have*...
2 ....
3 ....
4 ....
5 ....
6 ....
7 ....
8 ....
9 ....
10 ....
11 ....

Country Club 366: Breakdown of guests by region

- ■ Germany, Austria and Switzerland
- ■ Italy
- □ N. America
- □ Rest of Europe
- ■ Rest of the world

Speaking

Discuss the following question in small groups.

What other information would it be useful to have before you propose any advertising activities to Antonija?

Talking point

1 **Work in pairs. Study the information sheet below which Antonija sent you. Discuss what the information shows, and which information is most useful when planning an advertising campaign.**

Writing

Write a short letter to Antonija in which you do the following:

- say you've received her letter
- ask for the information you need
- say that you will make proposals when you have the information.

Useful language

One thing this sheet shows is that …
It's (also) interesting (to see) that …
I can't help noticing that …
Have you noticed that …?
Talking about customers / reasons for choosing Club 366

Country Club 366

Turnover last year: €10m   Pre-tax profits: €2m   Spare capacity in the last six months: 30%

Customers by age

Under 30	30–45	46–55	56–65	66+
8%	27%	38%	22%	5%

Customers by length of stay

Under 3 days	3–5 days	6–8 days	8+ days
37%	39%	20%	4%

Reasons for choosing Country Club 366

	Main reason	Second reason
The quality of the facilities	46%	17%
The location	22%	42%
The staff	12%	31%
Value for money	9%	4%
Other	11%	6%

2 **Work in groups of four or five. On the basis of this information, hold a meeting and discuss the following points.**

- Are they planning to spend enough on advertising?
- How/where should they advertise to previous/existing customers?
- How/where should they advertise to attract new customers?
- What selling points should they emphasise in their advertisements?

Task tip

Choose one person to act as chair before you start. Also, spend some time studying the questions and planning what you will say before you begin.

Answer key

Photocopiable activity

Getting started

2 Suggested answer

The following forms of advertising are probably most suited to business-to-business campaigns: newspaper advertising, magazine advertising (especially in the trade press), direct mail and the Internet.

Reading

Suggested answers

1 have   2 is   3 As   4 ✓   5 also   6 ✓   7 all
8 was   9 ✓   10 its   11 for   12 therefore   13 own
14 one   15 these/those   16 for   17 would

Student's Book activities

Getting started

1 1 building   2 awareness   3 launch   4 boost
5 market   6 customer

The effectiveness of advertising

Vocabulary

1 1 banner (a)   2 classified (c)   3 street (d)
4 point-of-sale (c)   5 endorsement (b)

Reading

2 The writer believes advertising is becoming less effective because there are more types of media and consumers are becoming more sceptical.

3 1 A   2 C   3 B   4 A   5 B   6 D   7 D   8 B
9 C   10 D   11 A   12 B   13 C   14 B   15 A

Grammar workshop: *adverbs*

1 still, actually   2 actually   3 particularly, increasingly, highly   4 as never before
5 for instance, Hence   6 constantly   7 literally
8 within a minute

Listening

2 1 (the) most cost-effective / (possibly) the best
2 point of purchase   3 budget   4 mood
5 cosmetic brand   6 throughout the day

Measuring the effectiveness of advertising

Reading

2 Suggested answers

1 There is no reliable correlation between the amount of money spent on advertising and how this affects consumers' decisions to buy. Advertising campaigns are not carried out with just one advert in one medium, but as part of a larger marketing campaign, so even if sales increase, it is usually not possible to know which part of the combination has been more effective and which less effective.

2 Because it is a cost, and costs have to be justified. If you can measure the effectiveness of advertising, you can make informed decisions for future publicity.

3 Only approximately, by using market research, i.e. asking samples of customers and target audiences, by monitoring changes in sales figures coinciding with advertising campaigns.

3 1 A ... developed to detect inaudible codes placed in radio and TV commercials, as well as other forms of electronic media ranging from the cinema to background music in places like supermarkets.

2 E Two-thirds of consumers feel 'constantly bombarded' with too much advertising

3 D advertisers will also be able to limit the number of times an ad is shown to an individual in order to avoid irritating him.

4 B it has always been difficult to put it all together to establish a link between exposure to ads and buying behaviour. This is what Apollo is designed to achieve.

5 E People are increasingly able to filter out ads.

6 A To measure their exposure to electronic media, they will carry an Arbitron device

7 C The response to the ads increased significantly

8 C Individuals using the websites remain anonymous

Vocabulary

1 households   2 exposure to   3 inaudible
4 scanners   5 barcodes
6 (electronic) tracers/cookies   7 tracked
8 filter out / block   9 subjected to
10 bombarded (with)

I = interviewer, NI = Neil Ivey

I: What in your experience is the best way to advertise?

NI: That's a very difficult question to answer because there are different answers for different types of product. And in some cases, the most cost-effective can be the most expensive, so television still remains probably the most expensive medium, but is possibly the best way still of … of … of getting to people, and given that our biggest ambition is to sell as much product as we can, then we want to reach as many people as we can most effectively.

I: And is advertising always the most successful way of promoting a product?

NI: Not entirely. I think there are a number of people who believe that a decision about, a final decision about a brand is made actually at the point of purchase, so anything that can be done within the store to attract a person, whether it be some sort of promotional activity within the store or something that actually sits on the shelf and attracts your attention or just simply the price.

I: And who decides where something should be advertised?

NI: We in the media company make that decision. We put together a proposal based on the size of the budget, which is, um, a major factor, because television is obviously the most expensive medium we can use, but also the … sort of time of day or the sort of, er, mood that the person is in will affect the … the place that we'll advertise. So, for example, if we were advertising a cosmetic brand, we might think that women reading a … a glossy monthly magazine might find that a more appropriate place to see an advertisement for a cosmetic brand or a fragrance, for example, whereas Fairy Liquid might well be suited much more to the television and have less of … of an appeal to people reading a newspaper or a magazine.

I: And who decides when to go on air on television?

NI: The media company would … would decide on that, and we would have a budget which we would, which would mean that we would have to buy a certain number of, er, slots within prime time, which is generally from about 5.30 in the evening until about 10.30 in the evening, but then again, to get a … a broad range of potential consumers, we would advertise throughout the day. And, for example, the morning time is cheaper than evening time.

UNIT 10 Advertising and the Internet

This unit focuses on language connected with advertising and the Internet. It particularly concentrates on tasks to develop listening skills. It also provides an introduction to writing short reports based on statistical information.

Although none of the tasks in the unit exactly replicate exam questions, some are designed to give students the skills and practice needed to deal with them (see table below).

	BEC	BULATS
Listening: *Internet sales*	Listening Part 2	Listening Part 3
Reading: *Internet sales*	Reading Part 2	
Writing: *Advertisers and the Internet*	Writing Part 1	
Listening: *Advertisers and the Internet*	Listening Part 3	Listening Part 4
Talking point: *Advertisers and the Internet*	Speaking Part 3	Speaking Part 3
Photocopiable activity	Reading Part 6 Writing Part 1 Writing Part 2	Reading Part 2 Section 6

Notes on unit

Getting started

If your class has Internet access, you could visit websites for some of these products or services, e.g.: www.tesco.com, www.dell.com or www.amazon.com and discuss the advantages and disadvantages of using these sites for purchasing.

Reading: *Internet sales*

- As a follow-up to the reading exercise *Motoring online* you could undertake a mini-project where students research how the Internet has transformed other markets (e.g. books, groceries or computer sales).
1 Divide students into groups. Each group could research a different market.
2 Ask them to design a short questionnaire on the subject in order to survey other members of the class. You may have to help them with questions (e.g. for books: *Do you ever buy books online? / Do you consult online reviews when deciding whether to buy a book? / Are you prepared to use your credit card number online?*, etc.).
3 Students conduct interviews with other members of the class, in pairs.
4 They then collate their information with their group.

5 They can go online to find out further information, visit e-sales websites, etc.
6 Finally, they prepare a short presentation to give to the whole class.
- Alternatively, if your students have sufficient background knowledge, you could ask them to research ways companies use the Internet for procurement and sourcing.

Writing: *Advertisers and the Internet*

The chart refers to the USA. As an extra activity, you could:
- ask your students how much time they are exposed to each of these media
- if they work in a company and they have this sort of information, ask them what percentage of their advertising budget is spent on each type of media
- ask them to draw an alternative graph to illustrate this
- ask them to write a brief report based on their graphs.

Listening: *Advertisers and the Internet*

Alternatively, you can ask them first to take notes on:
- the effectiveness of Internet advertising
- how small e-commerce companies can compete. They can then do the multiple-choice questions as a follow-up.

Getting started

Discuss this question in small groups.

When companies find their markets stagnating, should they increase their advertising budgets to boost sales, or should they reduce their advertising budgets to cut costs and maintain profitability?

Reading

1 Read the following information and complete the notes on the right.

Fred-Winter-Homes (CEO Fred Winter) is a well-known construction firm which specialises in building first-time homes in Germany and middle-market holiday housing developments in Spain and Portugal. Due to the international nature of its activities and its management team, the company does much of its internal communicating in English.

As a result of a general stagnation in the housing market, it has not seen a rise in its turnover for the last two years, and last year its profits underwent a 30% decrease on the previous year.

Since the housing market is heavily dependent on macroeconomic factors such as interest rates and consumer confidence, Fred-Winter-Homes have had to retrench by selling assets such as development land and by cutting costs. One of the areas which has come in for attention is the advertising budget and Fred Winter has asked you in the Marketing Department to analyse the cost-effectiveness of Fred-Winter-Homes's advertising budget and suggest how cuts should be made.

Name of company:

Activities:

Markets:

Financial performance:

Cause of present problems:

Solutions:

2 Read this memo from the marketing director, Helena Peralta. In most lines there is one wrong preposition. However, some lines are correct. Cross out the wrong prepositions and write the correct ones in the column on the right. Put a tick (✓) by the line number if it is correct.

To: Marketing Department section heads
From: Marketing director
Subject: Advertising budget

Dear Colleagues,

Due to the downturn ~~of~~ the housing market and the company's poor results from the last two years, the board of directors has asked us to implement a cost-cutting exercise which will involve some fairly drastic cuts for our advertising budget for this and the coming financial year. In order to minimise the effects of these cuts about our marketing performance, I would like to initiate this process for investigating which advertising activities can be reduced to the least detrimental effect. This will involve us having to undertake an in-depth analysis into these activities, with a view of determining whether our actual audiences correspond to our target audiences, and in what extent our advertising efforts are translated across increased sales. This may involve commissioning studies for market research consultancies in your respective countries. With this in mind, could you therefore please take the necessary steps, so that a breakdown in the relevant figures can be presented at our team-leaders' meeting at the end of next month? Our objective is to shave €3m from our advertising budget on the next financial year.

Many thanks

Helena

1 _in_ ....
2 ....
3 ....
4 ....
5 ....
6 ....
7 ....
8 ....
9 ....
10 ....
11 ....
12 ....
13 ....
14 ....
15 ....
16 ....

Photocopiable activity   Case study: Fred-Winter-Homes

Speaking 1

Work in pairs. Each pair should study ONE of the four charts and answer the questions below.

Chart 1

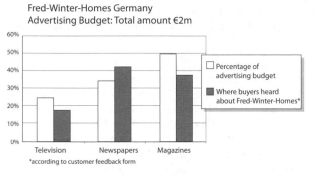

Fred-Winter-Homes Germany
Advertising Budget: Total amount €2m

*according to customer feedback form

Chart 2

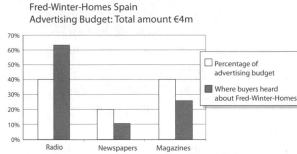

Fred-Winter-Homes Spain
Advertising Budget: Total amount €4m

*according to customer feedback form

Chart 3

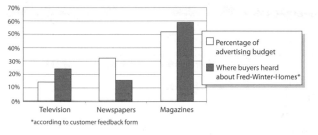

Fred-Winter-Homes Portugal
Advertising Budget: Total amount €1m

*according to customer feedback form

Chart 4

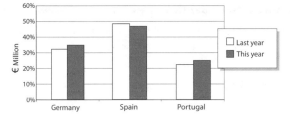

Fred-Winter-Homes Annual Sales

1 Analyse the figures and decide which areas of your advertising budget are most effective and which parts of your budget could be most painlessly cut, so as not to affect your sales performance.

2 Prepare to present your information in pairs to an informal meeting of the marketing department.

Writing 1

Work in pairs and write a brief report (100–150 words) summarising the information contained in the chart you studied.

Speaking 2

Work in groups of eight. (If there are uneven numbers in the class, make sure that in each group there is one person to talk about each chart.) Appoint a Chair for the group and hold a meeting following this agenda.

> **Agenda**
> 1 Chair's introduction
> 2 Presentation of advertising: UK team
> 3 Presentation of advertising: Spanish team
> 4 Presentation of advertising: Portuguese team
> 5 Presentation of Terry Homes's sales figures
> 6 Advertising cuts: plan of action
> 7 Chair's summary of decisions and conclusions reached

Writing 2

Use the results of your discussion in the last activity to write a proposal for the board of directors in which you do the following:

* explain which parts of the company's advertising activities appear to be most effective and which would cause least damage if they were cut
* outline the savings you suggest making in the advertising budget
* recommend a plan of action.

Write about 250 words.

Answer key

Photocopiable activity

Reading

1

Name of company: Fred-Winter-Homes	
Activities:	Construction of first-time homes in Germany and middle-market holiday housing in Spain and Portugal
Markets:	Germany, Spain and Portugal
Financial performance:	Profits down 30%, turnover flat
Cause of present problems:	Stagnation in housing market, interest rates, consumer confidence
Solutions:	Selling assets, cutting costs

2 1 ~~of~~ in   2 ~~from~~ in/over/during/of   3 ✓
4 ~~for~~ in/to   5 ~~about~~ on   6 ~~for~~ by   7 ~~to~~ with
8 ~~into~~ of   9 ~~of~~ to   10 ~~in~~ to   11 ~~across~~ into
12 ~~for~~ from   13 ✓   14 ~~in~~ of   15 ✓
16 ~~on~~ in/during

Writing 1

Sample answers

Chart 1

This report compares Fred-Winter-Homes's spending on advertising in Germany with figures on where house-buyers actually heard about the company. The company's total spending on advertising in Germany was €2 million. While 25% of the advertising budget was allocated to television advertising, only 18% of buyers heard about the company through that medium. On the other hand, the 35% of budget spent on newspaper advertising appears to have been more cost-effective, attracting 42% of buyers. The third medium, magazines, received 50% of the advertising budget, but drew the attention of just 38% of buyers. In conclusion, newspapers appear to be the most effective way of attracting new customers.

Chart 2

This report compares spending on advertising by Fred-Winter-Homes in Spain with where house-buyers actually heard about the company. Fred-Winter-Homes's advertising budget in Spain was €4 million. Of this, 40% was spent on radio advertisements which attracted 62% of buyers. In contrast, they allocated 20% of the advertising budget to newspapers, which attracted just 11% of customers. Finally, magazines received 40% of the budget, but only brought in 25% of buyers. To conclude, radio appears to be by far the most cost-effective advertising medium.

Chart 3

This report compares Fred-Winter-Homes's spending on advertising in Portugal with where buyers actually heard

about the company. From an advertising budget of €1 million, 15% was spent on television advertising, which attracted 25% of clients. In contrast, they spent 32% on newspaper advertising, which brought the company to the attention of just 15% of buyers. They spent 52% of the budget on magazine advertising, attracting 59% of buyers. It is clear therefore that television and magazine advertising are more effective in Portugal than newspaper advertising.

Chart 4

This is a report on Fred-Winter-Homes's annual sales in Germany, Spain and Portugal for this year and last year. In Germany, sales rose from €32 million last year to €34 million this year and in Portugal also there was an increase from €22 million to €24 million. Spain, however, underwent a slight decrease in sales, which fell from €48 million last year to €46 million this year. Nevertheless, Spain continues to be our principal market.

Student's Book activities

Internet sales

Listening

	Product/Service	Why used Internet
Bruce	3	a
Tanya	1	b
Paddy	7	e
Petra	2	f
Salim	4	d

Reading
1 1 c   2 g   3 a   4 f   5 e   6 d   7 b
2 1 H   2 E   3 G   4 F   5 C   6 A   7 B

Vocabulary
1 d   2 c   3 a   4 g   5 h   6 f   7 b   8 e

Grammar workshop: *although, however, despite,* etc.
1 1 although, while   2 despite, in spite of
3 however, in contrast   4 while   5 in contrast
2 1 While few people buy cars on the Internet, many people research them there.
2 Although people study new cars on the Internet, they go to showrooms to buy them.
3 It's difficult to measure advertising's effectiveness. However, few companies believe they can do without it.
4 Despite employing a consultancy, they couldn't improve their company's image.
5 Many dotcom companies have been struggling. In contrast, eBay has been growing by 40% a year.
6 In spite of (having) a / the / their large advertising budget, they kept their product prices low.

Answer key

Advertisers and the Internet

Writing

2   1 between   2 each   3 their   4 even/far/much
   5 with   6 spend

3   Suggested answer
   As the chart shows, there is a disparity between
   the quantity US advertisers spend on advertising in
   each of the main media and US consumers' use of
   the media.
   While advertisers spend 38% of their budget on
   television advertising, US households nowadays
   spend only 32% of their time watching television.
   The difference between advertising spending and
   consumption of newspapers is even more
   accentuated with advertising taking up 36% of the
   budget, although people spend an average of just
   9% of their time reading them. Magazines reflect a
   smaller disparity with spending of 8% by
   advertisers whereas consumers spend only 6% of
   their time reading them.
   In contrast, advertisers tend to spend less on radio
   advertising (14%) in relation to audience (19%).
   The most surprising difference of all, however, is
   between the time people spend using the Internet
   (34% of their media consumption) compared with
   advertising spending on the Internet, which comes
   to just 4% of the total advertising budget.

Listening

1 A   2 C   3 B   4 B   5 C

Transcripts

17 Listening page 50

Presenter: Good evening. I'm Serena Godby, and tonight
on *Your Computer*, we're talking about how you
can use the Internet to buy things and what sort
of things the Internet can really help you to
purchase. Now that questions of security and
Internet fraud are no longer such an issue, e-
commerce and e-shopping are becoming an
increasingly attractive option to both businesses
and consumers. I have five people with me in
the studio: the writer and broadcaster Bruce
Myers, up-and-coming young actress Tanya
Balham, computer programmer Paddy Smith,
Petra Ferriero, the fashion critic, and of course
our regular expert on this programme, Salim
Mahmud. Now, if I could just kick off by asking
each of you about something you bought
recently and why you used the Internet to buy
it. What about you, Bruce?

Bruce: Well, you know, I use the Internet quite a lot for
my work – I research articles and the like, stuff
on the economy, background facts and what
have you. Anyway, I'd been thinking for some
time that it was time for me to get away from it
all and take a break. Normally I just call in at
my local travel agent's while I'm in the High
Street, and they book the tickets and send them
round. Anyway, almost subconsciously the other
day, while I was reading the online edition of
the *Financial Times*, I clicked on this banner ad,
just to see how much things might cost, you
know. I certainly wasn't thinking of booking
anything up there and then. Still, it came as a
bit of a shock, I must say, to see how much
cheaper things are online and how much money
I could have been saving.

Tanya: Yes, they say you can pick up some great
bargains on the Internet, but I still think that
unless you shop around plenty, you can get
taken for a pretty big ride.

Presenter: Tell us about it, Tanya.

Tanya: Well, before I buy something I like to see it,
touch it, get the feel of it, so I'm most likely to
use the Yellow Pages online to find the local
showroom and one or two others – which street
they're in, that sort of thing. It's not bad, because
nowadays you can filter out pop-up boxes and
such like. Then I go down there and check if they
have any special offers, see what's going, perhaps
kick the tyres and take a test drive if they'll let
me. I mean, I don't think we'll ever want to
make a purchase like that online, do you?

Presenter: Well, not as yet, but you never know. It could
come, I suppose. Paddy, you're next.

Transcripts

Paddy: Er, well, I've just changed jobs, and that's been a pretty big thing for me. It means I've had to move and I've been using the web for <u>checking out estate agents</u> and what they've got on their books, <u>see what's going in the area</u> and look at a few photos before getting on the phone.

Presenter: Petra. How have you used the Internet for shopping?

Petra: Not for shopping, actually. Last time I was in London I bought <u>a new PC</u>, but they didn't have the one I wanted in stock – only a showroom model – so I arranged to have it sent on, which they did. I used my old one to <u>check where it had got to and when it was arriving</u>.

Tanya: I think that's wonderful, actually, to be able to do that.

Petra: So do I, because at least I knew it was coming – even if it didn't get here any quicker!

Presenter: Finally you, Salim.

Salim: Hmm, I've been thinking about doing <u>one of those online degrees</u>, you know, so initially I went to Google and typed in the words, and then actually I clicked on various sponsored links which were pretty good, because, you know, they took me direct to more or less what I was looking for and I was able to <u>look at the different options and what they were offering</u> all in less than an hour. I mean, ten years ago it would have taken me weeks!

Presenter: Great. So let's go on from there and just consider together what options there are for …

18 Listening page 53

I = interviewer, NI = Neil Ivey

I: How can advertisers use the Internet, do you think?

NI: The Internet is a … is a difficult one for advertisers at the moment because it's so new. I don't think a lot of people know quite how to use it. People tend to use the Internet for things that they're interested in … the places where the Internet can be very successful are in … in areas where there is high interest in the product involved, so for example, the motor-car industry, where you do a lot of research before you buy a car. Nowadays, most people do their research on the Internet, and therefore to advertise on the Internet is an obvious way to get people <u>when they're again in the right frame of mind to … to be advertised to</u>. And, that can be just simply brand advertising which tells people a little bit more about the car or redirects them to … to the website which will give them more information, or it can be <u>direct response advertising, which will encourage them to send off for a brochure or to send … to … to ask for a test-drive</u> which then gets them into the dealership in order to get the dealer himself then to persuade the … the customer that he might want to buy that particular model.

I: Can the Internet be used to advertise normal household products as well?

NI: There are ways that people try and get round that issue by the website or the advertisement on the Internet actually trying to give a solution to something, and … and what I'm thinking of here is that Persil, for example, the manufacturer of detergents, has a … has a part of its website which talks about tips and hints of how to get rid of stains out of clothes, so you might go and say, <u>you might … you might go into a search engine and … say I want to get rid of a stain on my shirt, a wine stain, and the search engine would then direct you to the Persil site</u> which would then possibly encourage you to buy Persil to get rid of that stain if it was the right solution.

I: So how would advertising on the Internet increase sales or attract new customers?

NI: Um, I suppose in … in the same way that advertising in any medium will work – it's … it's not a static medium, so it's probably mistaken to use static images on the Internet. It's … it's very much nearer, very much nearer … more akin to television in that respect, so that you can do a lot more with it. There's a lot of what are called 'viral ads' being put out now by fairly, um, normal major international companies, who are making ads to look like they're spoof ads, but they're actually made by big advertising agencies at vast expense, because <u>they might be a spoof on a … on an existing ad or they might do something that you wouldn't necessarily expect an advertiser to do, and then they're sent around to a few people, who will then pass them on to a hundred of their people in their mailing list, who will then pass them on and on and on</u>, and that's … that's an interesting way where advertising is developing, because at the end of the 30 seconds or whatever, you suddenly realise it is actually a brand message.

I: If a business wanted to set up an e-commerce operation or sell its products over the Internet, what would be the best way to go about it?

NI: I think it depends very much on what brand they're … they're trying to sell and, um, the danger is that there are now so many different websites that it would be a very difficult thing, I think, to set up a … an e-commerce site from scratch that … that could be successful because just about every market that you would want is catered for. The main reason that people go to the Internet, I think, is because they can shop around for price, and <u>if you're offering something that offers people better value for money, then there's an opportunity then to attract people's attention</u>. Otherwise I think small companies trying to set up e-commerce nowadays would find it very difficult to achieve, because most of the major manufacturers in the world are now savvy to … Internet and setting up their own websites which have a lot more, um, money spent on them.

UNIT 11 Sales reports

This unit teaches language connected with sales. It particularly concentrates on developing writing skills for reports. It also teaches vocabulary connected with describing charts and statistics. It provides grammar revision of the Present Perfect Simple and Continuous.

Although none of the tasks in the unit exactly replicate exam questions, some are designed to give students the skills and practice needed to deal with them (see table below).

	BEC	BULATS
Listening: *Evolving sales*	Listening Part 1	
Reading: *Evolving sales*	Reading Part 6	Reading Part 2 Section 6
Writing: *Evolving sales*	Writing Part 1	
Reading: *Report on a sales event*	Reading Part 4	Reading Part 2 Section 2
Writing: *Report on a sales event*	Writing Part 2	Writing Part 2
Photocopiable activity	Writing Part 2	Writing Part 2

Notes on unit

Getting started

If your class consists largely of pre-service students (who will talk about a company they know well), you can ask them to:

- work in groups on a company of their choice
- discuss and put together their ideas to answer the second and third question
- ask them to present their conclusions to someone from another group.

You could ask your students if they think the rules of effective selling are the same, irrespective of the product. Ask them to work in groups and produce some 'dos' and don'ts'. You could give some examples on the board, for example:

Do:

- know your product
- be honest.

Don't:

- press customers to buy things you know they don't need.

Finally, get feedback from the whole class.

Reading: *Evolving sales*

As an extra activity, you could ask your students to:

- work alone and draw a chart of the sales activities of

an imaginary company for now and ten years ago (as in the Student's Book)

- work in pairs and take turns to describe the information in their chart to their partner. Partners should listen and draw the chart described.

Reading: *Report on a sales event*

As a warmer for this reading activity, ask your students:

- if they ever go to sales events
- what activities occur during these events
- whether they enjoy them or not.

Talking point: *Report on a sales event*

If your students are working, you could ask them the following before approaching the questions in the Student's Book:

- whether they ever have to write reports in their own language for their job
- whether the reports they write would have a similar format
- why it's useful to write a report after a sales event (e.g. to improve organisation of future events)
- what activities and actions should follow a report inside an organisation (they may suggest meetings to discuss contents, action plans, further research, etc.)
- if their organisation has standard procedures for following up reports.

Photocopiable activity

A sales report

Getting started

Work in pairs. Study the table and decide which of these is generally a characteristic of formal written style in English, and which is generally a characteristic of informal written style. Write *formal* or *informal*.

1a	Phrasal verbs	*informal*	We had to put off the meeting till Friday.
1b	Longer one-word verbs	*formal.*	It was necessary to postpone the meeting until Friday.
2a	Long words e.g. *purchase*	....	Customers who wish to purchase rather than lease equipment …
2b	Short words e.g. *buy*	....	Customers who want to buy instead of lease equipment …
3a	Active voice	....	We've decided to cut the number of staff in the Customer Services Department.
3b	Passive voice	....	It has been decided that Customer Services Department staffing levels should be reduced.
4a	Compound nouns	....	staffing levels
4b	Other ways of expressing the same idea	....	number of staff
5a	Impersonal style	....	The G40 model sold well in the last quarter.
5b	Personal style	....	We sold a lot of G40s in the last three months of the year.
6a	Noun phrases	....	The decision to raise prices proved to be correct.
6b	Verb phrases	....	We did the right thing when we decided to put up prices.
7a	Contractions	....	Unfortunately, they didn't meet their deadline.
7b	No contractions	....	Unfortunately, they did not meet their deadline.

Reading

1 Skim the first half of the sales report your teacher will give you to find out how the company's different products performed and the reasons given for their performance.

2 Look at the words and phrases in italics. Choose the word or phrase which sounds MORE formal by deleting the less formal one.

Writing 1

1 Read the second half of the sales report which is written in a fairly informal style.

2 Rewrite the second half of the report in a more formal style. Then compare your answer with the sample answer your teacher will give you.

From *Business Benchmark Advanced/Higher* by Guy Brook-Hart © Cambridge University Press 2007 **PHOTOCOPIABLE** **UNIT 11**

Software Solutions: UK Sales Report

Introduction

~~The reason for writing~~ / *The purpose of* this report is to *summarise* / *sum up* sales for the different categories of product we have been selling in the UK over the past year and to *make recommendations for future sales activities* / *recommend ways to sell things in the future*.

Accounting software

We have sold a lot of our accounting software / *Our accounting software has sold well* over the last year in the UK with *an increase in sales* / *sales going up* from £120,000 to £145,000. *Existing clients* / *Clients we have now* have bought upgrades and *a number of new accounts were secured* / *we found some new customers* at the Accounting Fair at Olympia in April.

Stock control software

We are still selling more of our stock control software than any of our competitors / *Our stock control software continues to be a UK market leader* with sales of £950,000. *It is thought to fit* / *People think it fits* particularly well with UK stock control systems and most sales of the new 7.2 version were made to existing clients *through e-sales downloads* / *when they downloaded it off the Internet* or *when they were phoned by our call centre in Edinburgh* / *as a result of telephone sales from our Edinburgh call centre*.

CRM software

UK companies *continue to be wary of investing in* / *still don't want to spend money on* CRM and sales have been *sluggish* / *slow*.

Shipment tracking software

We decided to delay launching our new tracking software because we were having technical problems with it and we haven't sold as much of our existing tracking software as we hoped to, as you'll understand.

Payroll software

Sales of payroll software went up by 25% because we were quick to supply programs which dealt with changes in the tax rules. We also managed to boost sales by effectively combining telephone sales, e-sales and visits from our salespeople.

Conclusions and recommendations

In general, last year's sales were good, but I think we should stop selling by mail order as we don't make money on this in the UK any more. We also need to keep some cash in hand for when we launch the tracking software in the UK. The problems with it will have to be sorted out first, but we've talked about it with our clients and they seem keen to have it.

Talking point

Discuss the following questions in small groups.

- Why should reports be written in a fairly formal style?
- What other types of business writing need a formal style?
- What things do you need to consider when deciding if you need a formal or informal style of writing?

Writing 2

The company you work for is a distributor of materials for the building trade in your country. It sells construction materials, plumbing materials and materials for electrical installations. Your CEO has asked you to write a sales report for last year. In your report you should:

- outline the sales performance of the different product categories
- give reasons for their performance
- make recommendations for future sales activities.

Software Solutions: UK Sales Report

Introduction
The purpose of this report is to summarise sales for the different categories of product we have been selling in the UK over the past year and to make recommendations for future sales activities.

Accounting software
Our accounting software has sold well over the last year in the UK with an increase in sales from £120,000 to £145,000. Existing clients have bought upgrades and a number of new accounts were secured at the Accounting Fair at Olympia in April.

Stock control software
Our stock control software continues to be a UK market leader with sales of £950,000. It is thought to fit particularly well with UK stock control systems and most sales of the new 7.2 version were made to existing clients through e-sales downloads or as a result of telephone sales from our Edinburgh call centre.

CRM software
UK companies continue to be wary of investing in CRM and sales have been sluggish.

Shipment tracking software
The decision to launch our new tracking software has been delayed due to technical hitches and sales of existing tracking software have understandably been disappointing.

Payroll software
Sales of payroll software rose by 25% as a result of our agility in supplying programs which took into account changes in tax regulations. Sales were further boosted by an effective combination of telephone sales, e-sales and visits from sales personnel.

Conclusions and recommendations
Sales in the past year have been generally encouraging. However, I recommend that our mail order sales should be phased out as they are no longer cost-effective in the UK. Also, money should be reserved for the UK launch of the tracking software once the problems have been resolved as discussions with clients reveal that demand will be strong.

Answer key

Photocopiable activity

Getting started
1 a informal, b formal   2 a formal, b informal
3 a informal, b formal   4 a formal, b informal
5 a formal, b informal   6 a formal, b informal
7 a informal, b formal

Reading
2 See the sample answer on photocopiable page 70 which gives the more formal version of each sentence.

Writing 1
2 See the sample answer on photocopiable page 70.

Writing 2
Students' own answers

Student's Book activities

Evolving sales

Listening
1 retail sales (f)   2 e-sales (c)   3 mail order (b)
4 telephone sales (a)

Vocabulary
1 1 decrease   2 decrease   3 increase   4 increase
   5 decrease   6 decrease

Reading
1 1 ~~had~~ have   2 ~~of~~ from   3 ~~that~~ than   4 ~~too~~ to
   5 ~~In~~ On   6 ✓   7 ~~had~~ have
2 increase: expand, take off
   decrease: fall, halve, dwindle

Grammar workshop: *present perfect simple or continuous?*
1 1 present perfect continuous   2 present perfect simple
2 1 has been manufacturing   2 has risen
   3 She's been working   4 have gone

Writing
2 Suggested answer
Software Solutions: software sales by category
Over the last ten years, sales of our five main categories of software have undergone quite important changes. Ten years ago, our main product was accounting software, which constituted 55% of our total sales. This category has more than halved to just 20% nowadays. The other line which has not performed so successfully is stock-control software, whose sales have shrunk from 20% of the total to just 12%.
On the other hand, other categories have been remarkably successful. Our CRM software has soared from just 5% of the total to 27% at present. Similarly, our payroll software has trebled its sales, rising from 5% to 15%, while our shipment tracking packages have taken off and now account for 25% of sales where ten years ago they stood at just 15% of the total.

Report on a sales event

Reading
2 a Successful (orders and sales exceed investment in the event, attendees have asked for it to be repeated).
   b Outcomes: immediate orders of £1.6m and £2.2m in sales in the future.
     Reactions: need for EU payroll and accounting software, lack of interest in the CRM software, more informal presentations from clients, next event in a central European location.
3 1 B   2 A   3 D   4 C   5 C   6 A   7 D   8 C
   9 B   10 C

Transcript

19 Listening page 55

So, our company's been in existence for more than 15 years now, and during that time, we have, of course, I s'pose just like everyone else, experienced big changes. Probably more than most industries. Our products have evolved, and our production processes have changed out of all recognition. Our customers have also become more savvy and more demanding. And the whole global marketplace has been transformed, so, we've had to adapt our sales activities to meet the challenges. I mean, ten years ago, most of our sales were done by sales staff making personal visits to prospects and explaining our products, how they worked and their selling points. Now, all that area of activity has been declining because our customers know more now, and our products, of course, are much more intuitive. So there's not so much explanation needed. Sales by visiting reps have plummeted from about 40% to less than 20. And another big change that you can see on the chart, although not quite so big, is that people just don't buy our software in shops so much these days. Over-the-counter sales volumes are about 10% lower than they were ten years ago. On the other hand, though everyone hates being rung up about products, we find it surprisingly effective and comparatively cheap. Less time-consuming, no travel expenses. You know, what we do is actually call up prospects – that is, likely companies, potential customers – and make an intelligent sales pitch. Over the past ten years, these sales have soared from just a … a tenth of our total to around a quarter of our products, which is pretty good. Our … our other big success story, I s'pose, is fairly predictable because, of course, ten years ago, few companies – well, or perhaps almost none – were online and the whole concept of e-commerce was in its infancy. I'm proud to admit, though, that we were among the pioneers, and this has really now rocketed to become our most important sales activity. As a result, we can sell much higher volumes nowadays with just about the same staffing levels as a decade ago. That in turn means better margins, and these are really driving our profitability. The only other sales activity we do has been receding, and we're hard put to really know the reason: that's this one here, which has shrunk from 15 to just 3 per cent. People just don't fill in coupons or write in for things any more. I mean, we still advertise in the trade press and in specialist magazines, more than anything to maintain brand awareness, but I s'pose people like to go online and find things through Google, or some other search engine where they can download things instantly. Of course, people feel a bit more confident about using credit cards online as well …

12 The sales pitch

This unit focuses on talking to customers – making the first contact with them (*cold-calling*) and making a sales pitch. Students also revise ways of asking complex questions and they study the grammar of cleft sentences as a way of adding emphasis.

Although none of the tasks in the unit exactly replicate exam questions, some are designed to give students the skills and practice needed to deal with them (see table below).

	BEC	BULATS
Listening: *Cold-calling*	Listening Part 1	
Reading: *Providing services to large companies*	Reading Part 3	Reading Part 2 Section 5
Listening: *Making a sales pitch*	Listening Part 1	
Role-play 2: *Making a sales pitch*		Speaking Part 3

Notes on unit

Getting started

Here are some questions you could ask for further discussion:

- How do you feel when you have to cold-call someone? (Or how would you feel if you had to cold-call someone?)
- Which do you think is more difficult: cold-calling a prospective business customer or a private individual?
- What techniques do cold-callers have for avoiding being given the brush-off?
- What sort of cold-calling do you think is unethical? (E.g. phoning people to tell them they have won a prize when in fact the prize is worthless.)

Listening: *Cold-calling*

As an alternative, before students look at the note-taking exercise in the book, you could follow this procedure:

- ask students to listen and take their own notes on behalf of Rosa about Vogel Leblanc
- play the recording twice for them to do this
- complete the note-taking exercise in the Student's Book from memory and from their notes. (If necessary, play the recording again afterwards.)

Reading: *Providing services to large companies*

As a follow-up to the reading exercise, you could ask your students to:

- work in pairs and prepare a similar company-to-company sales problem to the one outlined in the speaking activity (perhaps one from their own experience)
- note the problem down on a piece of paper and exchange their problem with another pair of students
- discuss in pairs possible solutions to the problem given to them
- in groups of four, present their solutions to each other's problems and then discuss how viable the solutions are
- follow this up with a letter (perhaps written for homework) incorporating their solution to the problem – as if they were consultants.

Getting started

You will read an article for salespeople about how to improve their sales performance. The writer mentions the following five strategies.

1 Offer superior service
2 Provide unique value

3 Customise
4 'Sell through'

5 Build solid relationships

Before you read the article, work with a partner and discuss what you think the writer will say about each strategy.

Reading

1 Read the article. What ideas in the article did you predict in the Getting started activity?

Breakthrough Performance
By Barry Farber

Breakthrough selling is about creating relationships. Here are five proven strategies to do just that:
Offer superior service. Service is what keeps you in business for the long haul. It's your track record that **1** ...D..... current customers' confidence in you and attracts prospects to you.
Provide unique value. The best way to bring extra value to your customer is to understand his or her business better than anyone else. Get to know the customer's company, the people **2** .... and the industry as a whole. This kind of knowledge will be your **3** .... factor.
 The concept of adding value **4** .... no matter what you sell. Whenever you ask questions about your customers' needs and goals, you have another opportunity to look for ways you can support their vision. You'll become an **5** .... to the company, one that they will not easily **6** .... in for another vendor.

Customise. Even though your product or service may be similar to others on the market, make it as customer-specific as possible. Call customers **7** .... to find out how they're using your products. Then modify old products, and design new ones to match the information.
'Sell through.' Your objective should be to help customers sell more of **8** .... they sell. The more you help your customers sell, the more they're going to order from you.
Build solid relationships. Striving for the four factors above will definitely help you rise above the product parity that is so **9** .... today. But the most important factor is how well you connect with your customers. How many times have you heard of salespeople leaving one company to join another and **10** .... all their customers go with them? That's because each one of those customers had a special bond with the salespeople that was stronger than the bond to the product they sold.

From Entrepreneur

2 Choose the best answer, A, B, C or D, to complete the gaps in the article.

1 **A** constructs	**B** shapes	**C** encourages	**D** builds
2 **A** contained	**B** involved	**C** linked	**D** related
3 **A** differentiating	**B** discriminating	**C** distancing	**D** discerning
4 **A** connects	**B** implements	**C** applies	**D** relates
5 **A** advantage	**B** extra	**C** equity	**D** asset
6 **A** exchange	**B** trade	**C** change	**D** swap
7 **A** regularly	**B** persistently	**C** interminably	**D** constantly
8 **A** all	**B** whatever	**C** whichever	**D** that
9 **A** total	**B** overwhelming	**C** everywhere	**D** prevalent
10 **A** having	**B** letting	**C** getting	**D** making

Talking point / Writing

Discuss how important your relationship is with the sales person, when you buy a product.

2 Work in pairs. Write one more piece of sales advice like the five contained in the article. Then read it to the rest of the class.

Answer key

Photocopiable activity

Getting started
Students' own answers

Reading
1 Ideas mentioned in the article:
  1 Superior service keeps you in business for the long haul.
  2 Understanding your customer's business better than anyone else will make you unique.
  3 Call customers to find out how they are using your product or service so that you can modify them to make them more customer-specific.
  4 Sell more by showing your customer how your product can provide solutions to their challenges.
  5 There is a special bond between salespeople and their customers which can be stronger than the bond between customer and product.

2 1 D   2 B   3 A   4 C   5 D   6 B   7 A   8 B   9 D   10 A

Writing
Sample answer

Don't pressurise. You may achieve one-off sales by pressurising customers into buying your products, but you are unlikely to build a long-term relationship with them and this should be your aim. If your products are good and your sales service is good, your customers are quite capable of making up their own minds about whether to buy your products and the chances are that they will.

Student's Book activities

Cold-calling

Listening
1 1 Property-management companies generally let or lease or rent out properties on behalf of their owners. They find people or companies who want to rent the properties, they supervise the contract and also make sure that the people renting the property (or the owners, if it is their responsibility) maintain it in good condition.
2 1 physically threatened   2 visiting properties
  3 (large) mobile-phone   4 (call) the police
  5 (the) office   6 locate (the)   7 reception desk
3 1 False   2 False   3 True   4 False   5 True
5 1 e   2 a   3 c   4 b   5 d

Providing services to large companies

Speaking
1 He wants to service and repair their employees' cars by collecting them and returning them while the employees are at work.
2 He wants suggestions about how to get a chance to make his sales pitch to the companies' human resources departments.

Reading
2 1 C One way we solicit referrals is by identifying the decision-makers in a big company and then determining if we know someone who knows them. We then educate the person that we know about the things we can offer that the big company couldn't find somewhere else.
  2 B they tend to focus on the things that could go wrong
  3 B Can you track down the owners of those local businesses and gain insight into the relationship structure and the decision process that got them on board?
  4 A you'll be trying to crack a bigger bureaucracy

Vocabulary
1 g   2 d   3 a   4 f   5 c   6 b   7 e   8 h

Making a sales pitch

Listening
1 24 / twenty-four   2 (are) specially trained
3 press a button   4 give (them) advice
5 the (potential) problem   6 a few metres
7 contact number   8 five or ten / 5–10
9 leasing (the) equipment   10 (fixed) monthly charge

Grammar workshop: *cleft sentences*
1 1 b   2 a   3 a   4 b
2 1 b   2 a   3 a   4 b
3 1 What we do is deliver the pizzas to your home.
  2 All you have to do is provide the venue.
  3 It's the paperwork (that) we find too time-consuming.
  4 The last thing you should do is settle the invoice before you've received the goods.

Answer key

GRAMMAR WORKSHOP 3

Position of adverbs
Suggested answers
(The second and third alternative answers, where given, are possible, but perhaps not used so frequently.)

1 The advertising campaign which we carried out in major European newspapers last month has proved a great success.
   The advertising campaign in major European newspapers which we carried out last month has proved a great success.

2 Interestingly, brand awareness rose by 5% in the first three months.
   Interestingly, in the first three months, brand awareness rose by 5%.

3 In my opinion, this is due to our having targeted our audience very carefully before we started.
   This, in my opinion, is due to our having very carefully targeted our audience before we started.
   This is due, in my opinion, to our having targeted our audience very carefully before we started.

4 Consequently, we have already managed to meet our sales targets for several lines.
   Consequently, we have managed to meet our sales targets for several lines already.

5 For example, sales of our most popular brands have risen spectacularly since we began advertising.
   Sales of our most popular brands, for example, have risen spectacularly since we began advertising.
   Since we began advertising, sales of our most popular brands, for example, have risen spectacularly.

6 Unfortunately, however, our top-of-the-range brands have not performed so impressively.
   However, unfortunately, our top-of-the-range brands have not performed so impressively.

Unfortunately, our top-of-the-range brands have not performed so impressively, however.
However, our top-of-the-range brands have unfortunately not performed so impressively.

7 Sales of these have stayed at the same level, or even dropped slightly.

8 As a result, I think we should meet soon to discuss this.
   As a result, I think we should meet to discuss this soon.

9 We need to find a solution urgently, although it shouldn't prove especially difficult.
   We urgently need to find a solution, although it shouldn't prove especially difficult.

10 Could you call me later today on my mobile?
   Could you call me on my mobile later today?

Present perfect simple and continuous
1 has just decided   2 I've been trying
3 he's worked   4 he's made   5 Have you always occupied   6 haven't sent; have you been doing
7 I've been working   8 I've phoned
9 have been getting

Cleft sentences
1 What had a positive effect on sales was the CRM system.
2 What they did was outsource their production to Indonesia.
3 What they sold was/were paper products.
4 It's the time (which/that) it takes which/that is the problem.
5 It's Internet fraud which/that is our biggest problem.
6 All he does is complain.
7 All this shop sells is paint.
8 The last thing I want is your advice.

Transcripts

20 Listening page 58

Richard: Richard Slade speaking.
Rosa: Hello, Mr Slade. You don't know me. My name's Rosa Levy, and I work for CSS Security.
Richard: OK. I've only got a few minutes …
Rosa: Yes, I'm sure you're very busy, so I'll be brief. We specialise in providing security not just for buildings and properties, but also for employees so that they can do their jobs in the safest possible conditions and work with confidence.
Richard: So why do you think we need your services?
Rosa: I don't know at the moment, Mr Slade, but with your permission, I'd like to ask you a few very quick questions to see if there's anything we can do which your company could benefit from. Do you mind? It won't take long.
Richard: OK, go ahead, but make it quick.
Rosa: Thank you very much. First, <u>can you tell me: have any of your staff ever been attacked by members of the public or by clients of your company</u>?
Richard: Well, that's rather a sensitive question, so I'll only answer very generally. From time to time, we've had members of staff who've been shouted at, or on one or two occasions <u>physically threatened</u>.
Rosa: <u>And where have those incidents happened</u>: in the office or when, for example, they're showing a client a property?
Richard: From time to time, on the telephone, though our staff are trained to deal with that. On odd occasions, here on our premises and several times, as you say, when <u>visiting properties</u>.
Rosa: And these members of staff, <u>would I be right in thinking, when they visit properties are generally working on their own</u>?
Richard: Generally speaking, yes.
Rosa: <u>Can you tell me what protection you offer them when they're working alone outside the office?</u>
Richard: Well, we have an arrangement with a <u>large mobile-phone</u> company. If one of our staff members presses a number on their phone, a call comes straight through to us. We then ring the person concerned – you see, if they're in a dangerous situation they can press the number without anyone realising. If necessary, after that we <u>call the police</u>.
Rosa: I see. And one last question – do you find this works satisfactorily? Is there anything you would like to see improved?
Richard: Frankly, it's not too satisfactory because sometimes there's nobody in <u>the office</u>. And there was one occasion quite recently when the worker in question felt threatened – she wasn't actually physically attacked – but she didn't feel it was safe to answer her mobile and we were unable to <u>locate</u> her exactly.
Rosa: So, you'd like to be able to offer your workers round-the-clock protection and be able to locate them automatically if an incident occurs?
Richard: That would be ideal.
Rosa: Well, Mr Slade, that's exactly the sort of service we'd be able to offer you, and probably at a price that you would find very competitive with your present service. Would you be interested in hearing about what we have to offer?
Richard: Yes, I think so. Quite probably.
Rosa: Well, that's great. Perhaps we could set up a meeting and I could show you exactly what we can do.
Richard: OK.
Rosa: Would sometime this week suit you?
Richard: Let me have a look in my diary. I could do Friday afternoon at about 4 p.m.
Rosa: Friday at four. That's fine by me. I'll come to your offices, shall I?
Richard: Yes, I'll meet you at the <u>reception desk</u>.
Rosa: OK, fine. I'll look forward to meeting you then. And thank you very much for your time, Mr Slade.
Richard: You're welcome. Goodbye.
Rosa: Goodbye.

21 Listening page 61

Richard: So, come in and take a seat.
Rosa: Thanks, and thanks for finding the time to see me.
Richard: Not at all. Sorry it's a bit late on a Friday afternoon.
Rosa: No, that's fine. I'm used to working all hours.
Richard: Right. Now, tell me about your company's staff protection service. What does it consist of?
Rosa: OK. Now, as I understood from our phone conversation, you already have a service with a mobile-phone operator. They alert you when a member of your staff presses a button to signal that they've got a problem.
Richard: That's right, but the service has its limitations, as I mentioned to you on the phone.
Rosa: Right, so what we do is provide a more complete service. When a member of staff feels threatened or in danger, they press a button and alert us. Our service operates <u>24</u> hours a day, seven days a week, which means first that your staff know that they'll always get a response, second that the response will always be immediate, and third that the people dealing with the call – that's us – <u>are specially trained</u> to deal with these types of situations.

Transcripts

Richard: OK so far, but what do you do when you get an emergency call?

Rosa: Well, it's not exactly an emergency call. The employee doesn't have to call us. All he or she has to do is <u>press a button</u> and that alerts us. We then call the employee and if they answer, we ask them the nature of the problem and take it from there.

Richard: Take it from there?

Rosa: Well, clearly, in some situations the worker may just want to let someone know that the client is acting strangely, but they don't feel in any immediate danger. In this case, they have a code word, and we can <u>give them advice</u>, you know, tell them how they should proceed and perhaps just generally to calm them down so that they don't feel quite so threatened. You know, it really helps in these situations if they know there's someone there if they need them. We can also alert your office of <u>the potential problem</u>, and if the situation warrants it, we can call the police.

Richard: How will the police know where to go?

Rosa: Because your staff will be supplied with equipment which is basically a slightly adapted mobile phone, but which also contains a satellite tracking system, so we know where they are to within <u>a few metres</u>. Of course, we make sure that the employees know this and sign an acceptance form when they get the equipment – you don't want to be accused of spying on them when they're not working!

Richard: No, of course not – that's a good point. But I'll tell you why I'm interested. In the last year or so, we've had a couple of incidents involving staff. Of course, they're given some training in how to handle difficult customers or tenants, but about three months ago, a member of staff was visiting one of the properties we manage, and he was actually physically attacked by the tenant of the property. You may have read about it in the local press. He had no opportunity to make a phone call, let alone have a phone conversation. Fortunately, he wasn't badly hurt, but he was badly shaken and was off work for a month after that. It's that sort of situation that we want to avoid.

Rosa: Precisely, and in that case he'd just have pressed the button and not responded to our phone call. Often just the fact that the phone rings is enough to make a potential attacker desist. We'd then have alerted your office, or if there was no one in the office, we'd call a <u>contact number</u> you'd have supplied us with, and at the same time we'd have phoned the police.

Richard: That sounds fine, but the other incident we had was when one of our workers called in saying she was being threatened, and we responded by calling the police. The police, however, took nearly 45 minutes to come to her rescue. Again, fortunately, nothing very serious happened to her, but it could have been very serious.

Rosa: We actually try to keep track of the police. I mean, we direct them to the location, we phone every <u>five or ten minutes</u> to find out what the situation is and if they've resolved it. Our aim is to provide the completest possible protection without actually giving your staff bodyguards. But if the police have been informed, it's the police who have to deal with the situation. You and we have done everything we can.

Richard: And the cost of this? What's the bottom line?

Rosa: That's the interesting part. It really isn't going to hurt. The costs you'll have are for <u>leasing the equipment</u> – a more sophisticated mobile phone. The charge you'll have to pay for that is really not very high, especially when you consider it in the context of the confidence and security it will give your staff. All you have to pay apart from that is a <u>fixed monthly charge</u>, about the same as you'd pay if your burglar alarm was connected to us and nothing else. There are no extra costs and no hidden charges.

Richard: Not even when one of our staff presses the emergency button?

Rosa: Certainly not. The last thing we want is people to be calculating the cost of calling for help. Look, I have a list of our charges here.

Richard: And can you tell me the names of other clients you have, other companies who use this service?

13 Forecasts and results

This unit teaches language and vocabulary connected with making financial forecasts and other aspects of company finances. It also revises conditionals in the context of making sales forecasts.

Although none of the tasks in the unit exactly replicate exam questions, some are designed to give students the skills and practice needed to deal with them (see table below).

	BEC	BULATS
Listening: *Forecasting sales*	Listening Part 2	Listening Part 3 Section 1
Talking point: *Forecasting sales*	Speaking Part 3	Speaking Part 3
Reading: *Forecasting sales*	Reading Part 2	
Speaking: *Forecasting sales*	Speaking Part 2	Speaking Part 2

Notes on unit

Getting started

As a lead-in to this activity, you could ask the class:

• Why is it important for companies to make sales forecasts? What do forecasts help them to do?

Listening: *Forecasting sales*

As a way of getting your students to focus on the reasons for inaccuracy, you could ask them *either* to:

• paraphrase the eight sentences *or*:
• give examples of how each of these things could lead to a forecasting inaccuracy.

Talking point: *Forecasting sales*

As a follow-up to the group discussion, you could *either*:

• mix the groups and ask students to take turns to present the conclusions of their discussion *or*:
• choose a student from each group to present their conclusions to the whole class.

Reading: *Forecasting sales*

An alternative warmer, especially if you are starting a new lesson at this point, is to ask students to work in pairs and:

• list the different types of financial forecasts that companies make
• briefly say why each type of forecast is useful
• explain the difference between a *forecast* and a *target*.

Grammar workshop: *Conditional sentences*

As a follow-up to the work in the Student's Book, you could ask your students to work in pairs and:

• choose one of the five types of forecaster and write their own statement for that forecaster
• then read their statement to the rest of the class, who have to deduce which type of forecaster they chose.

Vocabulary: *Reporting results*

Since accounting systems vary between countries and some of this vocabulary is quite technical, you could:

• refer students to the Word list in the Personal Study Book to help them with this
• suggest they use a bilingual dictionary and
• if convenient, download financial reports from the students' own countries to compare with this one.

The financial report for Presto Bearings is very simplified. For more detailed examples, you can use the Internet. Public limited companies have financial information on their websites. Another place to look is: http://www.cwcu.org/youth/financialvocab.htm.

Photocopiable activity

If your students do not have access to the Internet, you will have to download and print out parts of the financial reports for them.

Photocopiable activity

Project: Investigating a company

Getting started

1 At present you are negotiating a valuable contract to supply another company with your products/services. If you accept the terms of the contract, this will mean substantial expansion of your company's operations and considerable investment.

Discuss in groups of four which of these things you think it would be useful to know about the company before you agree to sign the contract. Put a tick (✓) by those things you think it would be useful to know.

1 Something about the company's history ❏

2 The company's main activities and products/brands ❏

3 The company's recent new activities/ projects ❏

4 The company's attitude to corporate social responsibility ❏

5 Who the Chair and CEO are, and how much they earn ❏

6 The principal shareholders ❏

7 The location of the company's head offices ❏

8 Which countries/regions the company is active in ❏

9 Number of employees worldwide ❏

10 The company's
    a turnover ❏
    b profits/losses ❏
    c earnings per share ❏
    d assets and liabilities ❏
    e value ❏

2 When you have finished, give feedback to the rest of the class on what you decided.

Reading

1 Work in your group of four. You are going to investigate a company by looking at their website. Either choose a company from this list or one which interests you.

- **Tesco**: http://www.tescocorporate.com
- **Costain**: http://www.costain.com/finance/annual.htm
- **Quantas**: http://www.qantas.com.au/info/about/investors/fullYearResults2005
- **Astra Zeneca**: http://www.astrazeneca.com
- **Fletcher Building**:http://www.fletcherbuilding.co.nz/2_investing_in_us/Results&Reports.asp
- **Telcom SA**:http://www.telkom.co.za/minisites/ir/annual_reports.html

2 Divide into two pairs and decide which information from the list in the Getting started activity each pair is going to look for.

3 Work in pairs. Visit the website and find the information you need.*

4 Return to your group of four and prepare a presentation about the company you have studied.**

5 Give your presentation to the rest of the class.

---

* Large companies tend to have very extensive websites. If you are looking for financial information (which public companies must publish by law) you may find it under *investors* or *financial* or *annual reports*. Public companies must by law also publish what they pay members of the board of directors. This will also be in the annual report and may be called *emoluments*.

Please note that companies change names, go out of business or are taken over, so these websites may be changed.

** If you have a data projector in your class, you can download images and charts from the website to use in your presentation.

Answer key

Photocopiable activity

Getting started

1 In reality, all these would be useful to know, especially if the contract is a big one. The more information you have about prospective business partners the better, and many or most of these things can be found out by visiting a good company website.

Student's Book activities

Forecasting sales

Listening

1/2

	Contribution	Reason for inaccuracy
Olivia	(2) predictions about interest rates	(a) There was a shift in fashion.
Jaime	(6) the success of competitors' products	(f) Our publicity was more effective than we expected.
Gary	(4) intuition	(b) We were affected by a press report.
Sylvie	(8) the marketing budget	(c) There was an unexpected disaster.
Nesreen	(3) reports from sales teams	(h) We experienced a shortage of qualified staff.

Vocabulary 1

1 c   2 g   3 d   4 e   5 b   6 a   7 f

Reading

2 1 It's emotionally difficult for people to do negative scenarios. (paragraph 1)

2 it is useful to bring together people from various departments who think about the future in different ways. (paragraph 3)

3 "We compare the machine forecasts to the human forecasts every month … The numbers have got to be in sync with each other." If they're not, Wise wants to know why. But when in doubt, he says the human forecast … wins. (paragraph 4)

4 Ertel prods them instead to look for ways they can take advantage of competitors' inactivity or retrenchments. The goal isn't to predict what's ahead precisely but to imagine both positive and negative outcomes, understand what might prompt them and consider how you might handle each one. (paragraph 5)

3 1 H   2 F   3 C   4 E   5 D   6 B   7 G

Vocabulary 2

1 go bust   2 stock price   3 earnings shortfalls
4 layoffs   5 in sync   6 cross-section
7 discontinuities   8 resilient   9 prods
10 retrenchments

Grammar workshop: *conditional sentences*

1 1 e   2 c   3 a   4 b   5 d

2 1 a, c and e refer to present/future time; b and d refer to past time.

2 *If* + past perfect, *would/could have* + past participle

3 *If* + present, future simple/continuous; *If* + past, *would/could* + base form (simple or continuous)

Reporting results

Vocabulary

1 1 loss   2 turnover   3 pre-tax profits
4 dividends   5 profit and loss for the period
6 equity   7 debtors   8 equipment
9 liabilities

2 1 premises   2 depreciation   3 overdraft
4 retained earnings   5 assets   6 stock
7 goodwill

Talking point

Suggested answers

1 **The share price** – especially in relation to the value of the company. A low share price may lay the company open to a takeover bid.
How much profit has been made and what the company can afford, especially in relation to the company's other expenditures.
Shareholders' expectations

2 They can spend money before it registers as profits, for example by reinvesting it in company operations, or by spending it on things which are tax deductible, such as charities.

3 Goodwill includes the good reputation of the company, the reputation of its brands and its brand names and brand equity, and the value of its customer relations.

Presenter: Good evening and welcome to *Business Growth*, the weekly programme about business and finance. My name is Max Edwards, and tonight we're going to look at that recurring nightmare, the sales forecast, where sales and finance directors bang their heads together, supposedly gaze into a crystal ball and then pull some figures out of the air. Or perhaps it's not quite like that! We asked five company directors to tell us how they do it and how accurate their forecasts have been in the past. First, Olivia Howe of SPG Holidays. How do you do it?

Olivia: Well, I'm basically an economist, so sales forecasts are really not my speciality. But I am asked about how general circumstances might affect our sales figures and I usually give a projection for bank rates and how they'll affect demand. Last year, though, the company actually underestimated its sales forecast quite considerably when the holidays we sell suddenly rather unexpectedly caught on, and everyone, it seemed, was wanting to go on one. I mean, we used to think of our holidays as a niche product and suddenly they seemed to be mainstream.

Presenter: So, you were running to catch up with demand?

Olivia: Exactly.

Presenter: Jaime Almendro, you're a director of the up-and-coming Spanish clothing retailers, Próximo, which is appearing in every shopping mall in Europe. How do you predict sales?

Jaime: Oh, in any number of ways, but my particular contribution comes from my involvement with marketing and market research. I and my team track our rivals' activities and likely sales, and, on the basis that whatever they can do, we can do better, we work out what they're selling and add on a percentage. Like Olivia, we also fell short of our forecast last year when a Spanish Formula One driver won the championship and at the same time we talked him into wearing our clothes. That really was a knock-out, and we hurriedly had to source extra suppliers.

Presenter: Fabulous. Gary Summerwell, managing director of the bicycle importers, 'Free Wheel', how do you do your sales forecast?

Gary: Hard to tell, really. I mean, I've been to business school and learnt all the conventional techniques, like making computer extrapolations based on past sales and such like, but honestly I think, in the end, I just go on a hunch and, as you so nicely put it, pull a figure out of the air. You know, what I imagine will be the sales for next year, because however much calculating you do, you're never going to get it quite right. It's always, in my opinion, better to be optimistic and plan for more sales than fewer. Sometimes you have a hiccup, though, like the time a year or two ago when someone comparing bikes in a magazine said ours were overpriced for what they were. Completely untrue, of course, but sales took a bit of a nose-dive for several months. We survived, though. I think good quality and good service always survive if you stick in there and believe in what you're doing.

Presenter: Thanks, Gary. Sylvie Lemaître, your company, 'La Chaise', is a leading player in the French furniture market. How do you go about making sales predictions?

Sylvie: It's a complex process as you know, Max, and I really don't agree with Gary about computer extrapolations. I do think they have a place. But my role is more to look at how our promotional activities can affect sales figures and what we can do as a company to increase our sales. So, I look at the money we're thinking of spending and what bearing this will have on how much we sell. I really believe that what you spend in that area should have a quantifiable effect on what you sell. You've got to know that your investment is paying off. Of course, there are always the things you can't predict, like the fire that destroyed our factory in Cognac last winter and meant we couldn't complete all our orders on time.

Presenter: Bad luck, in other words.

Sylvie: Very.

Presenter: Thank you, Sylvie. Finally, Nesreen Nasr. You're director of one of the Middle East's most important translation and interpretation consultancies. How important are sales forecasts for a company like yours?

Transcript

Nesreen: Very important, though I should say that, though we make annual forecasts, we do adjust them on a monthly basis, as I expect all the rest of you do. They're important because we have to get our staffing levels right, we have to be training the right number of new personnel, and we have, like everyone else, to keep a tight control on our cashflow. So we do sales forecasts and cashflow forecasts, and my part is to get our agents in the field to tell us what their likely needs are going to be. I then collate this information and pass it on. Even so, over the past few years, demand has been growing faster than we can train new personnel and retain them – a lot of staff after a time tend to go freelance – and this has meant that rather too frequently recently we've had to turn down lucrative contracts that we'd counted on in our forecasts.

Presenter: Very frustrating.

Nesreen: Very, and in a labour-intensive industry like ours, not one with an easy solution.

14 Financing the arts

This unit focuses on finance in the theatre and corporate sponsorship of the arts in general. It also revises when to use the infinitive and when to use the verb + –ing form.

Although none of the tasks in the unit exactly replicate exam questions, some are designed to give students the skills and practice needed to deal with them (see table below).

	BEC	BULATS
Listening: *The theatre business*	Listening Part 3	Listening Part 4
Talking point: *Sponsoring the arts*	Speaking Part 3	Speaking Part 3
Grammar workshop: *Infinitive and verb + –ing*	Writing Part 2	
Listening: *Sponsoring the arts*	Listening Part 3	Listening Part 4
Role-play: *Sponsoring the arts*	Speaking Part 3	Speaking Part 3
Writing: *Sponsoring the arts*	Writing Part 2	

Notes on unit

Listening: *The theatre business*

As an alternative treatment here, you could:

- ask your students how they think the theatre business is different to other types of business
- tell them to listen and take notes on this point
- after they have listened twice, ask them to check their notes in pairs
- ask them to read the multiple-choice questions in the Student's Book and decide on the answers
- listen once more to check their answers.

If you decide to follow this procedure, you could also do the vocabulary exercise before the listening activity as a pre-listening task.

Talking point: *Sponsoring the arts*

- If your students need help with this activity, you could suggest that instead of talking about arts sponsorship, they could talk about sports sponsorship.
- Ask them about a sports team or sports competition they know well and the advantages and dangers for a company of sponsoring the team or the competition.

Grammar workshop: *Infinitive and verb + –ing*

Alternatively, students can study the explanation in the Grammar workshop on page 80 before they do the exercise on page 70.

Listening: *Sponsoring the arts*

Here are two alternatives for this activity.
Either:

- ask your students to take notes on:
  1 the advantages for companies of sponsoring the arts
  2 what things companies should take into consideration when offering sponsorships
- They then compare their notes, and afterwards do the multiple-choice exercise in the book.
  Or:
- ask your students to work in pairs and:
  1 read the multiple-choice questions before they listen
  2 discuss together which they think is the most likely answer to each question
- They then listen and check if their ideas were right.

As a follow-up to either approach, you could ask your students if there is any arts or sports event they would like their company to sponsor.

Photocopiable activity

You will need to make sure there are equal numbers of students with the instructions for Pair A and Pair B.

As a possible follow-up, you could:

- ask your students which of the situations seemed most realistic to them
- ask if they have ever had to face a similar situation
- ask them to prepare another similar dilemma and propose it to the rest of the class (if appropriate, this could be from their own experience).

Speaking

1 Work in pairs and read the instructions for Pair A.

> **Instructions for Pair A**
>
> As business people, you are always faced with choices.
>
> - In this activity, you have three situations (1–3). For each situation, you have decided that there are only two reasonable options (A or B). You should discuss them together and decide which option to choose.
> - Another pair has three different situations (4–6) which they will be discussing separately.
> - The language objective of the activity is to practise using conditional sentences, so you should say things like: *If we give her 90 days, we'll have to go to the bank for an extension of our overdraft. / If we made her pay cash, we might lose her as a customer.*
>   ➲ page 80 in your Student's Book (conditional sentences)

1

You run a small business. One of your business customers has told you that she'll order twice as many of your products if you allow her to pay in 90 days. This may cause you cashflow problems. Do you …

A sell the goods and give her 90 days?

B insist she pays cash and sell her less?

2

In the event of a recession, it could be quite risky for your company to be employing so many customer service staff. Recently one member of the management team suggested axing the customer service department and outsourcing their function. Do you …

A outsource?

B keep the function in-house?

3

While working for your present company, you've noticed a great business opportunity. Do you …

A … tell them about it in the hope that they'll put you in charge of a project team to exploit the opening?

B … leave the company and set up on your own to exploit the opportunity?

ONE YEAR LATER …

2 When you have finished discussing, join the other pair and take turns to explain each situation and the decision you reached.

3 Look at the box headed 'One year later …' to find out the consequences for the other pair. Take it in turns to explain the consequence of each decision.

> In this part of the activity, the language objective is the third conditional, so you should say things like:
> *If you'd become a late payer, you'd have been put on a blacklist.*

ONE YEAR LATER …

Consequences for Pair B

4 **A** The bank felt you were being too lenient on your customer and refused to give you an overdraft. You lost the customer and are still waiting for their payment.

   B Unfortunately, your suppliers put you on a blacklist, and it's been very difficult to get parts as a result.

5 **A** She doesn't accept the offer. You lose one of your best workers.

   B This really worked. She came back full of good new ideas and highly motivated. This is already showing results in the profitability of your division.

6 **A** At the departmental meeting you all agreed a reasonable time to leave the office. This didn't stop you being a workaholic and now you take work home.

   B Your staff were frightened of you and one by one the best workers left when they found alternative jobs elsewhere.

Photocopiable activity   Business options

Speaking

1 Work in pairs and read the instructions for Pair B.

> **Instructions for Pair B**
> As business people, you are always faced with choices.
> • In this activity, you have three situations (4–6). For each situation, you have decided that there are only two reasonable options (A or B). You should discuss them together and decide which option to choose.
> • Another pair has three different situations (1–3) which they will be discussing separately.
> • The language objective of the activity is to practise using conditional sentences, so you should say things like: *If we give them more time, we will increase our costs. / If we became late payers ourselves, we would have problems with our suppliers.*
> �'❯ page 80 in your Student's Book (conditional sentences)

4
One of your best customers has run into cashflow problems and is unable to settle their account with your company. This could give you similar problems with your suppliers.
Do you …
A go to your bank for an overdraft?
B become a late-payer yourself?

5
You're a divisional manager of a large company. One of the brightest and most effective members of your team has told you that she's decided to go off to Wharton Business School to do an MBA. Do you …
A offer her a pay rise and promotion to keep her?
B offer to pay for her course if she agrees to come back at the end of it?

6
You're head of your department and a bit of a workaholic. The problem is that you've noticed your staff tend to stay working at their desks until you decide it's time for you to go home and you don't want to go home before they do either. Do you …
A have a departmental meeting to discuss the problem?
B leave things as they are because it's more productive?

ONE YEAR LATER …

2 When you have finished discussing, join the other pair and take turns to explain each situation and the decision you reached.

3 Look at the box headed 'One year later …' to find out the consequences for the other pair. Take it in turns to explain the consequence of each decision.

> In this part of the activity, the language objective is the third conditional, so you should say things like:
> *If you'd become a late payer, you'd have been put on a blacklist.*

ONE YEAR LATER …
Consequences for Pair A
1 **A** You sold her the goods and she went bankrupt. You lost a lot of money.
   B She went to one of your rivals and bought the goods. Then she went bankrupt and your rival lost a lot of money.

2 **A** When the downturn came, your company survived.

B When the downturn came, you had to make a lot of employees redundant, which was expensive, causing severe financial difficulties for the company.

3 **A** Your company is delighted with you. They did exactly as you hoped and the new project is going really well.
   B Your new business has been extremely successful and is making a lot of money.

From *Business Benchmark Advanced/Higher* by Guy Brook-Hart © Cambridge University Press 2007   **PHOTOCOPIABLE** UNIT 14

Answer key

Student's Book activities

The theatre business

Listening

1   1 d   2 c   3 a   4 e   5 b   6 f
2   1 B   2 A   3 B   4 B   5 A   6 C   7 A

Vocabulary

1   1 f   2 b   3 h   4 e   5 c   6 d   7 g   8 a
2   1 break down   2 running costs   3 backers; put
    up   4 break even   5 sue

Sponsoring the arts

Grammar workshop: *infinitive and verb + –ing*

1   1   Because it represents a low-cost opportunity to
        enhance the company's image both locally and
        nationally; sponsorshop can be offset against
        tax.
    2   It would involve investing £10,000; in return,
        the company would have its name and logo on
        all publicity material and theatre programmes,
        and the logo would appear in the theatre.

2   1 sponsoring   2 to examine   3 doing
    4 promoting   5 to give   6 backing   7
    Sponsoring   8 hiring   9 to receive   10 To cover
    11 to include   12 to be agreed   13 to fund
    14 to enhance   15 to offset

3   1   (to) sponsoring (1), (of) doing, (to) promoting,
        (by) backing
    2   Sponsoring (7)
    3   include hiring
    4   tend to give, expect to receive, undertake to
        include, agree to fund
    5   to examine, To cover
    6   opportunity to enhance
    7   to be agreed

Listening

1 B   2 C   3 B   4 A   5 C   6 A   7 A   8 A

Transcripts

23 Listening page 69

I = *interviewer*; PF = *Philip Franks*

I: How do you think the theatre business is different from other businesses?

PF: Um, well, probably in no way at all. But the theatre business isn't just a business. The business side of it, i.e. something which has to produce a product that people want and which people are prepared to pay for, is exactly the same as any other business. It must be planned, it must be budgeted, it must be marketed and it must be successful in order to survive. However, the theatre's also an art form, and you can't, um, apply strict business standards to art. You just can't. The theatre has to have, in some way shape or form, the right to fail and the right to be unpopular.

I: And when a new production is going to be put on, where does the initial impulse come from?

PF: A commercial producer, er, for whom money is absolutely paramount, because they're not supported by the state in any way, um, will find a star, somebody maybe with a high film and/or television profile, and try and build a production round him or her.

I: How would you go about, um, setting, putting on a commercial play?

PF: Well, if … if I was, if … if I had a play in my head that I wanted to direct, and it had a cast of more than, say,

ten, um, I'd be pretty foolish to take it to a commercial management, because they would just say, I'm sorry we can't afford it, unless you have Brad Pitt in it, in which case we'll fill every theatre in the country. Um, we simply can't afford it. You have to be practical about these things. You have to know your audience, you have to know your producer. And most commercial, most theatre managers spend most of their time trying to second-guess what an audience will like. And more often than not, the things that are huge runaway successes both artistically and commercially, you couldn't have predicted in a million years.

I: How would you go about making financial forecasts and budgeting for a new production?

PF: How would I go about making financial forecasts? Um, I suppose if you knew that you had a certain bankable star, um, then your forecasts would be higher than if you were just taking the risk on a new play. If … you were performing a brand-new play with a good but not necessarily bankable cast, you would limit the number of performances. I think it would seem wise to do maybe 20 or 24 performances of … of a new play, not try and run it forever. Um, and be very careful about the size of cast, because an awful lot of the … the budget of a production goes in, um, actors' wages.

Transcripts

I: Yes, when you've got a budget, say you've got a production that you're going to mount and you're doing the budget, how does it break down?

PF: It breaks down into, um, creative team's fees, i.e. director, designer, lighting designer, sound designer, choreographer maybe – this is at sort of full stretch – actors' fees, a set budget for … for building, making and maintaining the set, a costume budget for either hire or making of the costumes, um, a properties budget, i.e. the things that are on the set, the objects that you will either have to, again, either hire or buy, um, and certain, some of those will be called 'running props'. That might be things that are consumed, er, cigarettes that are smoked, food that's eaten, plates that are broken. That has to be budgeted for as well. Um, and then, er, it's the running costs of the building, and that differs from, if it's again, if it's, if it's a subsidised repertory house or if it's not, if it's commercial. For instance, many subsidised reps have their own workshops where things are built, so you don't have to budget that over and above. Commercial projects which don't have a fixed building home, you would have to budget for having your set built out and then transported in to wherever you go.

I: And … a budget then has to be reduced, are there certain things that you would always go to first to cut?

PF: Um, I think you would look at, you would look very, very, very carefully at how many people you could afford, because to change that at a late stage is fraught with peril, er, not … not only from a sensitive and emotional side, but from a legal side – if somebody is … is sacked without deserving it simply because you can't afford to hire them, then they would be well within their rights – and I'm sure Equity would, Equity, the actors' union, would help them – to sue you and management for every penny they had. So you get the people right and you stick to it. Scenic elements are the next most expensive thing. You might find that a set has a piece of very expensive technical equipment for instance, a video screen or something like that which you might decide, we just can't afford it, or a revolving stage, we just can't afford the revolve. Or, for instance, many plays are set in rooms with three walls, obviously not four because you wouldn't be able to see.

I: So how would you finance a production? A commercial production, we're talking about.

PF: A commercial production, er, I would go to a producer. Assuming that I'm the director, I would go to a producer and say, 'I've got a marvellous idea. Let's do A Flea in her Ear by Feydeau … I've got actors X and Y lined up who are interested in being in it. Can you do it for me?' If the producer says, "Yes I think we might be able to do this", it is then his or her job to raise the money … They … they would either put up money of

their own, or, if they're the big ones and they own theatres, then that makes it a little bit simpler because you'd go into one of their theatres. … Or a smaller, more independent producer … would go to some rich backers, known as 'angels', and they would say to them, we have this production coming out, do you want to buy a share in it? Um, they might be sent, they might, for instance, sit down and say, 'OK, we'll … we'll send a hundred packages out to people who we think might be interested in investing in our production and they can invest in it at a level of their choice'. They can buy units, if you like, in the … in the production. And if … if you just fancy a flutter, you can buy a couple of units. If this is what you do and you want to take a big financial gamble in order, possibly, to reap a big financial reward, then you'll buy correspondingly a lot more units.

I: How long do you think a play has to run before it can break even in the West End?

PF: I think, um, a play that's been carefully budgeted and is not a hugely expensive one to front can probably break even in about 12 weeks.

I: Can you think of the proportion of London productions that make money versus the ones that don't make money?

PF: Um, no, I don't … no I don't know the answer to that. I would have thought that the ones that don't make money are … massively outweigh the ones that do. However, if you get one that does, it can be a cash cow for years and years.

I: Mm, and also, presumably, if the production company don't make money, they don't get to produce much … much more because they haven't got the money to put it on.

PF: No, although producers are huge risk-takers.

24 Listening page 71

Jenny: First tonight, we talk to Paul Keene from the National Gallery in London about corporate sponsorship of arts events. Paul, is sponsorship growing or is it going out of fashion?

Paul: Huh! Definitely not going out of fashion, Jenny. Corporate sponsorship of the arts is up about 50% on ten years ago.

Jenny: So it obviously takes quite a whack out of their budget. Why do they do it?

Paul: Well, there are lots of advantages to it. It can be great publicity if you get the right event or activity. You can get to people who would normally be impervious to your advertising, you can leave a pretty permanent reminder of your company's existence in a high-class public place, for example a theatre bar might be named after you or have the company logo in it, and <u>you can associate yourself with some really high-class art or music or theatre which does no end of good for your company image. Actually, for big organisations, I'd say that last point is the one which really gets them on board.</u>

Jenny: We hear about companies sponsoring arts events which actually appeal to quite a narrow audience, such as opera or ballet. Why do they do that?

Paul: Mm, that's interesting, but you must remember it's not the quantity of the audience but the quality which counts. These elitist events tend to attract people with money – not necessarily company directors, though I suppose there are a few of them, but certainly people who are likely to put money into the stock exchange. I mean, <u>you may not sell more product, but you bring your company name to people who invest, and up goes your share price, hopefully</u>. Neat, isn't it?

Jenny: It sounds clever if it works like that. We've always heard about corporate sponsorship in the United States. Is it something which is catching on more in Europe?

Paul: In the last ten years or so, certainly. Governments used to subsidise the arts much more than they do nowadays, so arts institutions have to get out there and find backers. <u>Though they've really been helped in a lot of countries by bigger tax breaks</u>. You know, what costs the company in real terms just about £200,000 can mean income of up to a million for the organisation receiving it.

Jenny: What sort of activities do companies most like to sponsor?

Paul: <u>I'd say that exhibitions in world-class galleries like the Tate are just about the most popular</u>. It depends on what they're exhibiting though. Music concerts are still pretty popular, although not so much nowadays, because they're fairly one-off. Er, exhibitions, on the other hand, um, go on for months and have people strolling around and taking their time and can be very beneficial for corporate image. Wouldn't you like your company to be associated with Matisse or Picasso? Then you read in the papers about Barclays Bank sponsoring the National Theatre, so there are no clear trends.

Jenny: What gives an arts organisation an advantage in attracting money?

Paul: They need to be big and well known. <u>Nowadays, they have full time fund-raisers – perhaps as many as 20 or 30 – working for them, and I think that's</u> <u>the crucial point</u>. They're able to put a professionalism into it that smaller organisations find hard to compete with. Although it also helps to be located in somewhere like London, Paris or Berlin. Places out in the provinces are at a disadvantage unless they're really well known, like, um, the Salzburg Festival or that sort of thing.

Jenny: Now, what about smaller businesses? How can they benefit from sponsoring the arts?

Paul: In a number of ways, actually, and they can do it on quite a modest scale and still reap the benefits. Particularly, their employees feel that they're working to put something back into the local community and that the profits are not just going to the shareholders. <u>It makes them feel more motivated and more closely tied to the company</u>. A lesser point is that people in the local community may also view them differently, and companies may hope that they'll get more favourable treatment from their local politicians. But politicians are a changeable lot, and I wouldn't count on it.

Jenny: Now, say an organisation – a theatre or an orchestra – was going to approach a company for funds, how should they go about it?

Paul: Um, good question. One thing which is definitely not too effective is to flood people with glossy brochures and videos and the like. Company decision-makers see hundreds of them. No, the personal approach is better – one of your executives should go along and give a presentation <u>accompanied by a two-page executive summary explaining goals, needs, budgets and activities. Something snappy and … and businesslike</u>.

Jenny: OK, and one final question: when a company is looking for something to sponsor, what criteria should they use?

Paul: In my opinion, you shouldn't look too much at visitor numbers. It may be OK, but it can rebound on you – you know, those exhibitions which attract thousands of people, long queues, many of whom are tourists from overseas and are never going to be your customers anyway. <u>The main objective is that the event is compatible with the way you want people to see your company</u>. What the newspapers say doesn't matter because they're not going to mention your sponsorship. Basically, the event has got to look right for you. Nothing else.

Jenny: Thank you, Paul Keene. And now, troubles in the fixed-line phone industry. Is it an obsolete technology, or can it adapt to changing times?

UNIT 15 Late payers

This unit focuses on language and vocabulary connected with financial problems, especially those caused by late or non-payers. It provides practice in letter-writing skills. The unit also provides general revision of different grammatical structures which can produce complex sentences.

Although none of the tasks in the unit exactly replicate exam questions, some are designed to give students the skills and practice needed to deal with them (see table below).

	BEC	BULATS
Listening 1: *Letter to a late payer*	Listening Part 1	
Grammar workshop: *Complex sentences*	Writing Part 2	Writing Part 2
Listening 2: *Letter to a late payer*	Listening Part 1	
Speaking: *Letter to a late payer*	Speaking Part 2	Speaking Part 2
Writing: *Letter to a late payer*	Writing Part 2	Writing Part 2
Photocopiable activity 2	Writing Part 2	Writing Part 2

Notes on unit

Getting started
An extra question for this section could be:
- Do you think governments sometimes contribute to the problem by paying for public contracts late?

Reading: *Late payers and small businesses*
If you have a small class and it's not practical to divide students into three groups:
- divide them into two groups and ask them to deal with the first two extracts
- when they have finished the activity, ask them to look at the heading for the third extract and predict what it will say
- ask them to read the extract to check if their predictions were correct.

Listening 1: *Letter to a late payer*
You could follow up the listening activity by asking:
- how well Astrid and Rajiv handled the situation
- how your students would have handled the phone call (from both sides).

If this leads to a productive discussion, ask students to do a role-play of Astrid's and Rajiv's conversation.

Grammar workshop: *Complex sentences*
An alternative approach:
- ask your students to cover up the box containing the words and phrases
- tell them to work in pairs and guess what phrases should go in the spaces in Astrid's letter.

You could also draw students' attention to the following collocations in the letter:
- *awaiting payment, settle your account, taking out an overdraft, prompt payment, deeply regret, valued customer, sincerely hope*

Writing: *Letter to a late payer*
If you have time, it would be a good idea to do Photocopiable activity 1 before the writing task.

Photocopiable activity 1
One possible procedure for this activity is to:
- ask students to work in groups of three
- cut the Answers box from the bottom of the photocopiable activity page and give it to one student
- ask that student to give feedback to the other two students after they have answered each question.

Speaking

Test how much you know about writing business letters in English by doing this quiz with a partner. When you have finished, check your answers at the bottom of the page.

Letter-writing quiz

1 When you write to someone and you don't know if the person is male or female, it's best to write:

  A Dear Sir   **B** Dear Sir/Madam   **C** Dear friend

2 In a British business letter, the best way to write the date is:

  A 6th January 07   **B** 01/06/07   **C** 6th January 2007

3 When you start a letter with 'Dear Mr White,', you should finish the letter with:

  A Yours faithfully,   **B** Yours sincerely,   **C** Yours,

4 Which of these is *not* correct in a British business letter, but *is* correct in an American business letter?

  A Dear Mr White   **B** Dear Mr. White: **C** Dear Mr White,

5 When should you write the name of the person you are writing to (e.g. Dear *Mr White*,)?

  A Only if you have met the person.   **B** Always if you know the name.

6 When should you use someone's first name in a business letter to someone from an English-speaking country (e.g. Dear *Martin*,)? (Choose *all* the correct answers.)

  A Always if you know their first name.   **B** When invited to do so.   **C** When the person is younger than you.

  D Only with friends.   **E** With colleagues, business associates and people at the same level as you in the same or another company.

7 When you are not sure how to start a letter, the best idea is to start with:

  A How are you? I hope you are in good health.   **B** Hello. My name's … . I'm Personal Assistant to … and I'm writing to … (+ reason for writing the letter).   **C** I am writing to … (+ reason for writing the letter).

8 Where should you put your complete name (not your signature)?

  A Above your address   **B** Below your signature

9 Where should you put your job title?

  A Above your address   **B** Below your name   **C** Above your address *and* below your name

Answers

1 B   2 C (A is not correct because if you write '6th January' it is more consistent to write the date as '2007', not '07'. B is correct in the USA, where the month comes before the date, but in Britain, this date would mean the same as 1st June, 2007.)   3 B   4 B   5 B   6 B and usually E   7 C   8 B   9 B

Writing

Read this letter written in British English and correct five mistakes in its layout and content.

Fenny Industrial Protective Clothing

194 Stockton Road
Middlesborough

15th Jan 20......

Chief Buyer
Racanos Stores
346 Wolverhampton Road
Solihull
BM16 4HI

Dear Mrs Ryder:

<u>7th International Clothing Fair</u>

Our company is going to participate in the 7th International Clothing Fair to be held in Birmingham from 15th–20th February. I am writing to you to invite you to visit our stand on the opening day and also to have lunch with us.

If you decide to come, we would be delighted to take the opportunity to show you our new clothing range and to give you preferential treatment for any orders you decide to place with us while you are there.

If you think you would like to visit us at the fair, please let us know and we will send complimentary entrance tickets for you and your colleagues.

I very much hope to see you there.

Yours faithfully,

Martin Whitemore

Marketing Director

Writing

1 Here are some boxes containing useful phrases for writing business letters. In each sentence, put the verb in brackets into the correct form. You may have to put it into a tense, active or passive, an infinitive, verb + –ing form or + –ed form, or add a modal verb (may, could, might, etc.).

Starting a letter
- Thank you for your letter of 28th January, in which you 1 .enquire/enquired.. (enquire) about our insurance rates.
- I am writing to apply for the post of economist as 2 .... (advertise) in the Financial Times of 16th November.
- With reference to our telephone call this morning, I am writing to confirm the schedule of meetings we 3 .... (arrange) for you during your visit.
- We are a manufacturer of equipment for fish farms 4 .... (base) in Helensburgh, Scotland, and would like some information on your range of machines for moulding plastics.

Bad news
- We regret to inform you that the goods 5 .... (delay) owing to the air-traffic controllers' strike.
- I am sorry to inform you that we are unable to offer you the position of economist which you 6 .... (apply) for.
- I am afraid that we are unable to grant you the 10 per cent discount you 7 .... (request).

Enclosures
- Please 8 .... (find) enclosed/attached a copy of the following documents:
- I 9 .... (enclose) our latest catalogue.

Good news
- We are writing 10 .... (inform) you that your order no. 234 for 15 laptop computers has been dispatched.
- We are pleased to announce that our prices 11 .... (cut) by 10 per cent.
- I am writing to invite you to our conference which 12 .... (hold) at the Grand Hotel on 21st April, Brighton.

Requests
- Could you please let us know whether these items 13 .... (be) still available?
- I would be grateful if you 14 .... (send) me your latest catalogue and price list.
- I would appreciate it if you 15 .... (recommend) a good hotel for my stay.

Complaints
- I am writing 16 .... (complain) about the delay in our order of 1st May.
- I regret 17 .... (say) that the delivery did not arrive in perfect condition.
- We are not satisfied with the way your company 18 .... (act) in this matter.

Apologies
- Please accept our apologies for any inconvenience this 19 .... (cause) you.
- I am very sorry about the delay in 20 .... (deliver) your order. This was caused by a shortage of components from our suppliers.
- We regret that this mistake was the result of the person who normally 21 .... (handle) your transactions 22 .... (be) on holiday.

2 Complete each of the gaps (1–13) in the sentences below with a word from the box.

> advance   advise   arrangements   convenient   discount   disregard   forward   further   hesitate
> hope   ~~quote~~   reference   suits

Orders
- We can **1**...*quote*........ you a unit price of €7.29 for orders of 50 units or more.
- We can offer you a **2**................. of three per cent for orders over €1,000.

Payment reminders
- With **3**................. to our invoice no. 247 for €557, we would like to **4**................. you that we still have not received your remittance for this amount.
- If your payment has already been made, please **5**................. this letter.

Appointments
- We will be in Munich next week and **6**................. that we can meet.
- I will be free on Monday. Please let me know if this **7**................. you.
- Please let me know if this would be **8**................. .
- I will call you next week to confirm our **9**................. .

Concluding
- If you have any **10**................. questions, please do not **11**................. to contact us.
- Thank you in **12**................. for your help.
- I look **13**................. to hearing from you.

3 Your manager has received the following letter.

> Dear Sir or Madam,
>
> You may be interested to hear that a delegation of business people from the Vancouver Chamber of Commerce, British Colombia, Canada, will be visiting your city next month with a view to exploring contacts both for import of goods from your region and exporting products from our region to your country.
>
> If you would like to take the opportunity to meet us, we shall be staying at the Marriott Hotel from ... .

She has asked you to reply saying:
- what your company does and giving a brief description of the company
- expressing interest in meeting business people from the same sector
- explaining what opportunities there might be to work together
- suggesting a time and place for a meeting.

Write 200–250 words.

Answer key

Photocopiable activity 1

Writing

Mistakes in the layout and content of the letter:

1 Write the date without the abbreviations i.e.: 15th January 20 ...... and place it below your address
2 Put the name of the addressee in the address i.e.:
Mrs Ryder
Chief Buyer, etc.
3 In British English, don't use a colon, use a comma after the salutation i.e.: *Dear Mrs Ryder,*
4 When you use the person's name, write *Yours sincerely,*. (*Yours faithfully*, is for when you started the letter *Dear Sir or Madam,*.)
5 Beneath your signature, print your name, and then beneath that your position, i.e.:
Yours sincerely,
Fedor Brosky
Fedor Brosky
Marketing Director

Photocopiable activity 2

Writing

1 1 enquire/enquired   2 advertised   3 arranged / have arranged / are arranging   4 based
5 were delayed / are delayed / have been delayed
6 applied / have applied   7 requested / have requested / are requesting   8 find   9 enclose / am enclosing   10 to inform   11 have been cut / are being cut / will be cut   12 is being held / will be held / we are holding   13 are / will still be
14 would / could send / sent   15 would/could recommend / recommended   16 to complain / in order to complain   17 to say   18 is acting / has been acting / has acted / acted   19 caused / has caused / may have caused / may cause / causes
20 delivering   21 handles   22 being
2 1 quote   2 discount   3 reference   4 advise
5 disregard   6 hope   7 suits   8 convenient
9 arrangements   10 further   11 hesitate
12 advance   13 forward

Student's Book activities

Late payers and small businesses

Vocabulary

1 h   2 j   3 e   4 k   5 a   6 g   7 i   8 d   9 b   10 f   11 c

Reading

3 1 Lack of cash (because you are a victim of late payment / falling order book / overtrading due to rapid growth) or poor financial management.

2 Cashflow problems, unauthorised overdrafts and high bank charges, time-consuming and stressful.
3 Businesses which are victims of late payment may refuse to do business, may only accept cash in advance, will not trust late payers in future.
4 Check credit worthiness, set credit limits, automate bookkeeping and monitor payments of invoices, keep your bank informed, have procedures for recovering debts.

4 1 constraints   2 unauthorised   3 punitive (bank) charges   4 undue   5 upfront   6 overdue
7 sound   8 root causes

Letter to a late payer

Listening 1

1 1 two (major) customers   2 cash-flow/cashflow difficulties   3 (our) overdraft   4 credit limit
5 (a) registered letter   6 11 days

Grammar workshop: *complex sentences*

1 1 According to   2 However   3 which   4 As
5 As a consequence   6 not only   7 but also
8 since   9 with whom   10 and that
2 1 The bank which normally handles our transactions has agreed to extend our overdraft for another month.
2 I regret to inform you that not only do we keep a list of late payers, but also we share this information with other suppliers. / ... but we also share this information with other suppliers.
3 We may have to put this matter in the hands of our lawyer, which we would regret having to do.
4 As I informed you in my previous letter, we shall not be supplying you with any further goods.
5 According to my accountant, we should set a credit limit of £5,000.

Vocabulary

1 in a position   2 deeply regret   3 unpleasantness
4 mutually profitable   5 further   6 settle your account with   7 assured   8 prompt   9 indicated
10 shortly   11 outstanding   12 awaiting

Listening 2

1 cash flow / cashflow   2 pay promptly
3 no good reason   4 (finance) team
5 (very) legitimate reasons   6 satisfied with

Writing

1 1 paragraph 1   2 paragraph 2   3 paragraph 2
4 paragraph 3   5 paragraph 3   6 paragraph 3
7 paragraph 4

Transcripts

Listening page 74

Astrid: Hello. Could I speak to Rajiv Narayan, please?
Rajiv: Speaking.
Astrid: Hello, Rajiv. It's Astrid Kloof here.
Rajiv: Hello, Astrid. Er, what can I do for you?
Astrid: It's about this invoice which you still haven't paid, and I was wondering when you were intending to pay it.
Rajiv: Oh that. Yes, I'm terribly sorry. We're hoping to pay it as soon as we possibly can.
Astrid: And when do you think that might be, Rajiv? It's beginning to cause us serious problems.
Rajiv: Well, the problem is that <u>two major customers</u> haven't paid us for what they owe us, and so we're also having <u>cashflow difficulties</u>.
Astrid: I see. So that's causing a sort of chain reaction, and we're at the end of it.
Rajiv: Yes, it's very embarrassing for us. We are hoping to pay you.
Astrid: Yes, but when?
Rajiv: Hopefully by the end of the month. Just as soon as we have some cash available. Our customers have promised to pay us by then.
Astrid: You know, Rajiv, the trouble is, it's beginning to cause us problems, too.
Rajiv: Oh dear.
Astrid: Yes, we've had to ask our bank to allow us to extend <u>our overdraft</u>, which is working out pretty expensive.
Rajiv: I'm sorry to hear that. In our case, to tell you the truth, we just can't ask the bank for any more money. We're right up to our <u>credit limit</u> now.
Astrid: I see – I'm sorry to hear it.
Rajiv: Look, Astrid, I'll keep you informed, and just as soon as the money comes in, I'll let you have what we owe you. Is ... is that all right?
Astrid: OK, Rajiv. I suppose it'll have to be. What I'd really like is a firm commitment to pay this month.
Rajiv: I think I can give you that, Astrid.
Astrid: I'd like that commitment in writing, Rajiv. Can you do that for me?
Rajiv: Sure. I don't see why not. I'll put a <u>registered letter</u> in the post to you today. You should get it tomorrow.
Astrid: OK, Rajiv. Today's the 20th. I look forward to receiving your cheque within the next <u>11 days</u>.
Rajiv: Fine, Astrid, and thanks for calling.
Astrid: You're welcome. Goodbye.
Rajiv: Goodbye.

Listening page 75

I = interviewer; WB = William Brook-Hart
I: Does Gifford's have problems with late payers or non-payers? And if so, how do you deal with them?
WB: Well, er, that has been a theme of recent years, and the need to, um, improve our <u>cashflow</u> is something which we've targeted during the last few years. We have a team of very friendly, um, people who contact our late payers amongst our clients and, um, politely remind them of the need to, er, <u>pay promptly</u>. Um, so it's very much done on a friendly, er, basis of encouraging to start with, um, but clearly if we have a client who, um, who's a very late payer and they had <u>no good reason</u> for ... for delaying payment, then ... then other measures have to be taken.
I: So this is outsourced from Gifford's, it's not a department within ...
WB: No, it's within Gifford, yep, so they're very much part of our team.
I: Part of the <u>finance team</u>.
WB: Part of the finance team who'll ... who'll look to recover late payment. And because we're looking to, um, have future jobs with clients, of course, um, it's preferably done on a very friendly, amicable basis.
I: But does it happen often that, um, that people are, that companies don't pay or that, um, I mean, they can be a slow payer? I suppose you get to know them.
WB: It's ... very rare that a company won't actually ever pay. There are some who are slow payers, but of course some of them may reckon that they've got very <u>legitimate reasons</u> for paying slowly. They may not be <u>satisfied with</u> the work we've done and they'll hold back payment until they're satisfied that we've done everything that we have to do.

UNIT 16 Negotiating a lease

This unit teaches some language and vocabulary needed for negotiating. It also revises alternative phrases for *if* in conditional sentences.

Although none of the tasks in the unit exactly replicate exam questions, some are designed to give students the skills and practice needed to deal with them (see table below).

	BEC	BULATS
Getting started	Speaking Part 2	Speaking Part 2
Listening: *Hard bargaining*	Listening Part 2	Listening Part 3
Listening: *Leasing office space*	Listening Part 1	
Role-play: *Leasing office space*		Speaking Part 3
Writing: *Leasing office space*	Writing Part 2	Writing Part 2
Photocopiable activity	Reading Part 1 Speaking Part 3	Reading Part 2 Section 1 Speaking Part 3

Notes on unit

Getting started

In many countries, and for many jobs, it may be difficult or unusual to negotiate your salary at a job interview. If this is the case, *either*:

- ask students to ignore this point *or*:
- tell them that this is quite common when applying for management positions in many European or North American companies. Ask them to imagine it is this type of job they are applying for.

All the situations may require some imagination from students. If necessary, to get them started, elicit (for the salary at a job interview):

- your present salary
- the salary for the post which is the industry standard/ what competitors pay
- what similar posts within the company are paid.

Listening: *Hard bargaining*

It is perhaps worth discussing the best approach to this task. Students can *either*:

- listen for the *type of negotiation* the first time they listen and the *problem* the second time *or*:
- listen for both items both times.

You can ask them to experiment by working in pairs. One student tries the first method and the other the second, and then they compare results and experiences. This may help them to find the best exam technique.

Reading: *Leasing office space*

As a warmer for this activity, ask your students:

- (if they work) whether they know if their offices are leased or owned by the organisation they work for
- what the advantages and disadvantages of leasing over ownership are (advantages: lower initial investment, capital available for other activities, less risk if business goes wrong, more flexibility if you want to move premises; disadvantages: high rents, loss of opportunity for investment in property if property market is rising)
- whether they have any experience of leasing office space and what the considerations and pitfalls were.

Writing: *Leasing office space*

If you have access to networked computers, ask students to do the writing task on computers and project their answers for the whole class to see (and possibly correct).

Photocopiable activity   Negotiation strategy: avoiding pitfalls

Getting started

Work together in groups of four. Brainstorm a list of advice for would-be negotiators.

Reading

Read the five extracts (A–E) from an article containing advice for negotiators. Decide which extract each sentence (1–8) below refers to. Write A, B, C, D or E in the boxes.

1 Avoid annoying your opponents: they may look for an opportunity for revenge. `E`
2 Consider your opponents' possible demands and what they may find acceptable. ☐
3 Don't give your opponents everything they ask for. ☐
4 Get your opponents to look at the deal from your point of view. ☐
5 It's not always necessary to compromise. ☐
6 Make what you're offering appear attractive to your opponents. ☐
7 Remember that your opponents today may be your colleagues tomorrow. ☐
8 You should decide in advance what is the lowest amount you are prepared to accept. ☐

A
Successful negotiators make detailed plans. They know their priorities and alternatives, should they fail to reach an agreement. You must know your bottom line. In addition, you need to understand time constraints and know whether this is the only time you will see your opponents in negotiation. After preparing your own agenda, outline the same for your opponents: what are their preferences, alternatives, and bottom line? Once at the bargaining table, test your hypotheses to determine what the opposition's priorities really are.

B
You may make the common mistake of thinking you cannot have everything when both parties want the same thing. For example: in the context of an overall negotiation involving salary, bonus and vacation, the boss wants to transfer a manager to San Francisco. The manager is eager, but frequently he will believe that, since the boss gave him a desired promotion, he must compromise on the transfer location. The employee might actually suggest a transfer to Atlanta. His psychology is: 'I can't expect to get everything I want, so I'll take the middle'.

C
Negotiators need to analyse the biases their opponents bring to the table. How will they evaluate your offers? One way to get inside your opponent's head and influence his attitude is to shape the issues for him, a technique called 'framing'. If you get your opponent to accept your view of the situation, then you can influence the amount of risk he is willing to take. A common mistake is negotiating from a negative frame: 'The other firm's deal offers $12, but we can afford only $11'. You must get them to focus on the point you are starting from — $10, not $12. You frame the issue positively by talking about all the ways your contract is different from the others. Your contract has some advantages outside of the hourly pay. The other side will be more willing to risk lower wages for the purported other benefits.

D
Accepting a well-priced deal too quickly can cause anger on the other side, too. If you list a used car for $5,000, you might really be thinking of accepting $4,500. But when your first buyer immediately writes you a check for $5,000 without trying to bargain, how do you feel? Disappointed. You'll think you sold it for too little. The lesson is: no matter what the price, even if it's fair, always offer less — if only to make your opponent feel good about the deal.

E
Finally, when you've got a result you're really delighted with, never do the dance of joy in public by turning to your opponents and telling them you would have done it for less. This will only drive your opponent to extract the difference from you sometime in the future. It is essential to keep on professional terms with your negotiating opponents. You may find yourself on the same side of the bargaining table one day.

From Negotiation strategy: Six common pitfalls to avoid by Margaret Neale

Talking point

Your manager has decided to run a one-day training course on basic negotiating skills for staff in your department. He has asked you to plan the course. Work in groups of three and decide the following:

- which skills staff should be taught
- what activities are most useful for learning negotiating skills
- what opportunities staff should be given to put their new skills into practice.

From *Business Benchmark Advanced/Higher* by Guy Brook-Hart © Cambridge University Press 2007   **PHOTOCOPIABLE**

Answer key

Photocopiable activity

Getting started
Suggested answer
1 Prepare carefully for any negotiation.
2 Obtain as much information as possible about your negotiating counterparts and their requirements.
3 Don't state all your demands at once.
4 Be sure what your bottom line is, but don't let your counterparts know what it is unless absolutely necessary.
5 Summarise what you have agreed.

Reading
1 E   2 A   3 D   4 C   5 B   6 C   7 E   8 A

Talking point
Suggested answers
1 Which skills staff should be taught: planning negotiations, strategies for testing your hypotheses about your opponents' priorities, deciding when to compromise, learning to 'frame' the negotiation (see extract C), negotiating behaviour and negotiating psychology
2 What activities are most useful for learning negotiating skills: theoretical lectures, role-plays and simulations
3 What opportunities staff should be given to put their new skills into practice: opportunities to be part of negotiating teams for procurement or for sales

Student's Book activities

Hard bargaining

Listening

	Type of negotiation	Problem
Vasili	C	J
Melinda	G	O
Glenn	D	L/P
Carla	H	I
Naomi	B	M

Vocabulary
1 a   2 h   3 b   4 c   5 g   6 d   7 f   8 e

Leasing office space

Reading
3 1 impact   2 meets   3 mind   4 stock   5 term
6 lock   7 interruption   8 come   9 restrictions
10 comes   11 unlimited   12 leverage

Listening
1 (an) (upfront) deposit   2 (commercial) activity
3 (the) inflation (rate)   4 alterations or repairs
5 renewable   6 (staff) parking space(s)

Grammar workshop: *conditional sentences: alternatives to if*
1 1 Supposing   2 unless   3 as long as
   4 provided   5 on condition that
2 Suggested answers
   1 Will we be able to undercut them?
   2 Imagine that you were suddenly made redundant.
   3 … you pay the additional premium.
   4 We'll reduce the rent by 5% …
   5 … you achieve all your performance targets.

Role-play
1 f, l;   2 c, e;   3 b, h, j;   4 a, m, n;   5 d, k;   6 o;   7 g, i

GRAMMAR WORKSHOP 4

Conditional sentences
1 launch; will almost certainly lose
2 went (were to go) / go; would be / will be
3 hadn't run; might have met
4 increases; will rise *or* increased; would rise
5 had been; could have made   6 could; would be

Infinitive and verb + –ing
1 Going; taking   2 to continue; going   3 to spot; running   4 To discourage; going; to close
5 to know; visiting   6 to hold; completing

Complex sentences
Suggested answers
1 We experienced a shortfall in earnings last year as a result of losing one of our most important customers, who started buying from our principal competitor.
2 I'm writing to thank you because the goods you dispatched to us last week arrived at our warehouse in record time, which means that our production is now ahead of schedule.
3 Martin Peters, whose appraisal, you may remember, was not very satisfactory, has decided to leave the company, so we will have to start recruiting a replacement as soon as we can.
4 While travelling home last night, I came up with a brilliant solution to our staffing problems, which I'm going to put in an informal proposal to be circulated among senior managers.
5 Unless Tasker Ltd offers its employees more attractive financial incentives, they will never manage to reach the productivity agreement which would put them ahead of the competition.

Answer key

6 There's a shortage of skilled workers in the chemical industry due to insufficient numbers of young people studying science subjects at school.

7 Redland Electronics have announced record profits for the fourth year running as a result of their partnership with Kawasaki Electronics of Japan.

Transcripts

Listening page 76

Tutor: So, let's initiate today's session by talking about negotiating problems and things we can do to get round them or get over them. Negotiating is a big part of all your jobs, er, so let's have a quick buzz session where each of you briefly describes a negotiating problem you've had in the past, and then we'll go on to look at how we can deal with these things. How does that sound to you? All right? So, um, who'd like to start? Vasili?

Vasili: Er, sure. Um, this wasn't in my present job, I'll start by saying. Er, I was working in procurement for a processed-food manufacturer at the time, you know a … a large multinational, and, er, working on a deal for a pretty large consignment of flour, and by that I mean several hundred tonnes. Of course, I wanted them to knock something off the price, I mean, taking into account the fact that we were buying in bulk. I was expecting to haggle a bit. You know, I'd ask for six and settle for three, reach a compromise, but when I put it to them, their sales people, I mean, they said that they didn't have the authority and would have to ask someone higher up. I mean, that's pretty frustrating when you think you're talking to the right people and then it … it turns out you're not.

Tutor: Um, so, pretty irritating. Er, who's next? Melinda?

Melinda: Yes. This was, er, before I was promoted, when I was still a fairly inexperienced office manager and we were talking about installing a new computer network in the office. I … I should say that we were running a pretty big but temporary operation to meet an order that had come in, so we were in larger temporary offices and, since it was just for a few months, we didn't want to buy the stuff, just hire it. Being relatively junior and fairly new in the job, I didn't have much leverage – you know, bargaining power. Well, when I met their reps, they only wanted to sell us the stuff and didn't seem to take in the fact that we wouldn't be needing it in six months' time. And they refused to take me seriously because I was so young.

Tutor: Um, ageism in reverse. And you, Glenn?

Glenn: I work in air-conditioning, and we were working on this deal with one of those big hotel chains where they'd buy the stuff and we'd install it. Then they insisted that the maintenance should be thrown in free, even when we'd already given them quite a hefty discount. I mean you can't do that; one thing is the price and another thing is the cost of labour and parts over years and years. Even when I told them what my bottom line was, they just refused to budge. I mean, their buildings manager said take it or leave it and that was it; we'd reached a deadlock. So, no deal.

Tutor: Very disappointing. Carla?

Carla: We import clothes from the Far East and really we have to have them in the stores by the beginning of October to make the winter season. These were a range of coats that we'd had designed and ordered and we were negotiating all the terms. The real sticking point was that if they were late delivering, we said they'd have to pay, or rather, they'd only get 50% of the final price. I think the real problem was that they didn't even know when they'd be able to get the things out and they were afraid of taking on something they couldn't do.

Tutor: Mm, frustrating. Finally you, Naomi.

Naomi: Well, these people had outlets all over the country, so we were hoping they'd agree to stock and sell our products. You know, they didn't have to do much more than that, except perhaps organise the publicity, which shouldn't have been a problem for them. Everything was going fine, you know, I was talking about the constraints on us caused by our suppliers' prices – it was just a bargaining point, really, because that's one of the enjoyable parts of my job, you know, the horse-trading – when suddenly my opposite number interrupted me by saying that it was too soon to be talking about this and that the market was not right yet. I was very put out because we'd already been discussing it for several months. I mean he could have come out with this information sooner.

Tutor: Um, well OK, thanks all of you. That was very good. Um, now, let's take all of these one at a time and analyse them and see exactly what's happening and what we can do about it …

RD = Regional Director; CS = Company Secretary

RD: So, um, let's go over what they're asking for again.

CS: Fine, I'll just get it up on the screen and then we can go through it point by point and see what we think. Um …

RD: That's it.

CS: OK, here it is. First, apart from the monthly rent, which we discussed before, they're asking for another half year as an <u>upfront deposit</u>. What do you think of that, Ramón?

RD: It's a bit steep. Supposing we offered them two months and settled for three. Do you think they'd accept that?

CS: Mm, it's possible, I suppose. We could try – after all, I don't think there are too many companies who'd be willing to shell out six months' rent as a lump sum.

RD: No, still, let's go through the rest and then we can put together a counter offer.

CS: Right. The next point, which shouldn't give us too many problems, I imagine, is that we'll have to keep to the same <u>commercial activity</u> unless we obtain the owner's approval in writing.

RD: Mm, no problem there. I suppose if we were to start doing something different, they could use it as an excuse to try to up the rent. I mean, we're an insurance company, and as long as we continue to be an insurance company, we won't have anything to worry about. We could perhaps use it as a bargaining point, though – you know, pretend that we might change and then haggle over it to get an advantage somewhere else.

CS: Um, possibly. Er, there's one thing here which I'm not too keen on – they want the right to raise the rent every year according to <u>the inflation rate</u>, and I think we'd be better going for a two-year deal on that.

RD: Mm, OK, but provided rents didn't rise by more than that, I'd be quite happy with that clause myself. I don't see it as a big issue, frankly.

CS: True, so perhaps we could let that one pass, though again we might use it as a bargaining point.

RD: Um, quite.

CS: Er, another point in this document is that we, the leaseholders, must foot the bill for any <u>alterations or repairs</u> we might decide to make. This is quite serious, as we have to be sure the building is in good condition before signing anything. We'll need a thorough survey, and we can only agree to this provided we're given a fairly long lease. I mean, we don't want to go to the expense of a lot of building work and then be evicted soon afterwards.

RD: Um, correct. So we should look for some guarantees there.

CS: Sure, and I think they'll be quite amenable on that one, because there aren't that many companies looking to lease round here at the moment. Er, the only thing about it that I don't like is that they want to reserve the right to change the conditions of the lease – i.e. making them <u>renewable</u> – after five years.

RD: Um, personally, I think we should go for ten.

CS: Mm, me too. In fact, I'd only take the lease on condition that we had a ten-year agreement.

RD: Good. Well, we have the basis for a counter-offer then. I think we should be able to negotiate something very much to our advantage. And the landlord should be happy, because we're prepared to offer him a pretty generous rent.

CS: True. And he's thrown in something which is quite attractive – it's not here on the document, but his secretary phoned to say that there was also the possibility of us renting <u>staff parking space</u> in the basement as part of the deal.

RD: Well, that's pretty attractive. If we were to get that, it would make life much easier for everyone. Did he mention a price or how many places were available?

CS: Mm … he told me there was room for up to 30 cars, which might mean we had some room for customers as well.

UNIT 17 Workplace atmosphere

This unit focuses on how workplace atmosphere can affect staff motivation and the issue of workplace stress. Students do further work on writing reports based on charts. They study the use of reference devices in written texts and language for expressing causes and results.

Although none of the tasks in the unit exactly replicate exam questions, some are designed to give students the skills and practice needed to deal with them (see table below).

	BEC	BULATS
Reading: *Motivating employees*	Reading Part 3	Reading Part 2 Section 5
Talking point: *Motivating employees*	Speaking Part 4	Speaking Part 4
Reading: *Stress in the workplace*	Reading Part 5	Reading Part 2 Section 3
Listening: *Stress in the workplace*	Listening Part 3	Listening Part 4
Writing: *Stress in the workplace*	Writing Part 1	
Photocopiable activity	Writing Part 2	

Notes on unit

Getting started

You could extend this by doing the photocopiable activity on the next page. Pre-service students may find this more manageable.

Reading: *Motivating employees*

As a further lead-in to this activity, you could ask your students to look at the title of Sirota's book in the first line and say:

- what attitude it reveals about the happiness of employees (*answer: that happy/enthusiastic employees increase company profits*)
- what this reveals about companies' and shareholders' attitudes to employees (*answer: that companies and shareholders are motivated by profit and that employee enthusiasm is a means to this end*).

You can then ask your students if the title reflects similar attitudes in their own country.

When students have done the reading activity, as a follow-up, you could ask them these questions:

- Is the article a reflection of particularly Western attitudes to work?
- How would they describe workplace relations in their own country, if they are different from those described in the article?

Grammar workshop: *Reference devices*

You could also explain that it is better English style to avoid repetition of vocabulary, where possible (this may not be true of all cultures or languages) and that reference devices help to do this.

Reading: *Stress in the workplace*

As a lead-in to this activity, you could ask students these questions:

- Is stress an issue in your country? Why? What causes it?
- Are workplace accidents an issue? What steps does your government take to reduce them?

Listening: *Stress in the workplace*

Instead of listening again to answer the multiple-choice questions, you could:

- ask your students to answer them from what they have understood so far
- play the recording again afterwards for them to check their choices.

Writing: *Stress in the workplace*

As a round-up for the whole unit, you could ask students these questions:

- What other factors related to human resources affect the efficiency of organisations?
- How much can organisations realistically do to deal with stress?
- What duties do organisations have to their employees beyond the basic terms of their contracts?

Reading

Work alone to answer the questions about your attitudes to work and workplaces.

Attitudes to work

How do you view your career, your colleagues and your workplace?

- **When you answer the questions, choose the answer which is closest to the truth for you.**
- **If you want to, you can choose more than one answer.**
- **Where none of them are exactly right for you, think how you would explain your situation.**

1 Which of these most closely reflects your attitude to timekeeping?
A I always make sure I arrive on time. If necessary, I'm early.
B It depends. If it's something important, I'll be on time but other times I may be a few minutes late.
C I may start late, I may stretch my breaks, but I get through my work and I meet my deadlines.
D I have no choice. If I'm late, I will be disciplined.

2 How long do you think people should stay in the same job?
A One year
B Three years
C Until they find something better
D All their working lives

3 When would you change jobs?
A I'm always looking for something better – I'd change if I found it.
B After a few years I might feel it's time to move on.
C Only if I was made redundant.
D If there were unwelcome changes in the place where I work.

4 Which of these most closely reflects your attitude to your colleagues?
A They're my friends.
B They're my rivals.
C They're my collaborators.
D They're useful to me.
E They just happen to share the same workplace.

5 Which of these most closely reflects your attitude to bosses?
A Bosses are colleagues. We should share common goals.
B Bosses are friends. We should enjoy each other's company.

C Bosses are supervisors. Their function is to make sure my work is up to standard.
D Bosses give instructions. I have to carry them out.

6 How do you view your career?
A I want to reach the top of my profession.
B I've planned my career and I'll follow that plan.
C At about 50, I'll want a career change.
D I'm happy as long as it provides me with an acceptable lifestyle.
E I'm not sure what my career is going to be yet.
F I've reached where I want to be.

7 Which of these do you think should be the most important aspect of your job?
A Your duties and responsibilities
B The companionship and respect of your colleagues
C Your salary
D The opportunities the job offers you

8 Which of these things do you think would motivate you to improve your work performance?
A The opportunity for more responsibility and promotion if you perform well
B Performance-related pay and bonuses
C Praise from your superiors
D A dynamic and stimulating workplace atmosphere

9 Which of these attitudes do you agree with?
A I want to feel proud of the organisation I work for and a part of it.
B If the organisation looks after me, I'll be loyal to it.
C Mine's a transactional relationship: I work in exchange for money and that's as far as it goes.
D I share my organisation's goals.

10 Which of these would you find most discouraging?
A An unfriendly boss
B Unfriendly or unmotivated colleagues
C Poor working conditions
D Low pay

Speaking

Work in pairs. Explain your answers to each other and give the reasons for them.

Answer key

Student's Book activities

Motivating employees

Reading

1 David Sirota would probably agree with 3, 5 and 6.
  He would probably disagree with 1, 2 and 4.
2 1 C firms where employee morale is high tend to
      outperform competitors.
  2 D they retrain workers
  3 B The team could look at quality and at what
      kind of maintenance and support were
      needed, and it could decide how to rotate
      workers.
  4 A Research has verified a system such as 'gain
      sharing', in which a group of workers judges
      its performance over time.
  5 C Then there is transactional ... The attitude is,
      'We paid you, now we are even ...' That's
      where most companies have gone today.

Grammar workshop: *reference devices*

1 1 *This* and *it* both refer to *camaraderie.*
  2 *they* refers to *some companies.*
2 for which (line 10) = the organisation
  it (line 10) = your job
  This (line 11) = camaraderie
  It ('s) (line 11) = camaraderie
  do (line 16) = laying off people
  they (line 18) = some companies
  that (line 25) = having groups of employees build
  an entire car
  it (line 29) = the team
  this approach (line 30) = Toyota said ... rotate
  workers
  thus (line 31) = as opposed to the usual top-down
  management
  this kind (line 35) = recognition, appreciative of
  good work
  such (line 42) = a reward
  That result (line 46) = greater efficiency
  This (line 47) = The result should be shared with
  workers
  the first one (line 50) = form of management
  Then there is (line 51) = form of management
  That's where (line 55) = the transactional form
  of management
  The fourth (line 57) = form of management
  It (line 58) = the partnership organisation
  that way (line 59) = because I paid you, now
  we're even

3 1 for which   2 This, that   3 do   4 that
  5 this approach   6 such   7 the first one, Then
  there is, The fourth   8 it, they

Stress in the workplace

Reading

2 1 the former   2 the same / this   3 the following
  4 They   5 this / the same   6 themselves
3 1 trends   2 pronounced   3 underwent   4 slight
  5 an all-time low   6 peaking

Listening

1 Suggested answers
  Causes of stress: perception of lack of control over
  one's life, harder work, close supervision,
  changing jobs, faster lifestyles, more intensive
  work, less social cohesion at work, work more
  invasive of non-working time, more time to worry
  about work, work more central to our lives and
  fashionable to complain about
2 1 B   2 A   3 B   4 C   5 B   6 A   7 C   8 B

Writing

3 Suggested answer
  This report summarises the findings of a survey of
  managers conducted to investigate the effects of
  stress on organisations.
  The main effect of stress is an increase in
  absenteeism, which 76% of managers reported.
  This is reflected in the figures for increased costs
  due to absenteeism in small companies, which
  have risen in companies with fewer than 100
  employees from €250 to €320 per employee over
  the last five years, while in companies of between
  100 and 249, these costs have increased from €310
  to €510 per employee.
  Stress also leads to decreased productivity
  (reported by 71% of managers), poor judgement
  and poor-quality products (54% each) and lower
  standards of customer care (41%). Managers also
  complain that staff leave the company more
  frequently, are less creative and have a higher rate
  of accidents.
  In conclusion, stress-related problems are a major
  cost for organisations.

Sue: Good evening and welcome to *Business Night*. Now, stress has been a favourite topic amongst workers and employers for a good number of years, and according to recent figures published by the Health and Safety Executive, it's still on the increase. The government is worried and has issued new guidelines to employers on how to deal with it. Tonight, we have in the studio Mariella Kinsky, an occupational psychologist who's just written a book about stress. Mariella, who is most likely to be affected by stress?

Mariella: Not an easy question to answer, because stress is such a subjective thing, and one person's stress is another person's excitement. Rather flippantly, I might suggest that housewives suffer the most from a fatal combination of boredom, isolation and low status, but there are no figures on this, because of course housewives don't come into data on work-related stress. The people who statistically come top of the league are routine office workers, which is surprising when you consider that, in many ways, their working lives are more comfortable than their predecessors' lives ever were. In general, their bosses seem to thrive on it, which perhaps explains in part how they became bosses in the first place. It also shows that it has its positive and negative sides. Positive stress is seen as a challenge which gives you a … a zest for living and doing more. Negative stress comes, I think, often from a perception one has of lack of control over one's life.

Sue: Mm … interesting. What is stress exactly? Can you give me a definition?

Mariella: Not easily, and that's the major problem doctors have when faced with a patient who says he's too stressed to go to work. I mean, how do you diagnose something you can't measure or examine? In that sense, it's a bit like pain; I mean, if you say you've got it, you've got it.

Sue: So, what do they do about it?

Mariella: Well, you can't just tell someone they're not really stressed and that they should pull themselves together and get on with things. Doctors do have a number of things in their armoury, though. They give people time off, they prescribe pills, in extreme cases they send them to a therapist …

Sue: Like you.

Mariella: Like me.

Sue: And are these things effective?

Mariella: In some cases. Not many.

Sue: So, how is stress affecting productivity, Mariella? Is it a major industrial problem or just something we all like to complain about?

Mariella: It's certainly something we like to complain about nowadays. In the old days, people had other ways of letting off their stress, I think. They weren't so supervised, so they could get their own back on their employers, you know, by not working too hard, perhaps even by stealing or damaging things at work, though I like to think that those were extreme cases, and this was part of the sort of 'them and us' battle which was fought out in the workplace. That's not so easy to do nowadays – I mean, it's socially frowned upon, and people can get found out more easily, especially as most of them spend their days sitting in front of a computer, not operating a machine at the back of a workshop. On the other hand, people change their jobs more frequently than was possible in the past, though it's hard to say what part stress plays in this, or whether it's due to other factors. After all, starting anew in a new place must be at least as stressful as staying put. What we can measure and what shows a sharp increase is sick leave due to workplace pressure.

Sue: Mm … and what's causing it? Is it boredom, or surveillance, or overwork, or what?

Mariella: Again, there's plenty of debate about this amongst occupational psychologists. We certainly don't spend so much time at work as we did in the past. All the figures will bear me out on that one. While we're at work, the pace has certainly hotted up: they give us perks like laptops and mobiles, and as a result we're always on call and we end up working very much more intensively than we did in the past. I think it has to be that. I mean, you mention that Big Brother bugbear – they can monitor your computer activity, they can record your phone calls and so on – all technically feasible, but it only happens in large companies with the resources to do this. Most companies really don't have the time or the personnel, while reports of workplace stress are pretty much across the board. So the cause has to be what I mentioned before.

Sue: Do you think the way our work is organised has changed, and that that's a stressor?

Mariella: Well, that's an interesting point. There's no doubt that our parents and grandparents in general lived harder lives, they worked more for less, but their work gave them a social cohesion which isn't so evident now. They got companionship from work, they were protected by their trade unions and

Transcript

professional associations in ways which disappeared 20-or-so years ago, and <u>when they stopped work, they stopped thinking about it and really devoted themselves to their family and freetime activities, and I think that last point is the one which has really made the difference</u>.

Sue: Mm … we often hear the consumer society cited as a reason for stress. What part does it play in the equation?

Mariella: Clearly, <u>we're better off than our parents and grandparents, and this means that we're liberated from a lot of the routine drudgery which they had to put up with in their non-working time. This means we have more time to worry</u>, and not only that, I think we even expect and want to worry about our work. Strange isn't it, considering that in most ways we're safer and more prosperous than was ever the case in the past?

Sue: Mm … you say we're expected to worry. What exactly do you mean by that?

Mariella: Yes, our <u>work has become very central to our identity, who we are as people, and work-related stress has become an acceptable, even a respectable thing to complain about</u>. You can do

it, and the fact that it's stressful is almost a sign of how difficult the job is and how hard you have to work, and therefore people will look up to you for doing something despite the difficulties.

Sue: So, finally, what can employers do to cut down on stress in the workplace?

Mariella: I don't think you're going to like my answer to this one, but, frankly, I think there's almost nothing to be done. It's a fashion and a reflection of our social climate. You know, you can, individually, get advice from professionals. In my experience, it's hardly ever cost-effective, or effective in any sense. Giving people social support by organising them in teams might, you would think, bring a favourable outcome, but it often results in more pressure on individuals prone to stress. <u>What the Health and Safety Executive, a … a government body, seem to think can improve things is getting people to take part in the change process within their workplaces. The idea is that they have a feeling of more control over their lives</u>. I personally see very little evidence for this being effective; people were less stressed in the past when they had even less control.

This unit presents language and vocabulary connected with different types of employment. Students are given language for expressing opinions and they also talk about their present jobs or a job they would like to do.

Although none of the tasks in the unit exactly replicate exam questions, some are designed to give students the skills and practice needed to deal with them (see table below).

	BEC	BULATS
Getting started	Speaking Part 1	Speaking Part 1
Reading: *The millennium generation*	Reading Part 1	Reading Part 2 Section 1
Talking point: *Job sharing*	Speaking Part 4	Speaking Part 4
Listening: *Job sharing*	Listening Part 1	
Speaking: *Job sharing*	Speaking Part 2	Speaking Part 2
Listening: *How people feel about their jobs*	Listening Part 2	Listening Part 3
Speaking: *How people feel about their jobs*	Speaking Part 1	Speaking Part 1
Photocopiable activity	Reading Part 2 Speaking Part 2	Speaking Part 2

Notes on unit

Reading: *The millennium generation*
Students doing the BEC Higher exam would have approximately ten minutes to complete the tasks connected with this text. You could:
- discuss with them what the most efficient approach to the text is
- draw their attention to the advice in the exam skills section on page 123 of the BEC edition
- set them a time limit for dealing with the text and questions.

Speaking: *Job sharing*
As an alternative, you could:
- give this activity as a project
- ask students to research one of these ways of working using the Internet, then prepare a presentation to be given during the following lesson.

Listening: *How people feel about their jobs*
At this stage in the course students will be familiar with this type of listening activity. As an alternative, they could follow this procedure:
1. Work in pairs, choose one of the names, one view of the present and one hope for the future.
2. Write a short monologue in which they incorporate the view of the present and the hope for the future.
3. Remind students not to include the actual words from the boxes and to include things in their monologues which may distract people, leading them to choose the wrong option.
4. Students then take turns to read their monologues to the rest of the class, who treat it as a listening exercise. Since it is normal to listen twice, each student in a pair can read the monologue once.
5. This is then followed by the listening activity in the Student's Book.

Photocopiable activity
Only do this activity if you are sure students won't express sexist opinions which other students may find offensive.

Getting started

Work in small groups and discuss these questions.

- Why do you think there are still fewer women than men in senior management posts?
- How would companies benefit from having more women in senior management?

Reading

1 Skim the following article (ignoring the gaps for the moment) to see if it contains the same ideas as your answer to the first question from the Getting started activity.

Why are so few women running big companies?

Business still male-dominated

A THE leaders of large public companies the world over are almost universally male. In America, only seven Fortune 500 CEOs are female; in Britain, only one woman runs a FTSE 100 company.
1 ....*b*........
Husbands and fathers are more likely to entrust the business to their widows or daughters than the markets are, but those companies are generally smaller.

B Why so few women? One answer is obvious: women are more likely than men to care for children. But to some extent it may be a question of time: women are now reaching positions just below CEO level in greater numbers than ever before, often rising through sales, marketing or finance. **2** ....

C However, women still face three big problems in climbing the corporate ladder, says Herminia Ibarra of INSEAD. First, they fail to get the really stretching jobs. **3** .... Getting into line management is important (and 90% of line managers at big American firms are male), but it is not enough: women also need tough, broad assignments to win experience and promotion.

D Second, women lack networks, not because they are deliberately excluded, but because people bond when they have much in common, and gender matters here. In particular, women lack the sort of networks that combine work and social life, which have proved hugely beneficial to men. **4** ....

E Third, women find it more difficult than men to develop an image compatible with leadership. There are fewer role models, and simply adopting a male style rarely works.
5 .... A study of business owners presented at this year's meeting of the Academy of Management found that 26% of male owners, but only 5% of female ones, wanted to be thought of as an authority figure.

F Sometimes women are their own worst enemies. A book by Linda Babcock and Sara Laschever called *Women Don't Ask* recently drew attention to their negotiating style. Ms Babcock noticed that male graduates with a master's degree from her university were paid starting salaries almost $4,000 above those of female students. On closer investigation, she found that the vast majority of the women had accepted the initial pay offer, but that 57% of the men (against only 7% of the women) had asked for more. **6** ....

G One senior headhunter says that boards frequently ask her to recruit women to top jobs. 'But when I get them there, the women say no. **7** ....' Maybe women have more sense than men.

From The Economist

From *Business Benchmark Advanced/Higher* by Guy Brook-Hart © Cambridge University Press 2007
PHOTOCOPIABLE   **UNIT 18**

2 Read the text again and decide what the main subject of each paragraph is. Write a note in the margin to help you remember.

3 Read the missing sentences (a–g) below and choose which sentence best fits in each gap (1–7). This task will show whether you have recognised the main points of each paragraph.

a 'Aggressive' male leaders are admired; female ones are disliked, especially by other women.

b An easier route for women to the top is to inherit.

c One study found that companies are much more likely to ask men than women to turn around a division in difficulties or to start a new one.

d They also tend to be concentrated in future-oriented sectors such as consumer products and technology.

e They look at what the job involves and think the price is too big to pay.

f Those who haggled raised their starting offer by an average of $4,053 – almost exactly the difference in men's and women's initial pay.

g Women are more likely to separate their working life from their home life, which makes it harder to go for a drink with the boss.

Vocabulary

Match the words from the text (1–8) with their meanings (a–h).

1 inherit

2 stretching jobs

3 assignments

4 networks

5 bond

6 role models

7 haggled

8 headhunter

a attempted to agree on a price or conditions by arguing

b form a close connection with other people

c contacts, friends and acquaintances who may help you professionally

d work which makes you learn new things and use your skills and experience more than you have done before

e person who tries to persuade someone to leave their job by offering them another job with more pay and a higher position

f receive something when someone dies

g pieces of work given to someone, typically as part of their studies or job

h people you admire and whose behaviour you try to copy

Talking point

Prepare a mini-presentation of about one minute on one of these subjects.

- **Management:** How to create more opportunities for women in company management.
- **The workplace:** How to eliminate different types of discrimination (ageism, sexism, racism) from the workplace.
- **Work:** The importance of equality of opportunity in the workplace.
- **Careers:** the importance of forming networks in career development.

Answer key

Photocopiable activity

Reading

1 Ideas expressed in the article as to why there are still fewer women than men in senior management posts: women are more likely to care for children; women fail to get the really stretching jobs; women lack networks; women find it difficult to develop an image compatible with leadership; they do not negotiate for themselves as much as men; the women decline top jobs when they are offered them

2 Suggested answers
Subjects of paragraphs: A: business still male-dominated; B: more senior women in the future; C: they fail to climb the corporate ladder; D: women lack networks; E: problem with leadership image; F: their own worst enemies; G: women decline top jobs

3 1 b   2 d   3 c   4 g   5 a   6 f   7 e

Vocabulary

1 f   2 d   3 g   4 c   5 b   6 h   7 a   8 e

Student's Book activities

Getting started

1 f   2 i   3 d   4 h   5 c   6 g   7 j   8 e   9 a
10 b

The millennium generation

Reading

2 1 E hungry for quick results
   2 C more young people have been striking out on their own.
   3 A They have less baggage and can therefore afford to take risks.
   4 C capital for the taking
   5 B They define themselves by their skills
   6 D You can always go back to college
   7 E intolerant of technophobes.
   8 E most will freelance

Vocabulary

1 less baggage   2 frenetic   3 obsolete   4 pervasive
5 places a premium on   6 roam   7 booming
8 striking out on (their) own

Job sharing

Talking point

1 1 f   2 e   3 c   4 a   5 b   6 d

Listening

1 career continuity / (flexibility)   2 family responsibilities   3 rejoin (the) workforce   4 go for promotion   5 less training   6 overtime   7 more productive / work harder   8 staff turnover
9 sickness absences   10 job functions
11 communication (problems)
12 more experienced partner

How people feel about their jobs

Listening

1

	Views of the present	Hopes for the future
Lechsinska	D	G
Ganesh	E	J
Francesca	F	I
Darron	C	L
Irenke	B	H

Vocabulary

1 1 apart   2 going   3 stuck   4 go   5 run
   6 dire   7 taken   8 good; cut

… and in actual fact, there are more than a million people in this country participating in some sort of job sharing scheme, so it's not all that unusual, really. What are its advantages and disadvantages? Well, for employees, if they have other things they want to do in life, for example, sing in a professional choir or do a university course as a mature student, career continuity is one of the main things in its favour. You don't have to totally give up one thing in order to do something else and, while you're satisfying your other longings, you can carry on working and earning a living. People who need to juggle their jobs and their family responsibilities get an element of flexibility which lets them carry on working when they might otherwise not be able to. Similarly, people who have had to give up working for one reason or other, can, through job sharing, rejoin the workforce in a way which they find practicable, er, especially if they can't work full-time.

There are a number of drawbacks for employees. First, for people who are a bit ambitious, job sharing lessens your chances of climbing the corporate ladder. The way round this is to put in your CV alongside that of your job-sharing colleague and go for promotion on a joint basis – and, er, this can work very well if both people in the partnership are performing well. Another drawback is that you're likely to come in for less training just because the cost of sending two people on a course is twice the cost of sending just one. Finally on this one, you'll probably never be paid overtime, as each of you is counted as a part-time worker, and you never get up to the maximum working hours.

There are quite a lot of advantages for employers to job sharing. Er, to start with, part-time workers generally work harder than full-time workers because they don't have to pace themselves through an eight-hour day or a five-day week. As a consequence, job sharers tend to be more productive, and this can reflect very favourably on the overall profitability of a department. Also, job-sharing schemes can make the difference between employees going off somewhere else and staying, so staff turnover on many occasions is lower in companies operating these schemes. Another thing: because job sharers have that extra flexibility to look after sick children or parents, they're less likely to take sickness absences than their full-time colleagues. Finally, to … to wind up, I'd better just point out the difficulties for employers when they want to implement a scheme like this, and it's not necessarily easy to do, even with the best will in the world. Because job sharers sometimes don't see each other, it can mean that job functions suffer – er, a task started by one person may not be continued by the other, so it takes longer to complete. Also, because working hours are different, bosses may not see the employees on the scheme regularly, and this can lead to communication problems. Finally, there's the training problem mentioned earlier and the costs involved in training two people instead of one. There is a way round this, which is to get the more experienced partner to train up the less experienced one.

However, I think that where employers and employees are willing to make the effort, job sharing can be a very positive experience for everyone involved and well worth giving a try. Thank you.

Transcripts

Presenter: In today's edition of *The Lowdown*, we talk about work and how it's changing. To start with, we invited five people from around the world to our studios to talk about their present jobs and their future ambitions. Here are some of the things they said.

Lechsinska: Well, my name's Lechsinska, and I'm an industrial electrician working in a large food-processing plant in Gdansk in Poland. Basically, I like my job, apart from the smell, but you can't have everything. I get on pretty well with my colleagues and I think they're pretty good to have placed their confidence in me, being a woman doing what's traditionally a man's job. On the other hand, I'm hardly getting what's the going rate for my job in this part of the world, and unless I get a more competitive wage, I think I'll soon be moving on, because I think, with my skills, I could make a better living being self-employed. I mean, I can't see myself working for them forever, even though I like the social side of things there.

Ganesh: I'm Ganesh and I work for the Indian subsidiary of a Swiss multinational as a pay clerk. Er, the job doesn't sound too exciting and it isn't. I've been in it for a few years now, and while computerisation has meant big changes in the way we work, I feel I'm stuck in a rut and stagnating. It's a sort of feeling of 'once a pay clerk, always a pay clerk'. I'm in my early thirties and with not too many commitments – I mean, I can easily make ends meet – so I'm thinking of doing one of those distance-learning courses where I can convert to being a proper accountant rather than what I'm doing now.

Francesca: My name's Francesca Morelli. My parents are Italian, though I was born and brought up in South London. Recently I've moved to Prague, where I work as a loss adjuster for a big insurance company. I'm on the go all the time and don't get much chance to wind down, not even at weekends, because they give me a mobile phone and I'm expected to be on call. Working hours are reasonable, in fact, but the job is pretty high pressure, and I sometimes worry that in the long run, it will affect my health. Well, basically I enjoy it, but I think I probably need a break from it for a year or so to take stock – just temporarily, I mean.

Darron: My name's Darron Corral, and I do temping for an agency just filling in for people off sick, or on maternity leave, or when there's a rush on. The place I'm working at the moment is pretty dire, actually – I mean, no one seems to speak to anyone, and when they do, it's only to complain – but, in general, I like temping because it suits my lifestyle. I can work when I want to work and I can concentrate on my career when I'm not. Er, in case you don't recognise me yet, I'm an aspiring actor waiting for my big break, and this job makes ends meet between the bit-parts I'm getting offered at the moment. My dream is to get taken on by the Royal Shakespeare Company and work for them till I retire in 40 years' time, 'cause this temping will become a bit of a strain if I carry it on for too long.

Irenke: So, I'm Irenke, and I'm from Hungary. At present, I'm working as a trainee stockbroker with a big firm in Budapest. We don't stop and there's lots of excitement because I'm buying and selling millions of euros' worth of shares every day. I think my boss supervises my work too much, which annoys me. I know he's worried I'll make a mistake, but I haven't so far. Still, I suppose it's his responsibility if I do. The money's good because we get a cut of the profits, and when I've made enough, I'll probably launch my own firm, but perhaps not a stockbroker's.

UNIT 19 Productivity

This unit focuses principally on report-writing. Students also learn vocabulary connected with productivity and grammatical structures to express cause and result. In the related Grammar workshop, they also revise modal verbs for certainty/uncertainty.

Although none of the tasks in the unit exactly replicate exam questions, some are designed to give students the skills and practice needed to deal with them (see table below).

	BEC	BULATS
Reading: *Productivity at Magro Toys*	Reading Part 6 Writing Part 2	Reading Part 2 Section 6 Writing Part 2
Listening: *Productivity concerns*	Listening Part 3	Listening Part 4
Speaking: *Productivity concerns*	Speaking Part 2	Speaking Part 2
Speaking: *Manufacturing and services*	Speaking Part 3	Speaking Part 3
Writing: *Manufacturing and services*	Writing Part 2	Writing Part 2
Photocopiable activity	Reading Part 2	

Notes on unit

Getting started

Productivity is not the only indicator of company performance – others are (for example): share price, market share, turnover, profits.

Speaking: *Productivity at Magro Toys*

After they have looked at the charts, but before they discuss them, ask students to:

- look at the Useful language
- do the work on modal verbs in Grammar workshop 5.

Reading: *Productivity at Magro Toys*

- As a follow-up to this, when students have done the writing exercise at the end of the unit, ask them to exchange reports and correct errors in each other's writing.
- For a reminder of formal/informal style, see the photocopiable activity in Unit 11 on page 68.

Listening: *Productivity concerns*

When students do the first task, encourage them to listen also for the ideas expressed, not just for the vocabulary items, then, as an alternative:

- encourage them to try to answer the multiple-choice questions before listening again
- play the recording again for them to check their answers.

Speaking: *Productivity concerns*

If you want to treat this activity as exam practice:

- ask students to choose one of the three topics
- give them one minute to prepare their talk
- give them one minute to speak on the subject to their partner
- meanwhile their partner should listen and think of a question to ask about the talk at the end.

Photocopiable activity

Getting started

Work in small groups. Brainstorm a list of factors which can limit or reduce productivity in a company (e.g. telephone interruptions, out-of-date equipment, etc.).

Reading

1 Read the following statements (1–9) made by different employees, ignoring the gaps for the moment. What are the factors affecting productivity mentioned in each case? Are there any extra ones which are not on the list you brainstormed?

1

'When I carried out a survey of our staff recently, I found that nearly 30% suffered either from occasional or chronic insomnia and admitted that in many cases it affected their output and their behaviour when they were at work. ....e........ Since this is a condition which is often caused by workplace stress, it would seem to me to be something of a vicious circle.'

Factor affecting productivity: *stress and insomnia*

2

'I spent a week with various delivery drivers and one thing I noticed was that at some of their destinations, rather than just leaving the goods, they stopped to pass the time of day and have a cup of tea or coffee. .... Then we would have to recruit untried and quite possibly unreliable replacements.'

Factor affecting productivity: ....

3

'Many of our office workers (i.e. 95% of staff) complained that we "impose" new, supposedly more efficient computer programs on them, without asking for their opinions. They then waste a lot of time struggling with the software. ....'

Factor affecting productivity: ....

4

'Head Office is near the city centre, which is where clients expect us to be. When I analysed our staff's home addresses and journey times, I found that many had journey times of way over half an hour to get from their homes on the outskirts and in dormitory towns to the city centre, and in some cases well over an hour. This means that many arrive tired and stressed before they have even sat down at their desks. ....'

Factor affecting productivity: ....

5

'I was musing on our productivity drive and it occurred to me that we put a lot of emphasis on staff productivity in general and almost none on managers' productivity. When I think about it, most managers spend most of the day either in meetings or on the telephone. ....'

Factor affecting productivity: ....

6

'Frankly, I stopped worrying about productivity some years back when we had one of those big shake-ups and agreed to reorganise our workforce in teams and set them targets. .... We set them tasks and we don't worry about how much time they put into them. Payment by results, you see.'

Factor affecting productivity: ....

7

'Why should I worry about productivity? I've got my job. It's the same job I've been doing for more than fifteen years. .... When those young managers come along with their ideas on efficiency, I send them away with a flea in their ear. Quite honestly, I do my job and I get paid for it and that's all that matters. I don't get a share of the profits, so why should I worry about them?'

Factor affecting productivity: ....

From *Business Benchmark Advanced/Higher* by Guy Brook-Hart © Cambridge University Press 2007 PHOTOCOPIABLE UNIT 19

Photocopiable activity

Constraints on productivity

8

'It's one of Parkinson's laws, isn't it, which says that work expands to fill the time available? Unfortunately, our bosses seem to have cottoned on to that one in a big way and little by little they reduce the time available for various tasks until we're running around like headless chickens. ....'

Factor affecting productivity: ....

9

'I love machines. .... They do the work they are designed to do at the speed their specifications say they will do it. They may break down from time to time, but the technician will tell you immediately when they'll be up and running again. Productivity goes up and up as machines get faster and faster. What more could you ask for?'

Factor affecting productivity: ....

2 Each of the statements (1–9) has a sentence missing. Fill each gap with a sentence (a–i) from the list below.

a All they have to do is meet the deadlines we set them.

b For the same reason, many are unwilling to stay late when required.

c I know it inside out and I do it well.

d It seems to me that much of what we do tends to be frustratingly ineffectual, especially when we're so demanding with our staff.

e Several also told me that it had also been the cause of accidents and, on occasions, of workplace rows.

f The stress is tremendous and I'm sure the sick leave records would show that management's productivity drive is totally counter-productive.

g They never answer back or complain.

h This actually means they get less done, at least initially, than if they had continued with the old programs.

i When I pointed out to them the negative effects of this on productivity, I was told in no uncertain terms that unless they were able to take these breaks, they would look for work elsewhere.

Talking point

Discuss these questions in small groups.

• Which of the factors mentioned in the statements (1–9) do you think are more serious, and which do you think are less serious?

• What can be done to reduce the effects of productivity problems, do you think?

Vocabulary

Match the adverbs from the statements (1–19) with their meanings (a–p). In some cases more than one answer is possible.

1 recently	a completely
2 on occasions	b frantically
3 in no uncertain terms	c gradually
4 elsewhere	d increasingly rapid
5 quite possibly	e it seems likely
6 supposedly	f annoyingly because we don't achieve our objectives
7 at least initially	g not long ago
8 frustratingly	h particularly
9 especially	i sometimes
10 frankly	j somewhere else
11 inside out	k straightaway
12 quite honestly	l they say they are, but I don't believe they are
13 unfortunately	m this is my honest and direct opinion (it may upset you)
14 little by little	n to start with anyway
15 like headless chickens	o very directly
16 totally	p I'm not happy with this
17 from time to time	
18 immediately	
19 faster and faster	

Writing

1 Work in pairs. Write another statement of three or four sentences like the ones you have read, explaining a factor which affects productivity. Try to include several of the adverbs you have just studied.

2 Read your statement to the rest of the class.

Answer key

Photocopiable activity

Getting started
Suggested answers
lack of equipment, uncomfortable office furniture and poor physical working conditions, inefficient office routines, long journey times for staff, insufficient training, poor company culture, lack of incentives to work more efficiently, etc.

Reading
1 Factors affecting productivity:
   1 stress and insomnia
   2 delivery drivers having too many breaks
   3 unfamiliar software
   4 long, tiring, stressful journeys to work
   5 meetings and telephone calls
   6 (productivity measures not applicable because employees paid by results)
   7 lack of motivation to improve productivity
   8 the time given for specific tasks
   9 the reliability of machines
2 1 e 2 i 3 h 4 b 5 d 6 a 7 c 8 f 9 g

Talking point
Students' own answers

Vocabulary
1 g 2 i 3 o 4 j 5 e 6 l 7 n 8 f 9 h 10 m
11 a 12 m 13 p 14 c 15 b 16 a 17 i 18 k
19 d

Student's Book activities

Productivity at Magro Toys

Reading
2 1 4   2 of   3 were   4 yet   5 the   6 4   7 in
  8 had   9 4   10 4   11 an   12 which   13 4
  14 4   15 up   16 it   17 4   18 on   19 are   20 the   21 4   22 forming   23 4   24 companies
  25 be   26 4
3 1 were achieved, have not been maintained, was decided, was carried out, should not be allowed
  2 the automation of our Villena plant, the implementation of this decision, a reduction of payroll costs, increase in turnover, increase in sales

Grammar workshop: *expressing causes and results*
1 The introduction of a new computer system led to an initial decrease in productivity. However, as a consequence of an intensive staff training programme, productivity soon rose to record levels.
2 resulted in, gave rise to, resulting from, one consequence of ... has been ..., this in turn has meant that ..., due to
3 1 b 2 a 3 e 4 f 5 c 6 d
4 Suggested answers
  1 Higher interest rates have resulted in cashflow problems.
  2 Our incentive scheme for sales staff has given rise to a 50% increase in sales.
  3 One consequence of doing market research has been that our products are even more suited to our customers.
  4 New environmental regulations have meant that we have had to reduce pollution from our plants.
  5 Due to the installation of new machines in the factory, we have managed to increase shop-floor productivity.
  6 As a consequence of our staff training programme, our employees are making more efficient use of the computer systems.

Productivity concerns

Vocabulary
1 f 2 g 3 h 4 a 5 e 6 c 7 b 8 i 9 d
10 j

Listening
1 C   2 B   3 B   4 A   5 C   6 A   7 A   8 C

Manufacturing and services

Reading
1 It expresses the opinion that manufacturing is growing and that this is a positive trend.
2 1 B   2 C   3 A   4 D   5 C   6 D   7 D   8 C
  9 C   10 C   11 B   12 A

Presenter: Tonight on *Business Night*, we look at productivity. With the advent of information technology, robots and the Internet, the drive towards increased productivity has become increasingly intense. I have in the studio three production managers, each from different industries: Lee Kah Seng of Radiolux, a manufacturer of household appliances, Ferenc Kovács from Kovács Shoes, and Mike Drewer from the producer of frozen convenience foods, Unifreeze. First, I'd like to ask Lee: should production managers always be looking for higher productivity?

Lee: It's one of the factors, but really they should be going for efficiency, reliability, quality, satisfying customer requirements and a whole range of requirements which are central to competing effectively, not just churning out products at the lowest possible price. In my company, in one factory, productivity actually went down quite sharply a year or so ago. Alarm bells started sounding at Head Office, but when they came for an explanation, there was a perfectly simple answer: <u>the gadgets we were making were more reliable and more complex, with more added features, so they took longer to produce</u>. But they met customer needs better and, while we produced less, we stopped producing things and stockpiling them because we couldn't shift them quickly enough. Our activities as a provider of unwanted goods with excess production capacity were cut short, and everyone was happier! So no, productivity is one of the factors to watch, but it's not the be-all-and-end-all of a production manager's life.

Presenter: In today's highly complex world, how reliable are traditional ways of measuring productivity?

Lee: Quite unreliable. You know, you're measuring output per worker, but in an industry like ours where we're constantly innovating, <u>large numbers of man hours are swallowed up in developing and modifying the product, designing, preparing and testing the production process for the new product, modifying the assembly line, and so on. It's a very complicated business, which in some cases can take months or years, and in other cases be comparatively quick</u>. You have also to take into account the parts you'll need to buy in, get these designed and budgeted for and ordered. So, with so many people involved in the process, productivity measures are bound to suffer.

Presenter: So what would you rate as the best measure?

Lee: Well, we've got to look at profitability and what we can bring to a product to make it worth buying at a price which is going to earn us revenue, I suppose. Though this may involve a loss of productivity and an increase in the time it takes per shop-floor worker to produce each product. Traditional production managers used to be very much product-led in their attitude to how the company should be run, <u>but we've moved on from there and become more centred on bringing the product to the end-user when and where they want it. And measures of how successfully and consistently you can do that are what I would rate most highly</u>. That's, after all, what's going to keep you in business and add value to your company.

Presenter: Ferenc, what's your view on this?

Ferenc: I'm also pretty sceptical about productivity measures. Trouble is <u>they tend to measure what's happened rather than what's happening</u>, and it takes up a whole load of your time and leads to nothing useful, even though you have to be highly trained to understand them. You could probably make the same or better decisions without them. On the other hand, I'm a big fan of automation. It's taken over a lot of the more unpleasant manufacturing jobs and made us less reliant on the vagaries of the labour market. It has its downside, of course, like anything else – you know, technical glitches, need to hire more expensive technical operators, that sort of thing, which all mean that <u>very often you're not saving on production costs at all; you're just stream-lining the process</u>.

Presenter: Mike Drewer?

Drewer: Can I just come in here to say that I think there's a serious hazard involved in industry's collective fascination, as it seems to me, with productivity. Productivity increases are usually at the expense of jobs, as companies replace workers with obedient technological marvels. What happens, though, to all those depressed redundant workers? Out of a job and no money to spend. Unlikely to find another job because companies prefer machines or outsourcing, so <u>they stop spending because they've got nothing to spend and, hey presto, we've lost our customer base!</u>

Presenter: But isn't that being a little alarmist?

Drewer: I don't think so. But to move onto another point: <u>a lot of our stuff is now not made by us at all.</u>

Transcript

<u>We give that job to modern specialist producers</u> and then buy it in according to demand. It allows us to switch products, innovate relatively cheaply, since we don't have to retool and concentrate on marketing the product, an activity where productivity measures are largely irrelevant.

Presenter: Ferenc Kovács. Do you think productivity has a ceiling, or will it continue to grow?

Ferenc: It'll grow, and in Europe it's got to grow. I don't know if there's some great new thing on the horizon like the Internet has been in the last ten years, and outsourcing will undoubtedly erode our manufacturing base, but <u>I'm quite sure that sooner or later employment regulations in Europe will have to change to make it easier to hire and fire workers, reduce their holiday time</u> (as has happened in the United States), otherwise we just won't be able to compete, and productivity, you know, is really about making the product in the cheapest and most efficient way and increasing profit margins while giving customers the best value for money possible.

Presenter: Gentlemen, thank you. And now to France, where the French prime minister appeared on television last week to announce a shake-up in their telecommunications industry …

This unit has the format of a case study where students follow through a scenario of redeployment of staff at an insurance company. Students study vocabulary connected with industrial relations and study variations on conditional sentences.

Although none of the tasks in the unit exactly replicate exam questions, some are designed to give students the skills and practice needed to deal with them (see table below).

	BEC	BULATS
Listening: *Travelsafe Insurance*	Listening Part 2	Listening Part 3 Section 1
Reading: *Travelsafe Insurance*	Reading Part 5	Reading Part 2 Section 3
Listening: *Horse-trading at Travelsafe Insurance*	Listening Part 1	
Photocopiable activity	Writing Part 2	Writing Part 2

Notes on unit

Getting started

Here are some additional questions you could ask to follow up the discussion:

- How mobile do you think people should be prepared to be when looking for work, or if their company relocates?
- How can companies encourage mobility in their staff?

Listening: *Travelsafe Insurance*

As an alternative treatment, you could:

- play Wendy's part of the recording and ask students to identify her complaint and demand
- tell students that Demitri's complaint is A and his demand is J. Ask your students either alone, or in pairs, to write what they think he will say (remind them that he probably won't use the same combination of words as in the lists of complaints and demands)
- ask them to read out what they have written and then listen to compare it with the words in the recording
- ask them to work alone and write one complaint and demand, using the ideas in the lists, but expressing them in different words
- ask students to then read their complaint and demand to the rest of the class, who say which ideas from the lists they express
- finish off by playing the rest of the recording.

Reading: *Travelsafe Insurance*

If you have students who have experienced company restructuring, ask them to talk about it.

- What was involved?
- How was it handled?
- How did staff feel about it?

Grammar workshop: *Variations on conditional sentences 2*

As a follow-up to this, you could give your students the Getting started exercise from the photocopiable activity on the next page.

Role-play

- Allow plenty of time for this, probably 50 minutes in total.
- In the negotiation in Step 3, tell the negotiating teams that the objective is to reach agreement, not deadlock. Often in negotiation role-plays students become too competitive and unrealistic in the way they play their roles.

Getting started

1 Match these phrases to make conditional sentences which might be said during a negotiating session between staff and management representatives.

1 As long as we keep talking,
2 Had you offered us that percentage last year,
3 If it were not for the economic downturn,
4 If you agree to raise productivity by 5%,
5 If you give all our members permanent contracts,
6 If you were to offer us 5%,
7 In the event of a deadlock in these negotiations,
8 Provided our members vote in favour,
9 Unless you accept a 5% cut in the workforce,

a we won't be able to meet your demands.
b industrial action will unfortunately be inevitable.
c we might have accepted it, but inflation is higher this year.
d I'm sure we'll be able to find a solution which is acceptable to both parties.
e we'd be making more profits and we'd be in a position to make you a more generous offer.
f we'd call off our planned industrial action.
g we'll accept some of your flexibility proposals.
h we'll raise your salaries by 3%.
i we'll sign the agreement.

2 Decide which of the statements above (1–9) would have been said by the following people, A, B or C.

A Staff representatives   B Management representatives   C Either

Role-play

1 Read the background information and complete the notes on the right.

SFL AG

SFL AG is a large manufacturing company based in Klagenfurt, Austria, with a workforce of 7,500 people and two factories in the city. They produce bearings and other components for heavy machinery and have been in business since 1947. They have a loyal and hard-working workforce in a region where the cost of living is 15% below the national average. The company's order books are full, with sales last year of 400m and pre-tax profits up 20% at 90m. Their salary bill, excluding members of the board, was 150m. The time has come for the annual pay round. Taking into account the company's healthy situation, the company's staff representatives have prepared a high pay claim. Management are keen to keep the goodwill of their workers, but at the same time they also have to maintain the competitiveness of the company, as well as profitability for their shareholders.

SFL AG
Established: 1 ....
Based in: 2 ....
....
Turnover: 3 ....
Pre-tax profits: 4 ....
No. of employees: 5 ....

2 Work in groups of four and divide into pairs. Each pair works together. One pair takes the role of *management negotiators* and the other pair the role of *staff/union representatives*.

Study your role card and take between five and ten minutes to prepare your negotiating position with your partner. While you are preparing your negotiating position, decide on the following.

1 What bargaining points can you make?
2 What leverage do you have?
3 What constraints are there on your position?
4 What is your bottom line?
5 How would you be prepared to compromise?

3 Work with the other pair and negotiate a work agreement.

Photocopiable activity

Writing

1 Write an email to your colleagues (fellow managers or fellow workers), summarising what you agreed in your negotiations. You can start your email as shown.

2 Compare your email with other students' emails. Decide which pair got the best deal.

> Dear colleagues,
>
> I am writing to inform you about the results of ...

Management negotiators

	Present conditions	What you can offer	Estimated cost to the company
Working week	42 hours	40 hours	€1.5m
Paid annual leave	20 working days per year rising after three years' service by one day a year every two years to a maximum of 25 working days per year (i.e. after 11 years' service)	22 working days per year rising to maximum of 28	€1m
Salaries	5% below the industry average	2% increase	€3m
Annual increments	on a 10-point scale, subject to performance	no change	€0
Working hours	8 a.m. – 5 p.m. with a one-hour lunch break at 12.00 a.m. and two 20-minute breaks at 10.00 a.m. and 3.00 p.m.	flexible start and finish times; possibility of working through lunch break	€0
Benefits	health insurance, sports facilities, subsidised canteen	Performance related pay of up to 5% of salary, depending on performance	€?

Staff/union representatives

	Present conditions	What you want
Working week	42 hours	37 hours
Paid annual leave	20 working days per year rising after three years' service by one day a year every two years to a maximum of 25 working days per year (i.e. after 11 years' service)	20 working days per year rising to a maximum of 25
Salaries	5% below the industry average	10% increase
Annual increments	on a 10-point scale, subject to performance	on an automatic 10-point scale (i.e. not subject to performance)
Working hours	8 a.m. – 5 p.m. with a one-hour lunch break at 12.00 a.m. and two 20-minute breaks at 10.00 a.m. and 3.00 p.m.	flexible start and finish times; possibility of working through lunch break
Benefits	health insurance, sports facilities, subsidised canteen	annual bonus equivalent to 5% of profits

---

Answer key

Photocopiable activity

Getting started
1 1 d 2 c 3 e 4 h 5 g or i 6 f 7 b 8 i 9 a
2 1 C 2 A 3 B 4 B 5 A 6 A 7 A 8 A 9 B

Role-play
1 1 1947 2 Klagenfurt, Austria 3 €400m
   4 €90m 5 7,500

Student's Book activities

Travelsafe Insurance

Listening
2

	Complaint	Demand
Wendy	H	I
Demitri	A	J
Naline	F	P
Claudio	C	K
Toya	B	M

Vocabulary
1 b 2 c 3 a 4 g 5 e 6 h 7 d 8 f

Grammar workshop: *variations on conditional sentences 1*
1 a, c, d, e
2 b
3 *in the event of, provided* (other possibilities: *providing, suppose, supposing, imagine, as long as, unless, on condition that*)
4 a
5 b
6 e

Reading
2 1 part 2 view 3 This 4 by 5 above/earlier
   6 in 7 for 8 more/details 9 during/at/in
   10 have/make/offer

Grammar workshop: *variations on conditional sentences 2*
1 1 c 2 h 3 b 4 f 5 a 6 g 7 d 8 e
3 Suggested answers
   1 … not been given promotion.
   2 … I'm given more responsibility.
   3 … the amount of work he has to get through.
   4 … a factory closure.
   5 … I have a chance to put my training into practice.
   6 … he's given a pay rise.

Horse-trading at Travelsafe Insurance

Listening
1 20% / twenty per cent 2 financial incentives
3 salary increase 4 one-off payment 5 paid leave
6 legal entitlement 7 outplacement service

Role-play
2 A: 1, 2, 12 B: 10, 11, 13 C: 3, 5, 6 D: 4, 8, 9, 14 E: 7, 15

GRAMMAR WORKSHOP 5

Reference devices
1 does 2 one; It / Another 3 done so 4 thus
5 One; the other; The former; The latter 6 This/It
7 This/It

Modal verbs to express degrees of certainty
1 can't have been cancelled
2 should/must have arrived
3 may/might/could be
4 can't be losing
5 must be holding
6 must have dialled
7 might not / may not / can't have had
8 should find / must have found

Variations on conditionals
1 If it weren't for the view, these offices would be perfect.
2 If it weren't for the transport costs, I'd place an order.
3 If the staff were to (go on) strike, the company would go bankrupt.
4 Had management been ready to negotiate seriously, there would have been no problem.
5 In the event of an interruption in/to/of our supply chain / In the event of our supply chain being interrupted, we'll need to be able to source alternative parts quickly.
6 Providing you pay me overtime, I'll do the extra work on Saturday morning.
7 As long as we replace the part, the customer has promised not to complain / the customer won't complain.
8 Supposing they raised the price, how would you react?

Transcripts

Peter: Hi, Wendy, have you got a few minutes?

Wendy: Er, sure, Pete. You got my email, then?

Peter: Yeah, and I'd just like to clarify a few things before my meeting with management next week. What exactly is it you want? It wasn't terribly clear from your email.

Wendy: Sorry, I wrote it in a bit of a rush. Um, my point is that we're all working round the clock here to make this company a success, and management don't give any sort of acknowledgement of our hard work. I mean, for what we do, I think we should all be moved up a point on the pay scale. I mean, if it weren't for us, this company would fold overnight, wouldn't it?

Peter: I agree with you and, er, I'll put it to them, but I don't think they'll jump at that one. Thanks anyway, Wendy.

Peter: Er, Demitri, I was looking at your comment before the meeting we've got with management next week. Could you talk me through it, please?

Demitri: Sure, Pete. You know the rumours about plans to open offices in other parts of the country? Well, I know they're only rumours, but, before they become reality, I just want to say that I don't want to be relocated to one of those against my will. I mean, I've got my home and family life here. Now, had the bosses spoken to us about this possibility, I'd have told them what I thought, but no doubt it never occurred to them, because they never ask us, and we're left to get hot under the collar and channel our complaints through you. It's them who should be asking us our opinions, not you!

Peter: Er, thanks, Demitri. So, er, next week I must go into the meeting and demand a complete change in management style! They'll love that! But you're right, of course.

Peter: Hi, Naline!

Naline: Hi, Pete. Here for one of your chats by the water dispenser?

Peter: Well, it seems a convenient moment. I've, um, got this meeting with management next week. What was your email all about?

Naline: Something which a lot of us think is a pretty big issue round here. We've got all this newly installed electrical and electronic equipment in the building, and no one seems to have much idea what it's for, but my question is what would we do in the event of a fire? And by the way, I think there's quite a good chance of one, the way this place is wired up. They could at least show us what to do, give some time to basic safety procedures and how to get out of this fire trap, don't you think?

Peter: Erm, you're right there. I was going to bring that up anyway, but, er, thanks all the same. I'll let you know what they say.

Peter: Hi, Claudio, er, is this a good moment?

Claudio: Good as any. What brings you to this remote workstation on the 7th floor ... Pete, isn't it?

Peter: That's right. Your staff rep.

Claudio: Now I know why you're here. It's that email I sent you a week or so ago, isn't it?

Peter: That's right, because we've got the meeting with management next week, so, um, could you fill me in a bit?

Claudio: Yes, I'll tell you. What I like to do is get my desk clear, know what I mean? And as a result they keep putting more on my plate. It's not as if I'm averse to a bit of hard work, but I do feel that I get picked on just because I'm a fast worker. I mean, I'd be happy to do all this provided other people were being asked to do the same amount. But the managers give the hard workers like myself extra stuff to do and they never say a word. I suppose they think that if they were to say something, then they'd have to put their money where their mouth is and give us a bonus. But as long as I'm not passed over when the next round of promotion comes along next year, I'll be happy. You got that clear?

Peter: Thanks, Claudio. Pretty clear, er, and it's not me you should be angry with, you know.

Peter: Toya! You got a mo'?

Toya: Hi, Pete. Long time no see. You been on holiday, then?

Peter: Er, not exactly. I've been completely caught up in a new project. Now, I ... I want to consult you about the meeting with the bosses next week, following your email.

Toya: Oh, right. Well, yes, it ... it's not such a big deal really, Pete. I just get a bit fed up with having the bosses breathing down my neck all day, and that goes for all of us round here. We wouldn't mind it if they just let us get on with things instead of continually checking what we're doing. I mean, I've been here a few years now and given the circumstances, I think that they should know that my work is consistently up to scratch, don't you?

Peter: Toya, you're not the first person I've consulted who is looking for a change in management style. Still, I'll find a way of suggesting some changes, I s'pose.

Transcripts

1

Man: Honestly! They could have given us more notice instead of springing this on us almost at the last moment! Really, those managers seem to live in their own little world and have very little idea of communication. I mean, in my case, had I known, I wouldn't have bought a new house here just six months ago!

2

Woman: For me personally, it would be a big upheaval. I mean, er, I've got my kids in local schools and so on. On the other hand, I guess several people in my department would be interested in relocating if the company were to offer the right package. It would have to be pretty generous, though.

3

Man: This is the sixth job I've had in five years and I've really had it up to here with these short-term contracts. I'd jump at the chance to move, providing I was offered some sort of permanent contract, but I guess it's just as likely that they'll just lay me off instead.

4

Woman: Well, you know Travelsafe's quite a small, limited place for someone who's interested in building a career, and I'd regard this as a great opportunity to go to a big city with more scope if it weren't for the fact that I have all my friends and family in this area.

5

Man: Actually, I'm originally from Liverpool, as you know, so for me the thing isn't as awful as some people seem to be trying to make out. I'll happily move back to Liverpool, as long as I'm given a section supervisor's job as an incentive. You see, I want to get on and I'm not prepared to move just for the sake of it.

6

Woman: My line manager told me that they had their eye on me to move to Glasgow and that I'd get a pretty decent promotion if I agreed to go. I'm not sure I like the way things are being handled, with people being taken on one side like this, but anyway, apart from promotion, I've told him I'll only move to Glasgow on condition that they give me a generous resettlement package as well, because I'm not prepared to end up out of pocket as a result of all this. I'd have to sell my house as well, you see.

7

Man: I'm quite a lowly employee in the hierarchy of Travelsafe Insurance and frankly I'm not the principal breadwinner in my household. That's my wife, who's running her own business here in the town. I mean, if it weren't for my wife's job, I'd consider moving as a possibility, but as it is, I can't expect her to close down her company and follow me. That would be totally unreasonable.

8

Woman: The trouble is, most of it's still just rumours, you know. For instance, one rumour that's been going the rounds is that they're going to close departments here completely and open them again in places like Plymouth. I don't honestly know how much truth there is in the rumour, but I must say that in the event of my entire department being relocated, I'll move with them to stay with the team. That's if they all agree to go, of course. Which is unlikely, I guess.

Transcripts

Frank: So, Peter, I called you in to just let you know in advance what our plans are for reformulating the company.

Peter: OK, Frank, go ahead. I'll just take notes and listen at this stage.

Frank: Fine. First, I'd like to start by saying that this re-formulation is an expansion of the company and an expansion of our operations. Our total projected number of staff is set to rise from 450 to 600, although a certain amount of decentralisation will take place as we open offices in different cities, and so there will be a certain amount of cutting back here at our head office in Norwich, where we plan to make cuts of 20% – that is, 90 out of our 450 staff. However, that said, I'd like to stress that nobody'll be out of a job unwillingly. We'd like a maximum of 60 employees to go to our new centres in Glasgow, Liverpool and Plymouth, and we'll give them financial incentives to do so. To start with, anyone who transfers will get a 5% salary increase straightaway, independently of whatever post they transfer to. Also, we know that there are a lot of costs involved in moving to another part of the country – you know, buying and selling houses and so on, so we're prepared to foot the bill by giving a one-off payment of £12,000 to anyone who goes to make sure that they're not out of pocket. Finally, to cover the time involved in uprooting themselves, all these people will get two extra weeks' paid leave when they transfer. We are, as you see, keen to get experienced and trustworthy staff from our head office into our new operations.

The other aspect of our reformulation is for those who don't want to or can't move, and here we're offering totally voluntary redundancies for people who want the opportunity for a career change or a career break. What I mean is to arrive at the correct number of posts, we'll pay people to leave to the tune of one month's gross salary on top of their legal entitlement. In other words, if they were to be made redundant for other reasons, they'd get whatever the law states, but we'll give them a month extra on top of that. And to help them find a new job if they wish to, we'll provide an outplacement service entirely free of charge so that they can do so.

I do want to emphasise most strongly that we want to make these changes with a maximum of goodwill and a minimum of friction. Now, Peter, what's your reaction? Are there any questions you'd like to ask?

21 Corporate ethics

This unit concentrates on business ethics and Corporate Social Responsibility. It also features fair trade as an alternative business model. Students work on adverbs and adverbial phrases and revise the grammar of definite and indefinite articles.

Although none of the tasks in the unit exactly replicate exam questions, some are designed to give students the skills and practice needed to deal with them (see table below).

	BEC	BULATS
Reading: *Corporate Social Responsibility (CSR)*	Reading Part 2	
Listening: *Fair trade*	Listening Part 3	Listening Part 4
Talking points 1 & 2: *Fair trade*	Speaking Part 4	Speaking Part 4
Writing: *A proposal*	Writing Part 2	Writing Part 2

Notes on unit

Getting started

As an extra lead-in to help develop the idea of Corporate Social Responsibility, you can ask/elicit what sorts of social activities large companies engage in (e.g. benefits programmes for their employees, charitable foundations, environmental protection, etc.).

Vocabulary 2: *Corporate Social Responsibility (CSR)*

As a possible follow-up, ask students to write their own sentences to give examples of how these adverbials are used.

Talking point: *Corporate Social Responsibility (CSR)*

As a follow-up, if suitable, ask students to prepare a short presentation on CSR in the organisation where they work/study. Tell them:
- they have about one minute to prepare their talk
- they should then speak to a partner for about one minute
- their partner should listen and ask a follow-up question at the end of the talk.

Listening: *Fair trade*

As an alternative treatment, you could ask your students to work in pairs and:
- read the multiple-choice questions and decide which is the most likely answer for each question

- imagine that they are Professor Hill, they then prepare a presentation of, say, two minutes on the subject of fair trade, in which they include information and arguments which will produce the answers they have chosen for the multiple-choice questions
- combine with another pair of students and take turns to give their presentations in pairs (one student gives the first half and the other the second half of the presentation)
- the students who are listening choose the answers from the alternatives offered in the multiple-choice exercise.

You then follow this by playing the recording, which is treated as a normal listening exercise.

Talking point 2: *Fair trade*

As a follow-up to the talking point, if it hasn't already arisen in discussion, you could ask students what benefit there is for business when poorer countries become richer. *(Suggested answer: it creates markets for goods, though the downside may be that the labour they employ there becomes more expensive and therefore drives down profit margins for goods sold in richer countries.)*

Writing: *A proposal*

You may have to elicit some of the points to be included in the writing task (e.g. benefits to companies of ethical trading: improved image with customers/potential customers, more loyal or motivated workforce, increased customer base, more sustainable supply base, etc.).

Teacher's Resource Book activity   Business quiz

This is not a photocopiable activity, so you, the teacher, will have to conduct it. (See the suggested procedure below.)

Suggested procedure

1 Divide the class into two, three or four teams, depending on class size.
2 Ask each team a question in turn from the list below. (Your students will know some of the answers from studying this course, but not all. Other answers may come from their general business knowledge.)
3 Award up to five points for each answer depending on:
  • how close they are to the answer you have
  • how well they express the answer.
  Use your discretion when awarding points.
4 If one team cannot answer a question, pass it to the next team as a bonus question.

Alternatively, you could continue asking the same team questions until they cannot answer one. At that point you pass to the next team.

Question	Answer
1 What is 'cashflow'?	*The amount of money moving into and out of a business*
2 What is the 'marketing mix'?	*The variety of marketing activities including product, price, place and promotion*
3 What is a 'non-executive director'?	*A director who does not have an executive management role, i.e. he or she is not involved in the day-to-day running of the company and has more of a consultative role*
4 When does a 'receiver' have to be appointed?	*When a company has gone bankrupt (this person sells the assets to pay the creditors)*
5 What are 'fixed assets'?	*Equipment and land owned by a company*
6 What is the 'balance sheet'?	*A statement that shows the value of a company's assets and its debts*
7 What is a 'hostile takeover bid'?	*When one company tries to buy enough shares to take control of another company against that company's will*
8 What is a 'majority shareholder'?	*The person or organisation which owns the largest number of shares in a company*
9 Give me another expression which means 'stock market'.	*'Stock exchange'*
10 What is a 'fixed-term deposit account'?	*A bank account where you leave money for a fixed length of time and you are paid interest on it*
11 When a company goes 'public', what is it doing?	*Selling shares on the stock market to the general public for the first time*
12 Explain the difference between a 'wholesaler' and a 'retailer'.	*Wholesaler: someone who buys goods in large amounts and then sells them to shops and businesses; Retailer: a person, shop or business that sells goods directly to the public*

Teacher's Resource Book activity   Business quiz

Question	Answer
13 When a firm goes 'upmarket', what is it doing?	*It starts selling more expensive, higher-quality goods*
14 What is a 'price war'?	*A situation where different companies compete with each other by lowering prices*
15 If your company tries 'brand stretching', what is it doing?	*It is using an existing brand name for a different product in the hope that it will help sell the new product*
16 If you are trying to 'break into' a new market, what are you trying to do?	*Start selling something in a market which is different from your existing ones*
17 What is a 'premium' brand?	*A high-quality brand at the top-end of the market*
18 Are overheads liabilities?	*Yes*
19 What is 'bookkeeping'?	*The job or activity of keeping an exact record of the money that has been spent or received by an organisation*
20 What is a supermarket's 'own brand'?	*A brand with the name of the supermarket on it*
21 Explain what is meant by 'economies of scale'.	*The advantages a large business has over a small business because it can spread its costs over more products*
22 If you 'hedge' your investments, what are you doing?	*Protecting yourself from loss by investing in more than one thing*
23 What was the 'dotcom collapse'?	*When Internet businesses went bankrupt in 2000*
24 When a 'bill of sale' is payable 'at sight', what does it mean?	*It is payable as soon as the correct documents are shown*
25 What do you call the time between the decision to develop a product and the time it actually arrives on the market?	*'Lead time'*
26 What is meant by 'self-employed'?	*Not working for an employer, but finding work for yourself or having your own business*
27 What is a 'franchise'?	*A right to sell a company's products using the company's name*
28 What is a 'merger'?	*When two or more companies join together*
29 What is a 'point-of-sale display'?	*A display of a product for promotional purposes in the place where it is sold*
30 What is a 'cut-price' product?	*A product sold at less than its usual price*
31 What is a market called when it is for a very specialised product?	*'Niche market'*
32 What is a market called when it is a market that most consumers are interested in?	*'Mass market'*
33 What do you call the loan you take out to buy a house?	*'Mortgage' or 'home loan'*

Question	Answer
34 If you pay a fixed amount every month for your house or car, what do you call this fixed monthly payment?	*'Instalment'*
35 What is a 'tax rebate'?	*An amount of money which is returned to you when you have paid too much tax*
36 What is a 'fringe benefit'?	*Something that you get because of your job which is additional to your pay, but is not in the form of money (e.g. health insurance)*
37 When a company 'goes into liquidation', what is happening?	*It closes so that its assets can be sold to pay its debts*
38 If you are 'overdrawn', what is your situation?	*You have taken more money out of your bank account than the account contained*
39 What is the difference between a 'debtor' and a 'creditor'?	*A 'debtor' owes money and a 'creditor' is owed money*
40 What is another expression for 'annual sales'?	*'(Annual) turnover'*
41 What is 'R&D'?	*'Research and development'*
42 When you tell a potential customer the price you are prepared to sell a product or service at, what is the name for this communication?	*'Price', 'quote', 'quotation' or 'estimate'*
43 What is a 'tax haven'?	*A place where people pay less tax than they would pay if they lived in their own country*
44 What is 'VAT'?	*Value-added tax*
45 What is a 'run on the bank'?	*A situation when people lose confidence in a bank and they all try to withdraw their money from it at the same time*
46 If you get a 'seat on the board', what has happened to you?	*You have become a member of the board of directors of a company*
47 What is a 'golden handshake'?	*A large payment made to someone when they leave their job*
48 If a number of people interview you for a job at the same time, what is this group of people called?	*'Selection board'/'Selection panel'*
49 What is the difference between a 'bonus' and a 'rise'?	*Bonus: an extra amount of money that is given to you as a reward, in addition to your annual salary; Rise: a salary increase*
50 What is an 'end-user'?	*The person or organisation that uses something (rather than the organisation which trades in it)*

Answer key

Student's Book activities

Corporate Social Responsibility (CSR)

Reading

1 1 Large companies must be socially responsible, not just profitable.

2 Examples of how to be socially responsible.

3 Corporations should recognise their obligations to society, either voluntarily through CSR or through government legislation.

4 How everyday business activities can be made to appear to give a social benefit.

5 Seemingly worthy actions can have an unseen detrimental effect.

6 Maybe it would be better if businesses concentrated on making profits and left governments to help other countries.

3 1 H   2 F   3 C   4 G   5 A   6 E   7 B

Vocabulary 1

1 f   2 a   3 h   4 d   5 e   6 c   7 g   8 b

Vocabulary 2

1 1 at least   2 merely   3 supposedly   4 all the while   5 thus   6 all things considered   7 simply put   8 unfortunately

2 1 Simply put   2 all the while / unfortunately   3 Unfortunately   4 all things considered   5 supposedly; merely   6 At least   7 thus

Fair trade

Listening

2 1 B   2 A   3 B   4 A   5 C

Grammar workshop: *articles*

1 a   2 –   3 a   4 the   5 the   6 –   7 the   8 a
9 –   10 the   11 –   12 –   13 the   14 the/–
15 –   16 –   17 a   18 –

Presenter: This week is fair-trade week, and tonight I have in the studio Professor Bernard Hill from the University of the South Bank, an expert in fair trade. Professor Hill, how does fair trade benefit third-world producers?

Hill: Er, producers are paid more for their produce, often cutting out the middle men who may take an enormous cut, and selling directly to ethically run businesses in richer countries. This is what, for example, has happened in the Maraba region of Rwanda, where, as a consequence, farmers can devote part of their land to growing a variety of crops to feed their families and another part of their land to a cash crop against which they can raise loans and develop their business, er, buy equipment and send their children to school. Er, it can and, in the case of Maraba, has, transformed the region.

Presenter: Fair trade has been taking off in this country. Growth in sales according to many reports has been in the region of 40 or 50 per cent over several years now. How have the big supermarkets reacted to it?

Hill: Supermarkets have a reputation for driving down prices from their providers, er, and they do this with a view to maximising profits and making the products they sell cheaper in turn. On the other hand, they all have to look good to their customers. Customer loyalty is something no supermarket can count on once they start getting a bad reputation, and in view of this, their mission statements and other literature usually pay lip-service to ethical trading and ethical treatment of their suppliers. Still, the main reason given me by someone speaking on behalf of one of our best-known chains, was that it's what people want, just the same as a few years ago they started looking for organic food, and that, rather than publicity-seeking, is why they carry these products on their shelves.

Presenter: And how do you account for the success of the fair-trade movement in this country? Programmes such as this one, perhaps?

Hill: Oh, these undoubtedly help, but they're comparatively few and far between, and frankly, I think the media have been a little slow on picking up on this story. Similarly, the fair-trade movement has been loath to spend money on spreading the word and, er, more interested in spending the money they have on developing their fair-trade activities. Really, this is one of those things which people have just told each other about. The idea has got round, and it's been helped by having fair-trade shops in the high streets and shopping centres.

Presenter: So is fair trade something which will continue to grow and eventually become a touchstone of the world trading system?

Hill: I'd like to think so. But there are many hurdles in its way. Eventually, trade tariffs and subsidies to rich world farmers will disappear, I think – I mean, they've got to, though that'll take time. What may prove a greater difficulty is that fair trade, almost by definition, means paying more than would be the case if the market was just allowed to find its own level, and it'll only bear these artificial levels, I mean consumers will only accept this in the long run, if they feel they're getting value for money in terms of quality. So, long term, it's a complicated question.
On the other hand, also in the long term, it's in the interests of all of us that this movement is successful. The current differences between rich and poor countries can't be maintained indefinitely. It's not reasonable to continue to pour aid into poorer regions forever. This movement helps people to stand on their own two feet and become self-supporting. Quite apart from that, many people in rich countries like the idea of paying a fair price. It makes them feel good – they feel they're co-operating and not exploiting. People become interested in the places their coffee and other products come from and they become interested to know about the lives of these producers. It's all part of a developing educational process.

Presenter: Bernard Hill, thank you.

Hill: It's been a pleasure.

UNIT 22 Expanding abroad

This unit focuses on Wolseley PLC (a highly successful international company which pursues a vigorous policy of expansion) and how it goes about expanding into overseas markets. It covers vocabulary connected with overseas expansion and adverbs of frequency.

Although none of the tasks in the unit exactly replicate exam questions, some are designed to give students the skills and practice needed to deal with them (see table below).

	BEC	BULATS
Reading: *Wolseley's strategy*	Reading Part 4	Reading Part 2 Section 2
Talking point 1: *Wolseley's strategy*	Speaking Part 1	Speaking Part 1
Listening: *Wolseley's strategy*	Listening Part 1	
Reading: *Wolseley's Chief Executive*	Reading Part 2	
Talking point: *Supervising overseas subsidiaries*	Speaking Part 4	Speaking Part 4
Listening: *Supervising overseas subsidiaries*	Listening Part 1	
Speaking: *Supervising overseas subsidiaries*	Speaking Parts 2 & 3	Speaking Parts 2 & 3

Notes on unit

Getting started

This unit focuses a lot of attention on the international expansion of one company – Wolseley PLC. Either at this stage, or near the end of the unit, you could ask students to:

*   think of a company from their country which has expanded abroad
*   research its expansion by visiting its website and finding articles about it published on the Internet
*   present the results of their research to the rest of the class.

In many countries, the take-over of national firms by overseas companies is a political issue. If suitable, you can discuss the pros and cons of this aspect of globalisation.

Talking point 1: *Wolseley's strategy*

*   After they have finished the Talking point activity, you could encourage students to visit www.Wolseley.com.
*   If you want a framework for this activity, you can ask them to find answers to the first section of the photocopiable activity from Unit 13 on page 80.
*   As a follow-up, they could be asked to write a report on Wolseley for their managing director.

Listening: *Wolseley's strategy*

Before listening, you can ask your students to work in pairs, study the notes carefully and:

*   predict possible answers
*   compare their predictions with the rest of the class
*   listen to find out how correct their predictions were.

Reading: *Wolseley's Chief Executive*

As a speaking activity to follow up the reading exercise, ask students to skim the text about Richard Branson in Unit 2 of the Student's Book on page 15 and discuss the following questions:

*   How are the two men similar and how are they different?
*   What insights do they give you into the nature of business leadership?

Listening: *Supervising overseas subsidiaries*

Especially with experienced business people, you can follow up the listening by discussing aspects of Wolseley's strategy and methods, for example:

*   are there any risks attached?
*   what prevents other companies from acting in the same way?

Photocopiable activity

Rather than being based on the subject of the unit, this is a revision activity for material studied during the whole course.

THE INVESTMENT GAME

This game is designed to help you revise vocabulary and expressions you have encountered during the whole of this course.

1 Work in pairs. Each pair has $200 to invest.

2 Below are 20 questions. You must invest a minimum of $1 on your answer to each question and you can invest a maximum of $30 per question. Write the amount of your investment in the column on the right.

3 If you get the answer wrong, you lose the money you have invested.

4 If you get the answer right, your money is multiplied by the number in brackets after the question e.g. if the question is followed by (3) and you have invested $15, you win $45.

5 The winners are the pair who finish with the most money.

6 You may not look at the Student's Book or use a dictionary.

SECTION 1   Investment

There is one wrong word in most of these sentences. However, some sentences may be correct. Cross out the wrong word and write the correct word. If you think the sentence is correct, put a tick (✓).

1 Having a competitive advantage involves being one step ahead of the competition. (3) ....

2 When government organisations put a public contract out to tender, they often ask competing companies to put in a sealed bid. (4) ....

3 Our sales this year went short of the target we had set. (2) ....

4 In bureaucratic organisations, it is often extremely important to do things by the manual and not cut corners. (3) ....

5 In our factory we churn up cheap plastic toys which we sell at a very low price. (4) ....

SECTION 2   Investment

Put one word in each gap in the following sentences.

6 It's important to get your staff .... board before making any drastic changes to working practices. (2) ....

7 His advice was expensive, but in terms of the money it saved us if we had made a mistake, it represents excellent value .... money. (2) ....

8 My boss got extremely hot under the .... when I suggested he should pay me a bonus for my work. (4) ....

9 When we have the new computer system up and ...., I think our operations will run much more smoothly. (4) ....

10 It seems a very strange product to me. I seriously doubt if anyone will buy it, but you never know – it may catch .... (2) ....

SECTION 3   Investment

Choose the best answer, A, B, C or D.

11 He didn't want to pay .... but when we took him to court he had to. (3)
A out   B back   C up   D off ....

12 Due to an earnings ...., the company has not been able to pay as high a dividend as it would have liked. (2)
A shortage B short cut C shortfall D short term ....

13 She's been working .... the clock to get the report finished in time for the annual conference. (2)
A round   B through   C across   D throughout ....

14 We'll never come to a decision if we all keep .... off the point. Can you all please just concentrate on the matter in hand? (3)
A walking B running C slipping D wandering ....

15 If our company can manage to .... out this recession, we should be strongly placed to expand when the upturn comes. (5)
A carry   B ride   C keep   D stay ....

SECTION 4   Investment

Choose one word or phrase from the box to complete each of these sentences.

> boils cut-and-dried cuts fall fire go
> ins and outs jump melts ups and downs
> nutshell problem summary trouble

16 The situation is extremely complex, so it will take you some time to understand all the .... (2) ....

17 To put the whole idea in a .... , going public is clearly the best way for us to raise capital. (3) ....

18 I should think that about 50% of my time as a manager is spent ....-shooting. (3) ....

19 In the end, the whole question .... down to a matter of money. (4) ....

20 It's a great opportunity and I'd have thought you'd .... at it. (3) ....

Answer key

Photocopiable activity

1 ✓   2 ✓   3 ~~went~~ fell   4 ~~manual~~ book   5 ~~up~~ out
6 on   7 for   8 collar   9 running   10 on   11 C   12 C
13 A   14 D   15 B   16 ins and outs   17 nutshell
18 trouble   19 boils   20 jump

Student's Book activities

Wolseley's strategy

Reading

1 1 Wolseley expands organically, i.e. by opening
      new branches, and through acquisitions.
   2 They achieve this through:
      • continuous improvement
      • using their international position both to sell
        and to purchase
      • providing customers with an increased
        choice of products, etc.
      • attracting the best employees.
2 1 B   2 B   3 D   4 D   5 C   6 A   7 C   8 D
   9 C   10 A   11 D   12 B

Vocabulary

1 acquisitions   2 sustained   3 complacent
4 leveraging   5 a diverse footprint   6 synergies

Listening

1 with experience   2 joint ventures
3 manufacturing   4 growth potential   5 expertise

6 outlets / financial performance   7 financial
performance / outlets   8 realise cash   9 lower
purchasing prices / experience and expertise
10 their own markets

Wolseley's Chief Executive

Reading

3 1 G   2 C   3 A   4 E   5 F   6 B

Vocabulary

1 surged   2 FTSE 100   3 topped   4 hard-driving
5 briefings   6 clutch   7 pay off   8 broaden our
customer base

Supervising overseas subsidiaries

Listening

2 1 discuss (the) objectives   2 (the) financial
   performance   3 senior management   4 annual
   conferences   5 (European) graduate programme
   6 mid-management level   7 own branch network
   8 awareness   9 (many) retailers
   10 economies of scale   11 service

Vocabulary

1 Order from most frequent to least frequent: every
   half hour, hourly, daily, twice weekly, fortnightly,
   monthly, every two months, quarterly,
   biannual(ly), annual(ly)
2 1 twice-weekly   2 annual   3 every half hour
   4 quarterly   5 fortnightly

Transcripts

Listening page 105

Interviewer: Can you tell me about how your company
breaks into new markets?

Richard: Mm, going into new markets, our company
tends to acquire businesses. Er, if you look,
for example, to the electronic market, a very
big market, or the construction industry
across Europe, it's an area in which we really
don't have a customer base, a supply base, so
what we use primarily is acquisition to
acquire people and a company <u>with
experience</u> in that sector.

Interviewer: Mm ... OK. Do you ever choose to have
distributors instead or form <u>joint ventures</u>
with other organisations?

Richard: We are a distributor ... what we ... we
wouldn't generally take on a joint venture, as
it'd be difficult to see what a joint-venture
partner would add to us. If we were taking
over a distributor, that would be our area of
expertise. We are primarily, as I say
distributors ... however, we don't do

<u>manufacturing</u>. The products we distribute, we
primarily source from a supplier or the
original manufacturer.

Interviewer: Mm, how does Wolseley identify the markets
it would like to expand into?

Richard: When you look at any market, you're looking
at size and <u>growth potential</u>. So when we look
across countries or we look to a new product
range we can get into, we're looking for
something where there's a big market and
which is also a growing market so we can, in
entering into that market, we can see lots of
potential for further growth of the business.

Interviewer: So once you have decided on a country, how
do you identify a company in that target
market which is suitable?

Richard: What we look for, what we acquire is
<u>expertise</u> in the management group, so what
you'd be looking for is a business that we
believe is well run. You can assess that by
how good their <u>outlets</u> are, their size, their
growth rate within that market, through
contact with the management and through the

Transcripts

finances of the business; is there healthy <u>financial performance</u> and is it growing?

Interviewer: So why would an overseas company want to be acquired by Wolseley?

Richard: The owners of an overseas company might want to sell because it allows them to <u>realise cash</u>. Management would potentially want to join Wolseley because being owned by a business that is in the same trade allows them to benefit from, for example, <u>lower purchasing prices</u>, from the experience and expertise that Wolseley has in other markets, to help them grow and develop in <u>their own markets</u> in a way that they potentially couldn't do on their own.

15 Listening page 107

Interviewer: And how do you supervise the companies once you've acquired them?

Richard: When you acquire a business, you … the first thing you need to do is share with them your view of the business plan you formed in advance that, as likely as not, you'll have discussed to some extent with them. You then set out the requirements of that, and then the supervision is done through regular contact that can be quarterly, semi-annually, where you'd meet with them face to face and <u>discuss the objectives</u> and how they're performing against those objectives, and then you have routine management reporting that comes in every month, which reports on <u>the financial performance</u> and that allows the business to report on the day-to-day running of the operations.

Interviewer: And how do you go about incorporating these companies into the Wolseley culture?

Richard: Ah, the important thing is about contact with <u>senior management</u>. Our senior management at a European level need to have contact with them, that's how you get alignment at a management level. There are then events and processes that they will get tied into … as I said, they'll tie into six-monthly reviews, they'll meet with group management, they will get tied into <u>annual conferences</u> that we hold, where management groups from across Europe come together, and slowly, over time, they come to see the way Wolseley works and the people within it.

Interviewer: So that's how you create an international culture then for your management, is it?

Richard: Yes, the international management culture comes really down from the senior management. There are also processes ongoing within the business to develop our international management and the culture. We're currently in the second year of a <u>European graduate programme</u>, where we take recently graduated individuals of high calibre and get them working within our business, trained and developed, to enable them to grow and work across our European network. We also recruit at senior and <u>mid-management level</u> to bring different expertise and different management potential. We're looking to then move certain people across Wolseley Europe at mid-management level.

Interviewer: Um, OK, and when you expand into a new market, what sort of activities does Wolseley undertake to build up its brand and make itself known to customers in the new market?

Richard: Mm, there's … the major form of expansion that you'd … um, we tend to take a business we've acquired and look to develop it through its <u>own branch network</u>. What we've tended to do is to retain the local brand. Wolseley believes in the power of the local brand, the individual business that we've acquired. So we'd retain that local brand that's operated by, um, in that market and then look to grow their branches. As we open new branches, we do leafleting and other sorts of marketing campaigns to increase <u>awareness</u> and develop a customer demand prior to opening.

Interviewer: So do you think that it's an option for any company to say no, we don't want to grow – become international we're happy as we are?

Richard: For other companies, that may be the case, it won't be the case for Wolseley, though.

Interviewer: So it is possible then?

Richard: You could … I could imagine a business that … um, would want to stay entirely local. If we're a service business, I know <u>many retailers</u> are actually … have entirely focused on national boundaries only and haven't sought to go international.

Interviewer: And they could survive like that?

Richard: I think, in the longer term, they'll find it more difficult. Generally, those that have gone further and developed further are bigger. Therefore they've achieved <u>economies of scale</u>. The reason why … um, one of the major factors in international development is to achieve greater economies of scale through, for example in our business, purchasing greater volume of product which would then achieve lower costs.

Interviewer: Uh-huh, what do you think it is that makes Wolseley products so successful?

Richard: Hmm! Wolseley is a <u>service</u> business, it's about the service that's provided to the professional contractor who visits our branches. What makes the service so successful is the experience and the service provided by the people in those branches, the availability of product, the service that's provided to deliver any products that aren't available the next day, and also other services, for example providing credit. So we primarily focus on service as opposed to price.

UNIT 23 An overseas partnership

This unit focuses on writing letters. It features further work on writing complex sentences and on tenses in future time clauses.

Although none of the tasks in the unit exactly replicate exam questions, some are designed to give students the skills and practice needed to deal with them (see table below).

	BEC	BULATS
Getting started	Speaking Part 2	Speaking Part 2
Listening: *Finding an overseas partner*	Listening Part 1 Reading Part 5 Writing Part 2	Reading Part 2 Section 3 Writing Part 2
Writing: *A trade sales letter*	Writing Part 2	Writing Part 2
Listening: *Going into new markets*	Listening Part 2	Listening Part 3 Section 1
Reading: *Replying to Magiczne Lustra's approach*	Reading Part 6	Reading Part 2 Section 6

Notes on unit

Getting started
Alternatively, you could ask students to do the preparation for homework and give their presentations in the following lesson.

Listening: *Finding an overseas partner*
Alternatively, after they have completed Marion's notes, ask them to write the letter and then compare their version with the gapped letter in the reading exercise which follows.

If any of your students have experience of this type of foreign business trip, you could ask them the following questions.
- How do you prepare for trips like this?
- What problems tend to arise on these trips?
- How successful are they, in general?

Another area you could explore in relation to both the sample letters in this unit is the use of marketing and promotional language in business letters of this type:
- ask students to find examples of such language (e.g. in the letter on page 109: *top quality*, *improved version*, *excellent sales projections*; in the letter on page 111: *leading local distributor, ground-breaking innovations*)
- ask them what effect this language has and to what extent it is employed. (Both companies are selling themselves, but promotional language is used quite sparingly, as other business people would see through it.)

Reading: *Replying to Magiczne Lustra's approach*
As a follow-up to the unit, you could ask students to role-play the first minute or two of the meeting between Aniela and Oliver (i.e. welcoming, introducing, establishing a relationship – the preliminary greetings before they start talking about business). You could follow this procedure:
- elicit what things they would probably talk about (Aniela's flight, her hotel, the weather, the traffic, each other's companies, etc.)
- give them roles and ask each of them to think of some 'small talk' before they start
- start the role-play, but cut them short after a minute or so
- round up by getting feedback on the problems that arise at this stage in a business meeting (e.g. not knowing how to greet in the country you are visiting, not knowing when it is appropriate to move on to business matters, etc.).

Answer key

Student's Book activities

Finding an overseas partner

Listening

1 1 same (basic) letter   2 formal style
    3 (some) sales figures   4 production capacity
    5 joint-venture partner   6 Asian tour
    7 provide (a) translation

Reading

1 1 other   2 As   3 capable   4 its   5 over/under
    6 Due/Owing/Thanks   7 in   8 with   9 or
    10 which/that   11 for   12 will   13 view
    14 let   15 most

Grammar workshop: *complex sentences*

1 1 based in   2 As you may have read in the trade
    press   3 in its original form
    4 Due/Owing/Thanks to our excellent sales
    projections   5 are now also in a position to begin
    6 with that objective in mind   7 in the pipeline
    8 with a view to

2 1 We are a large chemical company based in
       Bahrain.
    2 As you may have heard on the news, we are
       thinking of moving our offices to Abu Dhabi.
    3 In its original form, this book sold very
       successfully in the USA and Canada.
    4 We are launching an updated version of this
       product due to some technological innovations./
       Due to some technological innovations, we are
       launching an updated version of this product.
    5 Our training budget has been approved, so we
       are now in a position to run the course.
    6 We are hoping to increase our sales in India,
       and, with that (objective) in mind, we are
       launching a multi-million-rupee advertising
       campaign.
    7 We have various new products in the pipeline
       at the moment.
    8 We shall be launching a new publicity
       campaign with a view to increasing our share
       of the North American market.

Going into new markets

Listening

1 1 A global ambitions, move upmarket
       B cut costs, move a lot of product
       C affluence, spending power
       D undercut the competition, wage a price war
       E go into a whole new area, spread risks
       F an approach, write to accept
       G keep to targets, meet targets
       H an opening, a gap in the market
    2 Suggested answers
       I cut-throat, fierce rivalry
       J language problems, hard to get our ideas
          across
       K problems finding top-quality employees,
          good staff
       L change the way we work, accept their way of
          doing things
       M adapt appearance, change the packet
       N invest heavily, spend a lot of money
       O new publicity, new promotional material
       P seek a local partner, get assistance

2

Speaker	Reason	Problem
1	A	N
2	H	M
3	E	I
4	B	J
5	D	O

Grammar workshop: *tenses in future time clauses*

1 1 have got / 've got / (get)   2 gets
    3 sends / has sent   4 're selling / (sell)

Replying to Magiczne Lustra's approach

Reading

1 1 b   2 g   3 e   4 c   5 f   6 h   7 i   8 d
2 1 ~~that~~ which   2 ~~for~~ in   3 ~~Like~~ As   4 ✓
    5 ~~too~~ also   6 ~~For~~ In   7 ✓   8 ~~pieces~~ parts
    9 ~~are~~ were   10 ~~about~~ of   11 ~~could~~ would
    12 ~~seeing~~ see   13 ✓   14 ~~a~~ an   15 ✓
    16 ~~possible~~ possibility   17 ~~absence~~ absent
    18 ~~Although~~ However   19 ~~do~~ make   20 ✓
    21 ~~visiting~~ visit

Transcripts

16 Listening page 108

Aniela: Hello, Marion. Sorry to miss you this morning but I had to rush, as you know, so I thought I'd better just give you these instructions before I go, as I'd like to get this moving as soon as possible. You remember we were working on a list of contacts last Friday? Could you please draft the <u>same basic letter</u> to all of them, and then perhaps we'll be able to work out an itinerary when I get back from Shanghai? Write to them by name where possible – I know for some we only have the name of the company – and use a <u>formal style</u>. You're better than me at that, so it's better if you do the letter and you can email your draft to me later today if you want, and I'll send you any suggestions when I get to my hotel. I've got a few notes of what you should include in the letter. Give them details of our new product – the mirror, I mean – and also put in some <u>sales figures</u> from two or three years ago till now, as those should impress them a bit. I don't think you have to go into too much detail there – just the basics, really. Then tell them why we want to expand into Asia – I mean, we've increased our <u>production capacity</u> – and you know, we're now looking for other markets. Something fairly vague like that, but it sounds impressive. Also, you could put in something about our future plans, you know, marketing other products that we have in the pipeline, that sort of thing. Then you could also tell them that we may need someone to distribute our products in their country or even perhaps a <u>joint-venture partner</u>. I know that's not true in all cases, because it will really depend on the country and the type of operation they're running, but it could get some people interested, so that at least we can talk to them. You'd better also say that I'm hoping to go on an <u>Asian tour</u> in the next month or so, so we'll need expressions of interest from people pretty quickly and then we'll take things from there. I think that's all for now, Marion. Don't send the letters straightaway, because we might just think about asking someone, perhaps an agency, to <u>provide a translation</u> of the letter into some other European languages. Not sure which languages at the moment. Perhaps you've got some ideas on that one or you could look for an agency on the Web. Oh, that's my flight being called, so I'd better run. See you at the beginning of next week. Bye.

17 Listening page 110

1
Woman: <u>The initial investment is going to be pretty heavy</u>, because we'll be opening and equipping a whole chain of outlets, so that'll eat into profits in the first year or so. Still, we should be able to lure some pretty good local people, especially if we offer competitive salaries, and when we've got the whole operation going, we'll have taken one step further in <u>satisfying the company's ambition of becoming a global presence</u>. And once the operation really gets off the ground, there'll be plenty of profits for us there.

2
Man: Well, you know, <u>when there's an opening, you can't just pass it by</u> – and, er, with the things we have in the pipeline just now, we just have to be in the North American market, I mean, with the spending power they have there. Um, of course, <u>we'll have to present things a bit differently</u> to satisfy their rather different tastes, and, um, <u>we've got a design consultant working on the boxes</u> right now. I'll show you one as soon as he sends me a sample.

3
Woman: The competition in our main markets is just getting fiercer and fiercer, so I reckon that <u>unless we move into other areas and spread our risks, so to speak, we'll find ourselves in real danger</u>. Even so, <u>any new market we move into will also be pretty tough, so we'll have to run some very streamlined operations when we do so, otherwise we'll never undercut the local players</u>.

4
Man: People sometimes say that business is the same the world over, but frankly that's not my experience, and <u>it takes managers in the companies we take over some time to cotton on to our working methods. I expect that'll be the case this time, too. Often one of the most immediate problems is language</u>. On the other hand, <u>the effort will be worth it, because the enlarged distribution chains will allow us to cut costs</u> and sell our products considerably more cheaply than our local competitors.

5
Woman: Quite frankly, I reckon they're asking for it – <u>they've really pushed us into it with the price war they've been waging</u> – so it seems the most logical move is to take over one of their competitors as close to home for them as possible and try and rob market share from them there. <u>And we've got an agency working on the publicity already, because when we're selling our products there, we'll have to take account of the local culture</u>. Otherwise, all we'll succeed in doing is alienating a new market, and that would be a real flop.

A planning conference

This unit is designed to practise skills required for the Speaking Papers in BEC and BULATS (although students do this in the context of a planning conference at the company they work for, Ascendor). Non-exam students will also benefit from further practice in giving short presentations and participating in business discussions. The unit also focuses on the language of risk management and the grammar of concession (*although*, *despite*, etc.).

Although none of the tasks in the unit exactly replicate exam questions, some are designed to give students the skills and practice needed to deal with them (see table below).

	BEC	BULATS
Listening: *Making presentations to colleagues*	Listening Part 1	
Speaking: *Making presentations to colleagues*	Speaking Part 2	Speaking Part 2
Talking point 1: *Risk management*	Speaking Part 4	Speaking Part 4
Reading: *Risk management*	Reading Part 1	Reading Part 2 Section 1
Listening: *Risk management*	Listening Part 2	Listening Part 3
Talking point 2: *Risk management*	Speaking Part 3	Speaking Part 3

Notes on unit

Getting started

Below are some ideas for additional discussion:

- Talk about the best and worst presentations you have given / you have heard.
- What made them so good/bad?
- What should the presenter have done, in the case of the worst one, do you think?

Listening: *Making presentations to colleagues* and *Risk management*

As a reminder to students about presentations, especially if they are preparing for the BEC or BULATS exam:

- ask them to look at the transcripts for tracks 18 and 19 and look at ways in which the speaker:
  - structures the presentation
  - gives reasons and examples
- ask them to note down discourse markers such as *The second thing I'd like to say is …* or *In conclusion …*
- these can be practised using the photocopiable activity on the following pages.

Talking point 2: *Risk management*

As an extra activity, ask your students to investigate some corporate disasters on the Internet, for example:

- Mercedes Benz and the launch of the 'A class'
- Coca Cola and Dasani bottled water
- Ford and Firestone Tyres

If this is done for homework, it could then be the subject of presentations in a subsequent lesson.

Below are some questions students could consider while investigating:

- What mistakes did the company make?
- How did they handle the crisis?
- How could their handling of the crisis have been improved?

Photocopiable activity

If your students are BEC candidates, you should point out that:

- in the BEC Speaking Paper, the mini-presentation is NOT followed by scripted questions from the interlocutor – the other candidate has to listen to the presentation and ask a question of his/her own
- scripted questions from the interlocutor in the exam are in Part 4 of the Speaking Paper (i.e. following on from the joint task in Part 3).

(Practice for BEC Higher, Interview Part 2)

Student A

Work in groups of three (Student A, Student B and Student C). Each of you has a presentation card with three questions printed on it. Your questions are not the same as your partners'. Follow steps 1–4 below.

1 Choose one of the questions and take one minute to prepare a one-minute presentation answering the question.
2 Take turns to give your presentations. After each presentation, you should choose two or three questions from the list of follow-up questions to ask the person who has given the presentation (e.g. if Student B has talked about 'Production', choose two or three questions from that list to ask him/her).
3 You may also give your opinions in answer to the questions.
4 When you have each given your talk and answered the questions, you may repeat the process with another question from the presentation card.

- **Recruitment** – How can you attract the best quality staff?
- **Finance** – What can you do to avoid cashflow problems?
- **Marketing** – How important is brand image in a marketing strategy?

Follow-up questions for your partners' talks

Follow-up questions for Student B's talk

Human resources
- What factors should managers consider when allocating a training budget?
- Should staff pay for their own training? If so, when?
- What guarantees should be obtained from staff going on extended training?
- What are the advantages of secondment as a way of training staff?
- What methods can be used to identify staff training needs?

Production
- How important is it to have production facilities close to head office?
- Should production facilities be located close to target markets?
- How important is a reliable source of supplies for production?
- Are labour costs the most important factor when considering where to locate production facilities?

Marketing
- What are the characteristics of a good company website?
- What are the advantages of direct selling over the Internet?
- How many languages should a company website be in?

Follow-up questions for Student C's talk

Human resources
- How important are leadership qualities in a good manager?
- How much should managers delegate, and how much should they do themselves?
- Should managers' pay be related to profits?
- What factors should be taken into account when promoting an employee to a management post?
- How important is it that managers have good communication channels with their staff?

Finance
- For someone starting a new business, how important is it to have a business plan?
- What elements should a business plan contain?
- What are the disadvantages of selling shares when trying to raise finance?
- When should a company decide to stay small?
- What are the advantages of ploughing back profits?

Sales
- What is a suitable balance between sales and commissions?
- What balance should there be between technical knowledge and sales skills?
- What fringe benefits will attract good sales staff?
- How much contact should company representatives have with head office?

(Practice for BEC Higher, Interview Part 2)

Student B

Work in groups of three (Student A, Student B and Student C). Each of you has a presentation card with three questions printed on it. Your questions are not the same as your partners'. Follow steps 1–4 below.

1 Choose one of the questions and take one minute to prepare a one-minute presentation answering the question.
2 Take turns to give your presentations. After each presentation, you should choose two or three questions from the list of follow-up questions to ask the person who has given the presentation (e.g. if Student A has talked about 'Finance', choose two or three questions from that list to ask him/her).
3 You may also give your opinions in answer to the questions.
4 When you have each given your talk and answered the questions, you may repeat the process with another question from the presentation card.

- **Human resources** – To what extent is training staff in new skills a responsibility of the company rather than the individual?
- **Production** – What are the advantages and disadvantages of moving production facilities to another country?
- **Marketing** – How can a presence on the Internet make a difference to a company?

Follow-up questions for your partners' talks

Follow-up questions for Student A's talk

Recruitment
- What are the costs of recruitment?
- What are the disadvantages of putting job advertisements in newspapers?
- How important are working conditions in attracting good staff?
- How can offering fringe benefits help to attract staff?
- How important is staff mobility to the efficiency of a company?

Finance
- How can you encourage late payers to pay up?
- How can banks help if you have cashflow problems?
- How can a full order book lead to cashflow problems?
- How can a company reduce its exposure to risk in difficult economic times?
- What should you take into account when giving a customer credit?

Marketing
- What mistakes do companies make which damage brand image?
- How can companies improve their image?
- How does pricing affect brand image?
- How important is quality control?
- What is essential in after-sales service when thinking about the quality of the brand?

Follow up questions for Student C's talk

Human resources
- How important are leadership qualities in a good manager?
- How much should managers delegate, and how much should they do themselves?
- Should managers' pay be related to profits?
- What factors should be taken into account when promoting an employee to a management post?
- How important is it that managers have good communication channels with their staff?

Finance
- For someone starting a new business, how important is it to have a business plan?
- What elements should a business plan contain?
- What are the disadvantages of selling shares when trying to raise finance?
- When should a company decide to stay small?
- What are the advantages of ploughing back profits?

Sales
- What is a suitable balance between sales and commissions?
- What balance should there be between technical knowledge and sales skills?
- What fringe benefits will attract good sales staff?
- How much contact should company representatives have with head office?

(Practice for BEC Higher, Interview Part 2)

Student C

Work in groups of three (Student A, Student B and Student C). Each of you has a presentation card with three questions printed on it. Your questions are not the same as your partners'. Follow steps 1–4 below.

1 Choose one of the questions and take one minute to prepare a one-minute presentation answering the question.
2 Take turns to give your presentations. After each presentation, you should choose two or three questions from the list of follow-up questions to ask the person who has given the presentation (e.g. if Student B has talked about 'Production', choose two or three questions from that list to ask him/her).
3 You may also give your opinions in answer to the questions.
4 When you have each given your talk and answered the questions, you may repeat the process with another question from the presentation card.

- **Human resources** – What are the ingredients of a good management team?
- **Finance** – How can small businesses raise finance in order to expand?
- **Sales** – How can you motivate sales staff?

Follow-up questions for your partners' talks

Follow-up questions for Student A's talk

Recruitment
- What are the costs of recruitment?
- What are the disadvantages of putting job advertisements in newspapers?
- How important are working conditions in attracting good staff?
- How can offering fringe benefits help to attract staff?
- How important is staff mobility to the efficiency of a company?

Finance
- How can you encourage late payers to pay up?
- How can banks help if you have cashflow problems?
- How can a full order book lead to cashflow problems?
- How can a company reduce its exposure to risk in difficult economic times?
- What should you take into account when giving a customer credit?

Marketing
- What mistakes do companies make which damage brand image?
- How can companies improve their image?
- How does pricing affect brand image?
- How important is quality control?
- What is essential in after-sales service when thinking about the quality of the brand?

Follow-up questions for Student B's talk

Human resources
- What factors should managers consider when allocating a training budget?
- Should staff pay for their own training? If so, when?
- What guarantees should be obtained from staff going on extended training?
- What are the advantages of secondment as a way of training staff?
- What methods can be used to identify staff training needs?

Production
- How important is it to have production facilities close to head office?
- Should production facilities be located close to target markets?
- How important is a reliable source of supplies for production?
- Are labour costs the most important factor when considering where to locate production facilities?

Marketing
- What are the characteristics of a good company website?
- What are the advantages of direct selling over the Internet?
- How many languages should a company website be in?

Answer key

Student's Book activities

Making presentations to colleagues

Listening

1 1 good marketing activities   2 critical media coverage   3 customer expectations   4 cost-cutting exercises   5 polluting the environment   6 exploit (their) workers   7 marketing-led   8 prime objective

2 1 True   2 False   3 True   4 True   5 True   6 True   7 False   8 True

3 1 I'm going to talk to you, briefly, about …
   2 By way of introduction, I should say that …
   3 I think there are three main points in …
   4 First, …
   5 My third point concerns …
   6 In conclusion, …

Grammar workshop: concession

1 Even if a brand has a good reputation, it can be ruined overnight by critical media coverage.
2 Although there may be pressures from shareholders, the customer comes first in any business.
3 Despite your finance department wanting to implement cost-cutting exercises, brand quality should never be compromised.
4 People will just stop buying them, however many millions you spend on advertising.
5 No matter what you do in whatever area of corporate activity, you should first consider whether this could affect the health of the brand.

Risk management

Reading

2 1 B managers now have to be prepared for a range of risks that were unthinkable not long ago.
   2 E the misdeeds of one company can tarnish all its competitors as well.
   3 D If a company suffers a blow to its reputation, it can collapse with astonishing speed … Even if a company survives damage to its reputation, the loss of business can be devastating.
   4 B identify your risks. Be prepared for each of them individually
   5 C companies spent millions … to guard against the Y2K bug … Managing risks can seem a waste of time and money
   6 A Yet risk is trickier to handle than mergers or product launches.
   7 E the government, the public and the media, and, increasingly, the Internet, which has greatly improved transparency. Corporate secrets are becoming ever harder to keep.

8 E As they rely more on outsourcing, they may be held responsible for the sins of their subcontractors.

Listening

1 Increased risks from: natural disasters, international nature of business
   Reduced risks because of: insurance, limited-liability companies, government regulations, computer projections

2 1 B   2 B   3 A   4 C   5 C

GRAMMAR WORKSHOP 6

Articles

1 the   2 a   3 the   4 the   5 the   6 –   7 a   8 the   9 –   10 a   11 –   12 the   13 –   14 a   15 the   16 the   17 the   18 a / the   19 a   20 –

Future time clauses

1 1 finish / have finished   2 am working   3 is completed / has been completed   4 are visiting   5 speak / have spoken

2 Suggested answers
   1 … I am paid more for it.
   2 … I have perfected my pronunciation.
   3 … I retire.
   4 … they are retooling the factory, I'll take my annual holiday.

Concession

1 Profits are up, though productivity is down.
2 We won't be able to meet the deadline however hard we work. / However hard we work, we won't be able to meet the deadline.
3 No matter how high a salary you pay him, / No matter how much you pay him, he won't work harder.
4 Despite his good keynote speech / Despite his making a good keynote speech / Despite his having made a good keynote speech, the shareholders voted him off the board.
5 Even though interest rates are falling, consumer demand is not increasing. / Consumer demand is not increasing, even though interest rates are falling.
6 Whatever he asks (you), don't reveal our commercial plans.
7 In spite of our excellent psychometric tests / In spite of our running excellent psychometric tests, we never manage to recruit the ideal candidate.
8 However small our budget (is), the project will go ahead. / The project will go ahead, however small our budget (is).
9 Despite our model winning an innovation award / Despite the innovation award (which was) won by our model, sales never really took off. / Despite winning an innovation award, sales of our model never really took off.

Transcripts

Good morning. My name's Fedor Brodsky and, for those of you who don't know me, I'm marketing director for our consumer products division. <u>I'm going to talk to you, briefly, about how to protect your brand's reputation, a question which should interest all of you in this company</u>. By way of introduction, I should say that good reputations – both for brands and for people – don't come by accident but from <u>good marketing activities</u>, including particularly building up consistently high-quality, excellent packaging, shrewd pricing and, of course, effective promotional activities over a period of time. Remember, though, that however good a brand reputation is, it can be ruined overnight by <u>critical media coverage</u>, and companies have to do all in their power to avoid that.

I think <u>there are three main points</u> in defending one's brand. <u>First</u>, we have to make sure that we always satisfy <u>customer expectations</u>. Despite pressures from shareholders, the customer comes first in any business, and with good ongoing market research, we should always be aware of what our customers want from us. <u>Second</u>, we should never make sacrifices in quality. In particular, although your finance department may want to implement <u>cost-cutting exercises</u>, brand quality should never be compromised. Once it gets into the media that, for example, you're putting cheaper ingredients into your pies, people will just stop buying them, even though you spend millions on advertising. <u>My third point</u> concerns protecting the general image of the company because damage to company image will damage the brand. This is the area of corporate ethics; we know so many famous examples of companies <u>polluting the environment</u> – oil companies immediately spring to mind – though damage of this kind is often unintentional or accidental, or – another instance – companies passing part of their operations to subcontractors who then <u>exploit their workers</u> or don't pay attention to safety procedures.

<u>In conclusion</u>, the company has to be <u>marketing-led</u>. In other words, the company puts the customer and the customer's needs at the centre of all their strategies. This is really one of the golden rules of corporate culture, that whatever you do in whatever area of corporate activity, you should first consider whether this could affect the health of the brand, which must always be your <u>prime objective</u>.

Now, if you have any questions, I'd be happy to answer them.

So, following on from Fedor Brodsky's talk earlier today, I'm also going to talk about risk, but in more general terms. My first point is about risk in general. Many people have the perception that the world is a riskier place nowadays to do business. I'm not so sure that's entirely true. <u>We hear much more about disasters and the like from the media, and this leads to scares, which in turn can affect consumer confidence and share prices</u>. Then again, we keep hearing about global warming and how this is creating even more natural disasters, but these tend to affect business only in exceptional cases. <u>What's true, though, is that business is far more international than ever before, and this means that something that happens in one part of the world can have unforeseen consequences somewhere quite different. A hundred years ago, a disaster in Europe would almost certainly not have affected businesses in Japan or Argentina the way it might in today's world of global supply chains and global sourcing</u>.

The second thing I'd like to say is that in some ways, people in business run fewer risks. <u>They can take out insurance against many things, and insurance companies make a living from calculating what the probability of a risk is going to be. Business people set up limited-liability companies, where they are not responsible for all the company's debts if it fails financially. And government regulations, linked with technological breakthroughs, have made the world and the workplace safer places to live and work in</u>.

There are a number of problems connected with handling risk. While investors' willingness to accept risks varies according to their level of confidence at any one time, this is something which has always been part of the economic cycle. <u>The principal problem is that managers find it hard to assess the real degree of risk that they face in their activities</u>, and some risks seem far greater than they actually are, and so they waste resources preventing something which is unlikely to happen, while they're taken by surprise by something quite unexpected. We see the same with politicians, too.

<u>Nowadays, of course, computer projections can predict the probabilities of all sorts of untoward events occurring</u>, and these are the basis of how the insurance industry works. While there'll always be things computers can't predict, from rail strikes to storms, if used with confidence, they can be a useful tool. <u>Having said that, managers feel very often that they're paid to assess risks and take appropriate action, and they feel a certain loss of control if they put all their faith in the machine</u>.

Finally, I'd like to say that business is about taking risk; <u>you have to take risks to make money</u>, and it's this element of risk and gambling which attracts many people to become entrepreneurs. <u>Risk is part of life</u>, and our job as business people is to accept it and handle it responsibly. Thank you.

Exam skills and Exam practice answer key

BEC

Reading Part 1: Exam skills

1 1 Business schools are partly <u>responsible</u> for management's <u>failure to evolve</u>.
2 <u>Completing</u> a business course is <u>not so problematic as obtaining a place</u> on the course.
3 During their courses, students' <u>attitudes generally change in unintended ways</u>.
4 Many business students are <u>ill-equipped to take advantage</u> of their courses.
5 Many courses <u>do not teach the skills required</u> for running businesses.
6 Students <u>do not appear to benefit financially</u> from obtaining business qualifications.

3 1 C Rakesh Khurana, of Harvard Business School, is writing a book on why management has failed to develop as a profession.
2 A Of course, business schools may be important mainly as a screening mechanism – their basic skill may be choosing students, not teaching them. Once in, and the vast bill paid, few are ever thrown out for failing their exams.
3 C In 2002, the Aspen Institute surveyed 2,000 MBA students and found that their values altered during the course.
4 B Their students are often too young and inexperienced to learn skills …
5 B Conventional MBA programmes, he complains, ignore the extent to which management is a craft, requiring zest and intuition rather than merely an ability to analyse data and invent strategies.
6 A little evidence that getting an MBA had much effect on a graduate's salary

Reading Part 1: Exam practice

1 D   2 B   3 A   4 B   5 D   6 C   7 E   8 C

Reading Part 2: Exam skills

1 A <u>But</u> how do you measure the 'quality' of communication with workers or incentives for employees?
B <u>For instance</u>, under one heading a British consumer-products firm whose managers' only meaningful performance target was volume (with no mention of quality or waste) scored 1.
C <u>So, if poor management does not pay</u>, why does it last?
D There is little evidence, <u>though</u>, that competition raises standards by forcing managers to work better.
E <u>They</u> ascribe <u>some of the gaps</u> to differences in the quality of capital equipment, or in the development and installation of new technology.
F <u>Thus</u>, even among competing neighbours, there was huge variation in management practices.
G <u>A further reason</u> appears to be connected with something economists call 'management culture'.
H <u>In fact</u>, the system is nothing like as ruthless as it is cracked up to be.

2 1 A, C   2 D   3 E, F   4 B   5 H   6 A, C, H   7 E
3 1 E   2 A   3 B   4 F   5 C   6 D

Reading Part 2: Exam practice

9 C   10 F   11 A   12 G   13 E   14 B

Reading Part 3: Exam skills

1 1 paragraphs 1, 2 and 4
2 paragraphs 2, 3 and 4
3 paragraph 6
2 1 B high turnover rates
2 C positive emotions from home spilled over and caused people to be more engaged with work
3 A Negative emotions also spilled over and caused people to be more engaged with their work
4 B the hardest part of their job is that they know how to help the customer, but do not have the authority to take action
5 D An individual who avoids risk and accepts supervision is likely to feel satisfied and comfortable in the job

Reading Part 3: Exam practice

15 C   16 A   17 B   18 C   19 D   20 C

Reading Part 4: Exam skills

1 1 B   2 B   3 C
2 1 C   2 A   3 B   4 B   5 A   6 D
3 1 A   2 D   3 C

Reading Part 4: Exam practice

21 B   22 A   23 D   24 C   25 B   26 D   27 A
28 B   29 D   30 C

Reading Part 5: Exam skills

1   1 whose (relative pronoun)   2 despite
(preposition)   3 due/owing (preposition)
4 have (auxiliary verb)   5 be (verb)   6 off/back
(preposition)   7 as (preposition)   8 This
(pronoun)   9 such (determiner)   10 One
(pronoun)

2   1 as   2 according   3 hardly/scarcely/barely
4 despite/not withstanding   5 on   6 the/their
7 away   8 fall/fell   9 what   10 This/That

Reading Part 5: Exam practice

31 ahead   32 in/for   33 This/That   34 part
35 back   36 themselves   37 one   38 that/which
39 During/Throughout   40 on

Reading Part 6: Exam skills

1   1 will   2 up   3 we   4 being   5 a   6 of
7 then   8 in   9 they   10 so

2   1 hardly   2 still   3 when   4 forming   5 too
6 correct   7 put   8 correct   9 for   10 been
11 a   12 once

Reading Part 6: Exam practice

41 so   42 CORRECT   43 as   44 up   45 CORRECT
46 by   47 even   48 it   49 when   50 CORRECT
51 them   52 yet

Listening Part 1: Exam skills

3   1 brand portfolios   2 specialist   3 mergers and
acquisitions   4 (constantly) innovate   5 losing
market share   6 move up-market   7 edge/cost-
competitiveness   8 Manufacturing processes
9 (management) decisions   10 (operating) profits
11 (Rigorous) analysis   12 (continually)
streamlining

Listening Part 1: Exam practice

1 sleeping partner   2 45%   3 permanent   4 whole
process   5 (best) strategy   6 job fairs   7 internal
candidates   8 downsizing/outplacement training
9 long-term contracts   10 private equity group
11 float   12 three sectors

Listening Part 2: Exam skills

1a   Suggested answers
   A   key brands, running at a loss
   B   disappointing at first, the board, slow off the
       mark
   C   disappointing at first, not much take-up, slow
       off the mark

   D   helpline never stopped ringing, went over to the
       competition
   E   missed a deadline, slow off the mark
   F   called in a maintenance crew, system crashed
   G   top customer, went over to the competition, the
       board
   H   key files, system crashed, vanished completely,
       wiped off

7

	Problem	Cause
Speaker 1	D	P
Speaker 2	G	L
Speaker 3	C	J
Speaker 4	B	O

Listening Part 2: Exam practice

13E   14A   15F   16C   17B   18B   19E   20D   21C
22H

Listening Part 3: Exam skills

2   1 C   More to the point, though, is that managers
            start thinking that everything they are doing
            will go well and they tend to forget that they
            have rivals out there who might be even
            better than them. That's when things really
            start to go wrong.
    2 A   in a recent survey it was discovered that 40%
            of Americans thought that eventually they
            would end up in the top 1% of earners.
    3 B   the first price mentioned, the opening
            position, becomes the point of reference
            around which all discussions seem to revolve
    4 C   The problem really arises when managers
            spend too much time analysing the
            information for each decision. I mean some
            of the decisions are quite trivial
    5 A   they continue to pour money into
            researching and developing a no-hoper
    6 C   They just continue to live with them.
    7 B   especially if you're a serious investor,
            investing in a variety of markets and
            properties is a much safer and more
            reasonable decision.

Listening Part 3: Exam practice

23 A   24 B   25 A   26 C   27 A   28 B   29 A   30 C

Writing Part 1: Exam skills

2   1 a breakdown   2 Ten years ago   3 the following
eight years   4 In the last two years / (Since then)
5 In contrast   6 in other words   7 Since then
8 in total

3   1 summarises   2 was   3 had
    4 have been reduced / were reduced

5 has been taken / was taken

6 have increased / increased   7 had

8 have raised / raised   9 are / were

10 has risen / rose

5 Suggested answer

This report gives a breakdown of annual sales figures in each division of New Age Leather Goods Ltd over the last four years. While four years ago the clothing division achieved annual sales of £5 million, these rose to £5.5 million two years ago and are expected to reach £6.5 million this year. The shoe division has been even more successful, with sales rising from £4 million four years ago, and sales for this year forecast to reach £8.5 million.

In contrast, accessories are undergoing a slump in sales. Four years ago they stood at £2 million, rising to £4 million two years ago, but have since fallen back, so that this year they are not expected to exceed £2.5 million.

Writing Part 1: Exam practice

Suggested answer

This report compares gross income from domestic and export sales of the company and the company's fixed costs across a period of four years.

Income from domestic sales was consistently higher than that from export sales. Domestic income rose considerably in Year 2 but since then has fallen off and in Year 4 was not much higher than at the beginning of the period. In contrast, income from export sales has shown a steady rise since Year 2 and is now at almost the same level as income from domestic sales.

Over the same period fixed costs rose in Year 2, but have fallen since then to levels below that of Year 1. They have remained at the same level in the last two years of the period. This slight reduction in fixed costs over the period is likely to mean an increased profit margin.

Writing Part 2: Exam skills

1 Suggested answers

  1 Probably colleagues as well.

  2 Neutral, since it's for colleagues also.

  3 What the course consisted of, how useful it was, how it will benefit your company, advice for colleagues.

  4 Introduction, The course, Usefulness and benefits, Conclusion and recommendations

3 1 ~~Like~~ As   2 ~~week's~~ weeks   3 ~~in~~ of

  4 ~~improving~~ improve   5 ~~learn~~ learning

6 correct (though reduce could be changed to reducing)   7 ~~showing~~ shown   8 ~~no~~ not

9 ~~had~~ has   10 ~~enjoyable~~ enjoyably   11 correct

12 ~~of~~ from   13 ~~were~~ was   14 correct

15 correct   16 ~~some~~ a   17 ~~of~~ about   18 correct

19 ~~for~~ to   20 correct

Writing Part 2: Exam practice

Suggested answers

Question 2

Report

Introduction

The aim of this report is to detail changes that were made to our delivery systems and to discuss how the changes were monitored. It will also assess whether or not the changes were effective.

Changes to delivery systems

We made changes to the delivery systems in order to try and achieve a faster turnaround between ordering and delivery to the customer. A new computerised system was installed so that orders are now sent direct to the warehouse without having to be processed by the finance department first. Current staff received training in the new system and extra staff were employed to cope with the faster turnaround time.

Monitoring the changes

A control system was set up to double check that orders were received in the warehouse on time and were processed correctly. In addition, a member of staff monitored the warehouse on foot to see whether staffing was adequate and to check if any problems arose. Furthermore, customers were canvassed to get their views on the new system.

The success of the changes

Overall, the system proved effective, though there remain several teething problems to be ironed out. Staff do not always input the correct values if they are working too quickly so a control system needs to remain in place. In addition, we need to have a marking system for goods where payment is delayed to ensure these do not leave the factory before settlement. However, in general, staff and customers were satisfied with the improved service.

Question 3

Dear Mr Markin,

I am writing to you as I understand your consultancy can arrange training sessions in giving presentations. I am writing on behalf of our sales department as we feel that the presentations given by staff could be improved.

When giving presentations, staff tend to have a poor delivery method (speaking too quickly, etc.) and also fail to get across the main points that need addressing during the presentations. They also seem to handle questions from the audience very badly.

In general, most staff in the department have to give presentations at some stage but I am particularly concerned about our junior sales staff, who need to improve their presentation skills in order to achieve their sales targets. There are about eight of them who I would put forward for this training.

As we need to see substantial improvements, I would like staff to receive training over a period of several weeks. This ideally should include material to address the problems I have raised above, plus some sort of monitoring or testing system whereby staff can see any improvements they have made. This system should also make them aware of areas they still need to focus on. An off-site course would be preferable, so that staff can focus on the matter in hand.

If your consultancy is able to help us in this matter, please contact me so that we can discuss.

Yours sincerely,

Question 4
Proposal
Introduction
The purpose of this proposal is to comment on the market for our new MP3 player and to outline any problems with developing the product and suggest ways of addressing these.

Potential markets
The issue of whether to market the new MP3 player in Europe has already been discussed but there is more potential for growth if we expand our target market to include India and some of the Gulf States as well. Both these regions have a high proportion of young people who fit our customer profile. In addition, our competitors are offering players which have been on the market for a while and need upgrading. Our product would offer new features and therefore should eat into some of our competitors' market share.

Potential problems
One of the main problems we may encounter is the cost of arranging an adequate distribution system in markets where we have no presence at the moment. In addition, there may be a problem in all markets of managing repairs and after-sales service.

Suggested solutions
In order to arrange an effective distribution system it would be sensible to contact agents used by our parent company and investigate what they can offer us and at what cost. We would also need to check whether or not they were also operating for our competitors. Regarding after-sales service, I would suggest this is put to competitive tender.

Speaking Test Part 2: Exam skills
2 1 not just because   2 but also because   3 the main point I'd like to make is about   4 What I mean is   5 I think first that   6 for example
   7 It also includes   8 A third aspect of this
   9 Anyway   10 Finally and in conclusion

4 1 My talk is about …
   2 I think first …; It also includes …; A third aspect …
   3 This procedure must, for example, …
   4 … and I say 'boards' because …
   5 Finally and in conclusion, …
   6 procedures for internal recruitment, human resources, efficiency of the company, inter-staff relations, management and staff representatives, internal advertising of all posts, staff appraisal, personal files, recruitment boards, director or manager of the department, Human Resources department, elected staff representative

BULATS

Listening Paper Part 4: Exam skills

2   1   C   More to the point, though, is that managers start thinking that everything they are doing will go well and they tend to forget that they have rivals out there who might be even better than them. That's when things really start to go wrong.

2   A   in a recent survey it was discovered that 40% of Americans thought that eventually they would end up in the top 1% of earners.

3   B   the first price mentioned, the opening position, becomes the point of reference around which all discussions seem to revolve

4   C   The problem really arises when managers spend too much time analysing the information for each decision. I mean some of the decisions are quite trivial

5   A   they continue to pour money into researching and developing a no-hoper

6   C   They just continue to live with them.

7   B   especially if you're a serious investor, investing in a variety of markets and properties is a much safer and more reasonable decision.

Listening Paper Part 4: Exam practice

33 A	34 A	35 B	36 A	37 C	38 B	39 C
40 B	41 A	42 B	43 A	44 C	45 B	46 A
47 B	48 C	49 C	50 B			

Reading Paper Part 2 (Section 4): Exam skills

1   1 B   2 C   3 A   4 C   5 A   6 B
2   1 D   2 A   3 C
3   1 B   2 A   3 C

Reading Paper Part 2 (Section 4): Exam practice

1 C   2 A   3 D   4 B   5 B   6 A

Reading Paper Part 2 (Section 5): Exam skills

1   1   paragraphs 1, 2 and 4
    2   paragraphs 2, 3 and 4
    3   paragraph 6
2   1   B   high turnover rates
    2   C   positive emotions from home spilled over and caused people to be more engaged with work
    3   A   Negative emotions also spilled over and caused people to be more engaged with their work
    4   B   the hardest part of their job is that they know how to help the customer, but do not have the authority to take action

5   D   An individual who avoids risk and accepts supervision is likely to feel satisfied and comfortable in the job

Reading Paper Part 2 (Section 5): Exam practice

7 B   8 D   9 D   10 B   11 C   12 C

Reading Paper Part 2 (Section 6): Exam skills

1   1 ~~am~~ was   2 ✓   3 ~~arose~~ arisen   4 ~~would~~ had
    5 ~~will~~ would   6 ~~knows~~ know   7 ~~of~~ about
    8 ~~reached~~ reach
2   1 ~~of~~ in   2 ✓   3 ~~by~~ in   4 ~~on~~ in   5 ~~of~~ about
    6 ~~from~~ with   7 ~~to~~ for
3   1 ~~memory~~ remember   2 ~~extreme~~ extremely
    3 ~~interesting~~ interested   4 ~~expansion~~ expanding
    5 ~~brief~~ briefly   6 ~~discussion~~ discuss   7 ✓
    8 ~~possible~~ possibility   9 ~~fill~~ full   10 ✓

Reading Paper Part 2 (Section 6): Exam practice

13 ~~does~~ will   14 ~~for~~ to   15 ~~giving~~ given
16 ~~such~~ so   17 4   18 ~~has~~ have   19 ~~at~~ of

Writing Paper Part 2: Exam skills

1   Suggested answers
    1   Probably colleagues as well.
    2   Neutral, since it's for colleagues also.
    3   What the course consisted of, how useful it was, how it will benefit your company, advice for colleagues.
    4   Introduction, The course, Usefulness and benefits, Conclusion and recommendations

3   1 ~~Like~~ As   2 ~~week's~~ weeks   3 ~~in~~ of
    4 ~~improving~~ improve   5 ~~learn~~ learning   6 correct
    (though reduce could be changed to reducing)
    7 ~~showing~~ shown   8 ~~no~~ not   9 ~~had~~ has
    10 ~~enjoyable~~ enjoyably   11 correct   12 ~~of~~ from
    13 ~~were~~ was   14 correct   15 correct   16 ~~some~~ a
    17 ~~of~~ about   18 correct   19 ~~for~~ to   20 correct

Writing Paper Part 2: Exam practice

Sample answers
Task A
Report on accommodation for company visitors
Introduction
The aim of this report is to summarise the complaints visitors to our department have made about the accommodation we provided and to recommend changes.
Visitors' complaints
Several visitors complained that the Queen's Hotel, where we normally lodge visitors, is too far from our offices and that they spend too much time travelling here. Also, it is situated in a very noisy part of the city, and several people complained about difficulties in sleeping.

The need for a good hotel

Most of our visitors are important, lucrative clients, so it is essential for them to have the best possible experience of their visit to our company. By providing them with excellent accommodation, we will improve our company image.

Recommendation

I have investigated hotels in the area and found a new five-star hotel, the London Palace, which has recently opened just five minutes' walk from our offices. It is situated in a quiet area surrounded by gardens. I recommend we contact the hotel and negotiate special rates. I also suggest that in future we provide a taxi service for all visitors from the airport to the hotel and from the hotel to our offices.

Task B

Report on the company website

Introduction

The purpose of this report is to outline the shortcomings of the company website and to suggest improvements to make it more suitable.

Problems with the website

I have identified two main problems. Firstly, the website is in only two languages: English and Spanish. However, more than 50% of our customers are either Chinese or Japanese, and the website should also be available to them in their own languages. Secondly, although the website provides a full catalogue of our products, we do not include prices. This means potential customers have to contact us to obtain this information, which generates extra work for us.

Changes to the website

I recommend we make the website available in Japanese and Chinese. I also think it would be a good idea to include the prices of all the products listed on the site. In order to do this, we will have to:

1 engage a specialist translation service to provide a full translation of all pages of the site;
2 contact the web-design company we normally use and ask them to include the information about prices and set up the Chinese and Japanese versions when these are available.

Speaking Test Part 2: Exam skills

2 1 g   2 l   3 i   4 b   5 c   6 k   7 e   8 f   9 h
   10 j   11 d   12 a

3 1 I'm going to talk about the best office I've ever worked in.
   2 Firstly, the physical surroundings …
      The second thing which made it such a good office was that we, that is the trainees, felt so motivated …
      Finally, my fellow trainees …
   3 I mean, it had good carpets on the floors, … the latest computer equipment
   4 that is, the trainees
   5 All those things make that the best office I have ever worked in.
   6 graduate trainee, assistant human resources manager, ergonomic office furniture, etc.

Speaking Test Part 3: Exam skills

1 1 What types of car are available?
      Can/Could you tell me what types of car are available?
   2 How much do the cars cost?
      I'd like to know how much the cars cost.
   3 What are your terms of payment?
      What terms of payment can you offer?

Exam skills and Exam practice answer key

Exam skills and Exam practice transcripts

2 ▸ Listening Paper Part 1, Exercise 3 [BEC Exam skills]

In actual fact, all aspects of corporate life, especially in large corporations like Unipro, have become increasingly complex, and it's this need to manage complexity which is really sorting the sheep from the goats in the corporate marketplace, if you'll forgive the expression. Why is it that companies are becoming so much more complex? The answer to this really lies in the consumer boom which has been an ongoing process since the 1950s and which in recent years has led to tremendous enlargements of companies' brand portfolios – there's the famous example of a well-known ice-cream company which sells over 1,000 different flavours and varieties of ice-cream. Both the general public and corporate clients have come to expect this sort of choice, and to meet the demand, companies have had to become increasingly specialist in what they offer. This has certainly been the case in Unipro over the last few years.

On top of that, I should also draw attention to the ongoing process of market consolidation in our sector, where Unipro's culture, products and processes have gained additional complexity through mergers and acquisitions both of rivals and as we expand into new markets. Also, it has to be said that in today's marketplace, where your customers are always expecting something new or improved, if you are to maintain a competitive edge, you have to constantly innovate, and this in itself almost guarantees added complications.

We've heard recently of, er, some consumer-products companies actually reducing the number of products they sell in order to simplify their processes. The problem with doing this is that you lay yourself open to the risk of losing market share to your rivals – something that can be demoralising, while at the same time being detrimental to the bottom line. It has to be said also that, by bringing out new products rather than just reducing variety, companies have been able to move upmarket, and this is what we've been doing over the past three or four years.

The downside of complexity comes in three main areas, in my experience. Firstly, because we're no longer able to concentrate on just a few things which we do well, our products have undergone a slight but noticeable loss of edge in terms of cost-competitiveness, and this is something we're continually struggling to regain. Secondly, because we now produce 500 different products, whereas before we concentrated on just 50, our manufacturing processes have lost what little simplicity they might once have had. Of course, automation and computerisation compensate for this to some extent, but behind every machine ultimately there has to be a human hand, and this brings me to my third point; that as a result of all this complexity, management decisions are often reached more slowly, as managers have so many different tasks to concentrate on and aspects to consider.

Interestingly, at Unipro, we have no plans to reduce the number of products we sell. Er, quite the contrary. We plan to continue expanding aggressively, even though just a few of the many products we produce are actually responsible for the bulk of our operating profits. This is because we believe that we have the know-how and the energy to get ahead of our rivals and that the keys to managing complexity lie in just two things. On the one hand, we believe in a rigorous analysis of our markets and we believe that this will ensure that we bring the right products to the right people in the right place and at the right price. At the same time, we believe, in our organisation, that we have to make a sustained effort to be continually streamlining the development, marketing, production and customer relationship processes and systems in order to reduce costs and increase efficiency. Er, we believe that by doing this, we set a benchmark in complexity management for the entire industry.

3 ▸ Listening Paper Part 1 [BEC Exam practice]

This is the Cambridge Business English Certificate Higher, Listening Test.
You will hear an introduction to each part of the test and you'll have time to look at the questions before you listen.
You'll hear each piece twice.
While you're listening, you should write your answers on the question paper.
You'll have time at the end of the test to copy your answers onto the separate answer sheet.
There will now be a pause. Please ask any questions now, because you must not speak during the test.
Now open your question paper and look at Part One.

Part 1. Questions 1–12.

You will hear a woman, Anna Grant, giving a talk about her recruitment company, PKS. As you listen, for questions 1 to 12, complete the notes using up to three words or a number.

Anna: Good afternoon. I've been asked to come and talk to you about the company I set up a few years ago – PKS. We did something that was very innovative at the time and that is: we started offering an integrated recruitment service to companies. In other words, companies outsource their recruitment to us.

Like all great ideas, I didn't come up with this on my own. I set up the business with Alan Murton, who has now moved on to being a director of a new consultancy, though he is still a <u>sleeping partner</u> in my company, which I manage alone. And over the last seven years we've built up a huge business, with sales rising at roughly 15% per year and last year exceeding all expectations at <u>45%</u>. Our client list is wide-ranging, including several large multinational clients. We help some of the biggest UK companies – if they need temporary or casual staff, they often use their HR departments, but we now recruit all <u>permanent</u> staff for these companies in over fifty markets.

We recruit senior management staff as well as caretakers, so it's important we have good sources. So how do we find the right staff to match the company? We are different from the normal recruitment company because we're in charge of the <u>whole process</u> until the company makes the final recruitment decision. Sometimes we're responsible for hiring thousands of people for companies, especially for our multinational clients. To do this we will decide on the best <u>strategy</u> for going about that hiring – we might use a direct search company or go through suppliers or place recruitment adverts in newspapers or in a job centre. One of the most fruitful sources we have for hiring is at <u>job fairs</u> because they tend to attract the kind of high achievers we are usually looking for. And it's not always a question of searching outside the company – we are also often given the role of evaluating <u>internal candidates</u> for promotions within companies. This is evidence of how much the companies trust the service we offer.

We're also committed to helping staff in their career aspirations. So we don't just help people on their way into a company but also with how they advance within that company and we also offer support on their way out. For example, when a company is <u>downsizing</u>, we can offer <u>outplacement training</u>. Our unique selling point is that we offer a complete package and, in order to do that, we need to be in a position where we can really get to know a company and its staff. So we demand that our clients agree to <u>long-term contracts</u> – though that's not as rigid a commitment as it sounds, as we can be flexible within those agreements.

And what might the future hold for us? Are competitors nipping at our heels? Well, at the moment we're hoping to expand even further and, to facilitate that, we're talking to <u>a private equity group</u> about them taking a majority stake in the business. And I suppose if that is successful, my ultimate ambition would be to get to a point where, when many people would be thinking about whether they wanted to retire from work, I can consider whether or not to <u>float</u> the business. That would be a real reward for my hard work. As for the immediate expansion, the next stage of our development would be to utilise the clients we have who have very large customer bases and, through them, to add a further <u>three sectors</u> to our portfolio – though I'm not sure exactly which areas yet; maybe telecoms, retailing and financial services.

Now are there any questions?

Now you will hear the recording again.
That is the end of Part 1. You now have 20 seconds to check your answers

4 **Listening Paper Part 2, Exercise 2b**
[BEC Exam skills]

1
F1: This was a few years ago now. I don't suppose it's still happening because if it was, I imagine the company would be bankrupt by now, but the company I worked for was regularly delivering orders late. <u>Our clients were definitely not happy and they were saying so. More and more, and in no uncertain terms.</u> The helpline never seemed to stop ringing. <u>Trouble was, we had a number of new recruits on the job and they hadn't been shown how to do things properly.</u>

2
M1: So he rang up the marketing director and said, <u>'That's it. I'm taking my custom elsewhere!'</u> Frankly, <u>it was a disaster which could have been avoided so easily if we'd bothered to check things carefully as they came off the production line.</u> As it was, there were plenty of people standing around doing hardly anything, and they could have been usefully employed doing that.

3
F2: The launch was pretty dispiriting. <u>Almost no interest and almost no take-up in the first month.</u> The promotional budget was quite low, but, um, I don't think it was that. <u>In my view,</u>

the new product manager lacked the background for this type of product and activity.

4

M2: Well, the board took the decision to substitute all our Macs for PCs, and we really weren't ready for it – this was a few years ago now, but it led to a lot of headaches. Anyway, we lost a lot of files – only temporarily, I'm glad to say, and nothing too sensitive – but it took the various directors quite some time to realise we all needed training up with the new equipment.

5 (Listening Paper Part 2 [BEC Exam practice]

Part 2. Questions 13 to 22

You will hear five different people talking about their company's recent expansion.
For each extract there are two tasks. Look at Task One. For each question, 13 to 17, choose the way the company chose to expand from the list A–H. Now look at Task Two. For each question, 18 to 22, choose the challenge the company now faces from the list A–H.

You will hear the recording twice.
You have 30 seconds to read the two lists.
Now listen and do the two tasks.

1 We produce fitness products for gyms and private clients – we'd wanted to expand for a long time. We had a variety of options open to us. For example, our main competitors expanded by allowing other companies to make their products under a licensing agreement – a possibility for us in the future. We wanted to move slowly though, so we negotiated a partnership with a personal training firm, who gave us access to their list of contacts. It's really taken off beyond what we expected and we're struggling to find people with the right kind of background to manage our production teams. It's so frustrating as we've put a lot of money into the expansion but we're ending up with delays in our deliveries, which is bad for our reputation.

2 We sell sporting goods and we've got a very large customer base in several countries, so looking at how we could grow was difficult. We did it through a huge investment programme, which involved increasing the number of stores worldwide. Our brand is now so big that we plan to look at ways of franchising in the future, which will give us more expansion with limited risk. Something we'll have to sort out first though is how we're going to get the goods to so many different places in a cost-effective way. We've expanded so quickly that our current system isn't working very well and the costs are escalating. I think we need to take on someone to come in and restructure the whole system.

3 When we started looking at expansion we looked at how much money we might make out of franchising, which is the way a lot of companies have gone. In the end we felt it was more sensible to allow other companies to produce our goods under licence, so we had some control. It's very difficult though – there are so many administration issues that you have to get sorted in the contract and they're different for every country. We outsourced all that to a team of lawyers and we've got it all off the ground, but we've got several major schemes on the go at the same time and it's getting increasingly problematic to keep track of them all. We may need to take on more people.

4 Expansion is always a problem, especially in our business, which is electrical goods. We did it the easy way really – rather than invest in new products, which we perceived as a risk, we made a bid for one of our competitors and were successful, so we have access to all their warehousing and outlets. Plus we use their website for our retail operations. We've been monitoring everything closely and it's clear that getting the raw materials from abroad is causing delays. We can't depend on the steel manufacturers we currently use. So, although we've increased the efficiency of our own delivery system worldwide, we'll have to look elsewhere if we're to get materials into the factory in time for our production deadlines. It may push our costs up but it'll be worth it.

5 Our company sells packaged food in several very profitable regions in Europe. Last year we decided it was time to build on that and saw no reason why we shouldn't diversify – by offering frozen goods, for example. So we looked at what our main rival was doing and tried to increase our market share at their expense by undercutting them. Of course it's meant spending a lot more on machinery and re-training our production staff. But what we hadn't realised was how complicated it would be to make sure we satisfied all the standards set down by the various official bodies in each country – trading standards and so on – so in the end I'm not sure we will be able to undercut our competitors.

Now you will hear the recording again.
That is the end of Part 2.

6 (Listening Paper Part 3, Exercise 2 [BEC Exam skills]

2 (Listening Paper Part 4, Exercise 2 [BULATS Exam skills]

Interviewer: I have in the studio this evening Jeremy Pollock, lecturer in psychology from the University of Leeds, who has made a study into the psychological factors which influence poor decision-making in business. Jeremy, are business people such poor decision-makers?

Jeremy: Um, not all of them, but a lot of them could improve, and one of the reasons is that, while they invest a lot of money in fancy computer equipment to help them make decisions, a lot of them don't like what their computers tell them and so they rely on their intuition instead.

Interviewer: And how does intuition lead to bad decisions?

Jeremy: In a number of ways. The first one is over-optimism. When people are optimistic, this reflects heightened morale, and as a result people often do better-quality work and produce better outcomes. Obviously a good thing, and footballers are a great example of this. That's not a problem. The problem is over-optimism, and in business it may lead managers to put too much effort into something which is not going to produce such good results as they expect. They waste resources, and the business in general would benefit from a more modest approach. More to the point, though, is that managers start thinking that everything they are doing will go well, and they tend to forget that they have rivals out there who might be even better than them. That's when things really start to go wrong.

Interviewer: As a matter of anecdote, which nationality do you think is the most over-optimistic?

Jeremy: I guess the Americans. They think their houses are always going to appreciate in value, they never expect to lose money on shares and, most tellingly, in a recent survey it was discovered that 40% of Americans thought that eventually they would end up in the top 1% of earners. I mean, how unrealistic can you get?

Interviewer: What other psychological influences are there on decision-making?

Jeremy: The next one I'd like to mention is what's called the 'anchor effect'.

Interviewer: What's that?

Jeremy: Well, in negotiation, this is where the first price mentioned, the opening position, becomes the point of reference around which all discussions seem to revolve. Negotiations become distorted because negotiators should be looking at real values so that they reach realistic agreement, rather than one which is based on an outrageous opening bid.

Interviewer: Can you give an example?

Jeremy: Sure. You're interested in buying a house whose market value is really £200,000, but the sellers are asking a million. The chances are your discussions (if you have any) will centre round the million figure, not the 200,000 figure. It's clear if you reach a deal that you're going to lose out.

Interviewer: Many people find it hard to make decisions when there is a wealth of information, don't they?

Jeremy: Maybe, but you know for … for business managers, actually making decisions is a central part of what their job consists of, so that making decisions as such is not generally the problem, and as long as you can differentiate useful from useless information, having lots of information is a bonus. The problem really arises when managers spend too much time analysing the information for each decision. I mean, some of the decisions are quite trivial: where to place the photocopier, when to have the Christmas party. This distracts them from analysing information for big decisions like that looming merger, for example.

Interviewer: I know managers who, once they've made a decision, find it very difficult to admit that the decision was wrong. Is this something which came into your study?

Jeremy: Mm … very much so. This is the stubbornness factor. Pharmaceutical companies who find it hard to admit that the product they decided to develop has no future, so they continue to pour money into researching and developing a no-hoper. Er, another more typical example is the manager who recruits a new member of staff who turns out to be a dud – just no good at the job. What do they do? Well, it's hard to believe on a theoretical basis, although we all see it every day: they stick with them. They don't give them the boot and admit their mistake, and they don't send them off to some other part of the company as an advertisement for their bad judgement. They just continue to live with them. Amazing, isn't it?

Interviewer: Yes, but it does sound very familiar. Are there any other psychological factors that affect decision-making?

Jeremy: Mm, just one more, called 'home bias'. This is where people tend to put money into things in their region or in their country, rather than looking further afield – I'm talking about stock market investments and also business investments. Reasonable, you may say, after all you probably understand those things closer to home better. But you can also get your fingers burnt, and, especially if you're a serious investor, investing in a variety of markets and properties is a much safer and more reasonable decision.

Interviewer: Jeremy Pollock, thank you.

Jeremy: My pleasure.

7 ◖ Listening Paper Part 3 [BEC Exam practice]

Part 3. Questions 23–30

You will hear an interview with a consultant, Jason Copeland, on the competitiveness of small retail stores. For each question, 23 to 30, mark one letter A, B or C, for the correct answer.

You will hear the recording twice.

You now have 45 seconds to read through the questions.

Now listen and mark A, B or C.

Interviewer: Jason, you have substantial experience in retail and you're concerned at the takeover by the big retail chains, aren't you?

Jason: Yes. I do consultancy for smaller stores because I believe they can compete with the big hitters.

Interviewer: Well, what would you say a retail store's success depends on?

Jason: Many stores focus on getting a range of products that will appeal to their target customers and, of course, price is an important part of this equation. Naturally you need to find out what customers want – your store is defined by what you stock and what you charge. None of this matters if your customers don't know you exist. For example, the wrong promotional campaign can mean your message is not heard and the result is too few people through the door.

Interviewer: And how do you think it's possible for smaller stores to compete with large chains?

Jason: They need to make a realistic choice about what to compete on. The advantage for small stores is the fact that they are individual. This means they can offer something special and they need to maximise that feature. Small stores do have a different character and that atmosphere can appeal to some people. And the same goes for the type of service small stores can give their customers – it's very personalised, which people like – but you need to attract them to the store first.

Interviewer: So which type of customer do you think these stores should focus on – er, the big spenders?

Jason: Actually it's much more important to concentrate on customers who may not spend much, but who are regular. You may not make a fortune off them, unlike say, your typical, average-spending customers, but if they're regular, it means they're satisfied with the store and will probably tell everyone they know about it. You should nurture them as your most valuable customers as they could be your future.

Interviewer: Do you think that online shopping will put the small retailer out of business?

Jason: It's true it's important for all stores to have an online presence. This may just be an informational website as not all stores want to invest in the security systems which are needed for online ordering. This doesn't matter as there will always be customers who want to inspect the quality of products and this will preserve the brick and mortar retailers. Also hold-ups in delivery are often seen as a disadvantage with online shopping – but I feel this is negated by the fact that the online shopping experience is instant.

Interviewer: When small stores expand they often relocate – but then they can end up going under, can't they?

Jason: Yes, relocating a store is inevitably expensive. However, if you've thought it through, it can be the best thing for your bottom line. Obviously you want to expand your customer base and attract new customers in the new location. Having said that, this will not be enough to keep you afloat, unless you advertise the move well, so that you concentrate on keeping old customers.

Interviewer: And do you think the old saying that the customer is always right is true?

Jason: No, the customer is not always right. But of course you can't tell them that. Sometimes they make an honest mistake about something or want something for nothing. But even if they're not right, it's our job to make them believe that they are valued and essential to the store. After all, it's their purchasing decision that makes a store a success or failure.

Interviewer: The retail industry has very high staff turnover, doesn't it? Do you think retailers should invest more in trying to keep staff?

Jason: Yes, given how important customer service is, stores should make every effort to keep staff who are good at their job. But I think sometimes stores think anybody can do sales – it's not seen as a very highly trained job and so staff needs are seen as very low on the agenda. Also salaries tend to be very low and prospects for rising up the ranks are few – it's by addressing these latter issues that good staff can be retained.

Interviewer: So there is money to be made in the small retail store?

Jason: Oh, indeed. The profit margin may be small but good sales can generate a reasonably healthy income for someone operating on their own. Surviving is easier, I think, if you decide to focus on one or two particular areas and become well-known for that. The real money, though, lies in gambling on an investment in growth when it may seem most chancy. You may be surprised at what takes off.

Interviewer: OK, thank you for your help on this.

Now you will hear the recording again.
That is the end of Part 3. You now have ten minutes to transfer your answers to your Answer Sheet.
You have one more minute.
That is the end of the test.

8 Speaking Test Part 2, Exercise 3 [BEC Exam skills]

My talk is about procedures for internal recruitment. This is an essential area of human resources, not just because it has implications for the efficiency of the company, but also because of the effect it can have on inter-staff relations. So the main point I'd like to make is about transparency. What I mean is that the process must be fair and seen by all staff involved to be fair. How can this be achieved? I think first that there must be a clear procedure for internal recruitment which has been agreed between management and staff representatives. This procedure must, for example, include internal advertising of all posts and allowing all suitably qualified staff to apply. It also includes a regular system of staff appraisal, which is also open and transparent. Staff know how they have been appraised and know what comments are on their personal files. They also have a right to appeal if they feel that any aspect of their appraisal has been unfair. A third aspect of this transparency is the composition of recruitment boards, and I say 'boards' because really internal recruitment is too sensitive to be the responsibility of one person. Anyway, these boards should

really be made up of the director or manager of the department which has the vacant post, someone from the Human Resources department, and also, though this for many managers may sound rather controversial, an elected staff representative as well. Finally and in conclusion, I'd like to say that I think Human Resources should circulate among the staff involved the reasons for choosing the person they finally choose as this makes the process as transparent as possible, and makes it clear to staff what criteria were used.

3 Listening Paper Part 4 [BULATS Exam practice]

Section 1. Questions 33–38

You will hear a discussion between Brian, the managing director of a company, and Judy, its finance director, about premises for a new head office. For questions 33 to 38, circle one letter, A, B or C, for the correct answer. You will hear the discussion twice. You have 20 seconds to read the questions.

Now you will hear the discussion.

Brian: Well, Judy, now that we've both had a chance to visit the two buildings, let's compare notes. Do you think either of them would be suitable for our new head office?

Judy: I rather liked the location of the Carter House, Brian. About three kilometres from the town centre, but still within the built-up district, and mostly surrounded by housing. It seemed a very pleasant area.

Brian: … and not far from open country. Yes, I think that was very much in its favour. I could imagine working there. And it's in a reasonable state of repair, isn't it? Though it'll certainly need some work to make it suit our requirements. It's a bit small, but we could build onto it.

Judy: Don't you think we could get away with removing some walls, to turn two or three small rooms into one bigger one? Then we can use the existing space more efficiently.

Brian: Good idea. Anyway, there's space for an extension, if we decide we need it in the future.

Judy: We need to consider access, though. We don't want to have problems with that.

Brian: Mm. It wouldn't be difficult to reach the place from the motorway, which will help with deliveries, as well as staff getting to and from work.

Judy: I didn't like the fact that the only way into the car park was near a bend in the road. It might be worth changing that, to approach the car park from the other side of the building.

Brian: Yes, that might be better. Did you have time to talk to the agent about the price?

Judy: Yes, I did. The asking price is one and three quarter million. But the agent hinted that the company that owns it would be prepared to come down to one and a half. My guess is that if we made an offer in the next couple of weeks, we could get it for one and a quarter million. I really don't think it's worth more than that.

Brian: But do you think they'd accept that?

Judy: The agent gave me the impression that the owners want to complete the sale as soon as possible. Apparently one of their subsidiaries is planning to construct a new shopping centre in the town, and the holding company is trying to raise as much of the finance as they can from their assets, to avoid having to borrow it all from the bank and pay interest.

Brian: That certainly seems to work in our favour! Well, it's worth taking this further.

Judy: What do you think should be the next step? Our board members will want to have a look at the building before we purchase it, won't they?

Brian: Yes, but I think time is the most important factor here. I'll get onto the agent straight away and put in an offer. We can always withdraw it if the directors decide against it. If the owners accept it, I'll brief the board next week, and fix up a visit for them. Then we'll be in a strong position to go ahead with the purchase.

Judy: Good idea.

Now you will hear the discussion again.

4 **Section 2. Questions 39–44**
You will hear a radio interview with a man called Gary Waters about how advertising agencies can win new business. For questions 39 to 44, circle one letter, A, B or C, for the correct answer. You will hear the interview twice. You have 20 seconds to read the questions.

Now you will hear the interview.

Interviewer: With me tonight is advertising executive Gary Waters to talk about planning an advertising campaign. Gary, how does it start?

Gary: Say a company wants us to plan a campaign for a new product – it could be in magazines, on TV – whatever. We have regular clients, of course, but a lot of work comes from people who've seen work of ours and like it. Usually they call us first, and at this stage it's really exploratory, to see if you're on the same wavelength – we don't usually get into a discussion of money yet. Next they send a written brief, outlining what they want, and

we agree on a date to present our proposal to the company. That presentation's really important, because it'll help them decide whether or not to give us the job. So we must have good ideas, and present them convincingly.

Interviewer: How do you get ideas for your proposal?

Gary: I may do some background research, and play with a few ideas, but I make sure I have a preliminary meeting with the client – usually their marketing manager. That's when I pick up the image they have of the product, any problems they might be having, what they're really looking for, and what pressures they're under – say from their competitors. I need to get a feel for the company itself – that's actually more important than the product, and that's when the campaign usually takes shape in my mind.

Interviewer: What do you do next?

Gary: I put together a team. That way we get far better ideas than by working separately. Once we've got an idea we're happy with, we work on it till we know exactly how we see the campaign. Then we start planning the presentation we're going to give the client. That's an oral presentation, followed up by a written proposal package, but we prefer to do that part of the proposal individually. A lot of agencies write both the presentation and the back-up as team efforts, but the danger is that you can end up with a mixture of styles, which would make both your work and your agency seem disorganised.

Interviewer: Do you write out the presentation in full?

Gary: Some people do, but it's much more effective not to. I plan it carefully, and just write down key words to remind me of the points I want to cover. That way I can talk to the client in a much more natural way than if I'm reading aloud. I can also keep an eye on how they're responding, and modify the presentation if I see I'm losing them.

Interviewer: Do you ever get asked difficult questions?

Gary: Oh yes. We always practise giving the presentation to colleagues, to make sure everything's clear, and the people listening try to anticipate the clients' questions by asking as many as they can think of – particularly difficult ones. That way, we're hardly ever taken by surprise when we present to the clients.

Interviewer: Finally, Gary, what's the secret of an effective presentation?

Gary: <u>Some people like to make it funny, but I think it's important to keep it clear, short and simple. People can't usually concentrate for longer than about 20 minutes, and you can't cover everything in that time, anyway, so the detail can go in the written proposal package.</u>

Interviewer: Gary Waters, many thanks.

Now you will hear the interview again.

5 ◖ Section 3. Questions 45–50

You will hear a radio news item about Ben Miller being appointed as the new European Chairman of GTR, a big advertising group. For questions 45 to 50, circle one letter, A, B or C, for the correct answer. You will hear the news item twice. You have 20 seconds to read the questions.

Now you will hear the news item.

First some marketing news: Ben Miller, former Creative Director with American advertising group, Jackson Media, is expected to move to the GTR marketing group in the newly created role of European Chairman. The surprise move follows the launch of his own agency, Hudson, in the US earlier this year, in partnership with Susie Thomas. <u>Miller confirms that he quit Hudson last week, but declined to comment on his new job.</u> It's understood that he has yet to sign the contract.

Inside sources at GTR suggest that Ben Miller won't be welcomed by everyone in the group. This appointment is unsettling, especially since it comes at a time when GTR is still in a state of transition. The company was only created last year, as a result of a merger of three European and North American agencies, so it sorely needs stability and clear vision. <u>It's felt by certain key GTR staff that the decision to appoint Miller was taken at the group's New York headquarters, without any discussion with senior management of the European division,</u> whom Miller is expected to join in London.

<u>Miller's move to GTR will reunite him with the man he used to report to at Jackson Media, Mark West.</u> In fact, West recruited Miller to join him in Jackson's Manhattan office, having done business with him some time previously. West is now president and chief operating officer of GTR.

West was ousted from Jackson Media at the beginning of last year, after investigations into the agency's finances by the US Securities and Exchange Commission, and Ben Miller left the company soon afterwards. <u>Apparently, Miller didn't get on with West's successor</u>, and when he left, he took some of Jackson Media's biggest clients with him, which gave Miller's own agency, Hudson, a good start.

Hudson finds itself in trouble now that Miller has left. The agency was recently responsible for an advertising campaign on behalf of Yellowstone, the American food and drinks giant, and was expecting to pick up further business from the client. <u>The initial deal was down to Yellowstone's seven-year relationship with Miller, built up while he was at Jackson Media.</u> Yellowstone had subsequently moved their business to another agency, but Miller picked them up when he founded Hudson, this year.

Commentators are surprised at Miller's move, not only because it means leaving his own newly emerging agency, but also because there were rumours that he had been approached by the chairman of another big marketing agency, Outward Signs. <u>It's thought that Outward Signs was interested in acquiring Hudson from Miller and his partner, with a view to strengthening their own position.</u> The agency is now expected to look elsewhere. Now for news of the manufacturing industry.

Now you will hear the news item again.

6 ◖ Speaking Test Part 2, Exercise 2b [BULATS Exam skills]

Well, <u>I'm going to talk about</u> the best office I've ever worked in. <u>To start with, I should say that</u> this office was in Bangalore, that's a city in southern India, and it was an office in quite a modern office block, not far from the city centre. I was working there as a graduate trainee, basically learning general management skills – <u>that was before</u> I became an assistant human resources manager, which is the job I do now, but here in Chennai and for a different company. So, <u>as I was saying</u>, I was there basically learning the job or, <u>as you might say</u>, general management and, <u>to come to the main point of the question</u>, what I most liked about the office was a combination of things.

<u>Firstly</u>, the physical surroundings. It was a light, airy office on the seventh floor of the building. It was well decorated, <u>I mean</u> it had good carpets on the floors, interesting pictures on the walls and comfortable, ergonomic office furniture and of course the latest computer equipment, so pretty well perfect as an office. Interestingly, it also had areas for workers to relax – a good canteen and a comfortable rest area – <u>so you could say</u> we were quite spoiled, although I think we probably worked harder and were more motivated as a result of feeling so well treated.

<u>The second thing which made it such a good office was that</u> we, that is the trainees, felt so motivated and stimulated. The place had a real buzz, and at that time the company was growing really fast and we felt we were part of something which was going to give us great opportunities. Rightly, as it turned out.

<u>Finally</u>, my fellow trainees, who were some of the most talented people I have ever met. <u>All those things</u> make that the best office I have ever worked in.

The Common European Framework (CEF)

What is the Common European Framework (CEF)?

The CEF has been developed by the Council of Europe to describe what we *can do* with a language, and to give a framework for language learning and language achievement throughout Europe. It divides language achievement into six main levels, from A1 for beginners through to C2 for very advanced learners:

	CEF level	
proficient	C2	Mastery
	C1	Effective Operational Proficiency
independent	B2	Vantage
	B1	Threshold
basic	A2	Waystage
	A1	Breakthrough

These levels apply to all major European languages, not just English, and language learners may have a 'Language Passport' describing their language level in the different languages they have studied. This Language Passport may be used when applying for a job, or a course of studies and shows the holder's linguistic levels in the languages they speak.

A language learner's level is assessed by a series of descriptors showing what the learner can do with the language. These descriptors are called *Can Do statements*. The statements have been translated into all major European languages and are used to describe a learner's ability in those languages.

Who assesses language learners in the CEF?

Learners can read the *Can Do statements* and decide for themselves which of the abilities that are described they can do. They can also go through these statements with their teacher, who may also provide an assessment. A learner is considered to have achieved a CEF level if he/she can do 80% of the things described in the *Can Do statements* for that level.

How is *Business Benchmark Advanced/Higher* related to CEF?

Business Benchmark Advanced/Higher is a Business English course which covers descriptors in the CEF relevant to the needs and objectives of students studying Business English. It is pitched at a level of C1 (in other words, a student who successfully completes this course will have a level of C1). This is the same level as a successful candidate at BEC Higher (see the exam description on page 122 of the Student's Book, BEC Edition), or a BULATS candidate who achieves a score of 75–89 (BULATS is described on pages 122 and 123 of the Student's Book, BULATS Edition), or a successful candidate of the Certificate of Advanced English. These exams provide an objective assessment of a learner's level and are closely related to CEF.

The *Can Do statements*

On the next page you can see the CEF *Can Do statements* for level C1 which are relevant to this course.

	Your assessment	Your teacher's assessment

Listening

1 I can understand in detail what is said to me in standard spoken language, even in a noisy environment.

2 I can follow a lecture or talk within my own field, provided the subject matter is familiar and the presentation straightforward and clearly structured.

3 I can understand the main ideas in complex speech on both concrete and abstract topics delivered in a standard dialect, including technical discussions in my field of specialisation.

4 I can use a variety of strategies to achieve comprehension, including listening for main points; checking comprehension by using contextual clues.

Spoken interaction

5 I can initiate, maintain and end discourse naturally with effective turn-taking.

6 I can exchange considerable quantities of detailed factual information on matters within my fields of interest.

7 I can convey degrees of emotion and highlight the personal significance of events and experiences.

8 I can engage in extended conversation in a clearly participatory fashion on most general topics.

9 I can account for and sustain my opinions in discussion by providing relevant explanations, arguments and comments.

10 I can help a discussion along on familiar ground confirming comprehension, inviting others to join in, etc.

11 I can carry out a prepared interview, checking and confirming information, following up interesting replies.

Spoken production

12 I can give clear, detailed descriptions on a wide range of subjects related to my fields of interest.

13 I can understand and summarise orally short extracts from news items, interviews or documentaries containing opinions, argument and discussion.

14 I can construct a chain of reasoned argument, linking my ideas logically.

15 I can explain a viewpoint on a topical issue giving the advantages and disadvantages of various options.

16 I can speculate about causes, consequences and hypothetical situations.

Strategies

17 I can use standard phrases like 'That's a difficult question to answer' to gain time and keep the turn while formulating what to say.

18 I can make a note of 'favourite mistakes' and consciously monitor speech for them.

19 I can generally correct slips and errors if I become conscious of them or if they have led to misunderstandings.

Language quality

20 I can produce stretches of language with a fairly even tempo; although I can be hesitant as I search for patterns and expressions, there are few noticeably long pauses.

21 I can pass on detailed information reliably.

22 I have sufficient vocabulary to express myself on matters concerned with my field and on most general topics.

Reading

23 I can rapidly grasp the content and the significance of news, articles and reports on topics connected with my interests or my job, and decide if a closer reading is worthwhile.

24 I can read and understand articles and reports which express specific attitudes and opinions on current problems.

25 I can understand in detail texts within my field of interest or the area of my academic or professional speciality.

26 I can understand specialised articles outside my own field if I can occasionally check with a dictionary.

27 I can read letters on topics within my areas of academic or professional speciality or interest and grasp the most important points.

28 I can quickly look through a manual (for example for a computer program) and find and understand the relevant explanations and help for a specific problem.

29 I can communicate with reasonable accuracy and can correct mistakes if they have led to misunderstandings.

Writing

30 I can write clear and detailed texts (compositions, reports or texts of presentations) on various topics related to my field of interest.

31 I can summarise information from different sources and media. I can understand the overall meaning of varied text.

32 I can develop an argument systematically in a composition or report, emphasising decisive points and including supporting details.

33 I can write about events and real or fictional experiences in a detailed and easily readable way.

34 I can structure and produce reports, expressing both facts and opinions.

Adapted from National Language Standards (revised 2005) © CILT, the National Centre for Languages, 2005